# SEEKING SPIRITUAL DIRECTION

# Seeking
# Spiritual Direction

*How to Grow the Divine Life Within*

Thomas Dubay, S.M.

CHARIS

Servant Publications
Ann Arbor, Michigan

Scripture texts used in this work, unless otherwise indicated,
are taken from *The Jerusalem Bible,* copyright © 1966 by
Darton, Longman & Todd, Ltd. and Doubleday &
Company, Inc., and are used by permission. Occasionally,
Scripture texts are taken from *The New American Bible with
Revised New Testament,* copyright © 1986 by Confraternity
of Christian Doctrine, Such citations are noted by paren-
thetical reference (NAB).

Published by Servant Publications
P.O. Box 8617
Ann Arbor, Michigan 48107

Cover design by Steve Eames

03 04 05 15 14 13

Printed in the United States of America

ISBN 0-89283-810-8

**Library of Congress Cataloging-in-Publication Data**

Dubay, Thomas.
  Seeking spiritual direction : how to grow the divine life within
/ Thomas Dubay.
     p. cm.
  Includes bibliographical references.
  ISBN 0-89283-810-8
  1. Spiritual direction. 2. Spiritual life—Catholic Church.
3. Catholic Church—Doctrines. I. Title.
BX2350.7.D83   1993
253.5'3—dc20                                    93-26747

# Contents

# ACKNOWLEDGMENT

THIS VOLUME should not see the light of day without a sincere expression of gratitude to Sister Joseph Marie, H.T., both for her editorial expertise and for the long hours of labor that she devoted to improving the first draft. She likewise offered valuable suggestions bearing on the content of the book. For these, too, the author is grateful.

# Part One

# *A Foundation for*
# *Spiritual Direction*

# ONE

# Getting Our Bearings

A FEW YEARS AGO two blind men crossed paths in a drizzle on a neighborhood street in Falkirk, Scotland. The first enjoyed sensory vision and knew in a general way where his destination was, but he did not know how to negotiate the ever-winding streets which abound in old Scottish towns. His blindness was a lack of practical know-how: he was lost. The other man lacked sensory vision, but he was not lost. The first of these two individuals was I. As I drew near to the second, I discovered that he was literally blind, but nonetheless I presented my problem to him. With an extraordinary warmth I shall never forget, he took me by the arm and walked me to the brow of a hill. There he described to me how to find the monastery at which I was to give a series of lectures.

This volume is aimed at offering some help, mostly practical help, to the large number of sincere people in all states of life who want to know and love God and yet declare that they cannot find adequate spiritual guides. They seek someone to take them by the arm and show the way. These men and women may make a retreat dealing with the universal call to infused contemplation or perhaps they read a book on the subject. Earnest as they are, they spontaneously wonder where they can find the aid they need. Some of them tell me that they have widely inquired in their diocese and still cannot find a prayerful priest who is a competent guide and also is free enough of other pressing commitments to respond positively to their need.

What are they to do? The perceptive among them know well

that many of those who offer themselves as spiritual directors have only a meager knowledge and experience of advanced prayer and probably even less adequacy in the many areas of Scripture and theology required for a well-rounded competency. The less perceptive may dabble in Eastern techniques or in ever-changing Western fads. Some, perhaps many, in both groups get discouraged and give up the hope of finding guidance on a one-to-one basis. They may turn to books, but even in cases where solid spiritual reading is obtained, it is not enough.

This book attempts to answer the question of what a person might do in this case. An abundant supply of first-rate guides would be the ideal response, but the fact is that no such supply is available or likely to be available in the foreseeable future. As we shall note further on, for centuries saints have lamented the lack of individualized and competent help for people intent on knowing and serving God better. We plan in these pages to discuss many of the questions, theoretical and practical, that people ask about and within spiritual direction. We also take up the question as to whether there is any valid sense in which one may direct oneself.

Those who read this last sentence and are immediately inclined to turn to the chapter that deals with "self-direction" (and omit all the rest) are well advised to resist the temptation. Truth must be seen and appreciated in its context, and the chapter on this subject should be read only in the light of all that precedes and follows it.

We assume in these pages that our readers wish to scale the heights, to leave mediocrity far behind. Even though sincere and honest people may not have philosophized about the matter, they know deep down that nothing this world has to offer will satisfy the yearnings of their hearts. Nothing, they realize, is enough but the divine Enough. Not money, not possessions, not drugs, not sex, not power, not luxury. Some individuals claim to be perfectly content with their hedonistic lifestyle. But this brave protestation, notes Catholic apologist and philosopher Peter Kreeft, "verges on culpable dishonesty, the sin against the Holy Spirit, and requires something more like exorcism than refutation.... Even John Stuart Mill, one of the shallowest minds in the history of human thought, said that it was better to be Socrates dissatisfied than a pig satisfied."[1]

Yes, spiritual direction should aim at making saints, nothing less. Because such should be its aim, its apostolic power extends far beyond the directee immediately concerned. Even though British convert Arnold Lunn had spent years studying and writing about the Catholic Church he was to enter, the final impulse (following after his reasoned conviction) that sent him into her bosom was provided by "Catholicism in action," that is, by the lives of the saints. These he considered "the best of all arguments for the Catholic faith."[2] The Lord was of the same mind: "by their fruits you will know them" (Mt 7:20, NAB). Once within the barque of Peter, Lunn remarked, "when I find myself with a near saint virtue goes out of him, and I know that sanctity is the most impressive and the most beautiful thing in the world." Or as Augustine put it, "One loving soul sets another on fire." The focus of this volume is reflected in the title and subtitle, *Seeking Spiritual Direction: How to Grow the Divine Life Within.* It is to be hoped that those benefiting by it will be multiplied manyfold by the silent witness of its readers being enkindled by the one love that ignites others.

To say that spiritual direction is meant to assist the Holy Spirit in enkindling a love which transforms the face of the earth is to suggest the aesthetic side of the supernatural order, the experience of beauty, created and uncreated. Both mentor and disciple work together to be rid of the many clingings, major and minor, which block a capacity for beauty and love. Or to put the matter positively, spiritual direction aims at sensitizing a person for the perception of the divine loveliness reflected in the splendors of the universe, but mostly in the life of grace vibrantly lived. As Hans Urs von Balthasar put it, "Before the beautiful—no, not really *before* but *within* the beautiful—the whole person quivers. He not only 'finds' the beautiful moving; rather, he experiences himself as being moved and possessed by it. The more total this experience is, the less does a person seek and enjoy only the delight that comes through the senses or even through any act of his own."[3] A person who has come thus far has no trouble understanding the Gospel's insistence on the hard road and the narrow gate, no problem in grasping the *nada* of St. John of the Cross, no difficulty in seeing how and why the saints are so happy.

## A BOOK FOR THOSE SEEKING SPIRITUAL DIRECTION

Most current writing on spiritual direction deals, it seems, with the subject from the point of view of the mentor. Hence, we hear the names 'art of spiritual direction' or 'art of spiritual guidance.' We read about directive and non-directive counseling techniques and about Jungian insights into the workings of human personalities. While this volume touches lightly on these matters and others like them, most of our attention is centered on the directee. We focus on the needs, desires, and problems of those who seek spiritual guidance whether they have succeeded in finding a human master or not.

People who have sought unsuccessfully to discover a competent and prayerful director—and their number is not small—obviously need individualized aid in grasping the finer points of total Gospel living and in applying them wisely to their own particular circumstances. We envision them especially. But we also have in mind men and women who do have the blessing of a suitable guide, for as St. John of the Cross remarks, rare is the director who is competent to deal adequately with every question that can arise in a serious spiritual journey. People in both groups have problems that come in an extensive variety.

We provide in Chapter Two an understanding of spiritual direction as it is rooted in divine revelation, so that the directee may have a more full grasp of how to view this relationship. For this same reason we explore also the Christic and ecclesial aspects as well as the very concept of what spiritual direction is and is not in Chapters Two and Three. Useful likewise is an understanding of the need for this guidance (Chapter Four) as well as the problem of competency in the pool of available mentors (Chapter Five).

Part Two, "Practical Questions and Problems," is written in the informal manner of spiritual direction itself, and it takes up a large number of specific questions such as honesty and receptivity in seeking guidance, finding a competent director and profiting from the help offered, direction by mail, counseling approaches and methods, guidance within the Sacrament of Reconciliation, possibility of self-direction, finding God's will without illusion, profiting from spiritual reading, the saints as guides, judging alleged supernatural experiences, growing in contemplative prayer, balancing work and prayer in one's life, conditions for developing prayer depth, styles of prayer, solitude and community, liturgical prayer and personal growth, the universal call to contemplation, practical questions concerning a deepening communion with God. Likewise considered are commonly occuring questions concerned with methods of meditation, difficult and dry prayer, recognizing the beginnings of infused contemplation and the dark nights, conditions for growth, impediments to prayer, new prayer movements whether occidental or oriental, mortification and self-denial, feeling and willing, conscience and confession.

Part Three deals with results and performance. In Chapter Twelve we touch upon key factors in the spiritual life without which growth is impossible. Even though these factors may appear obvious, they are easily lost sight of in the pressures of daily living. The final chapter offers concrete criteria, based in Scripture, indicating clearly and with particulars how we may recognize whether and to what extent we are growing in our journey to God.

The stakes are high. We are destined to the endless ecstasy called heaven, not to the paltry pleasures of earth, which, no matter how intense they occasionally may be, soon fade away. We exist not to pursue the fatuous inflation of prestige and fame, but to "dance with joy" in the only lasting glorification—begun on earth and completed hereafter—that is given to the humble who are invited to "enter into the joy of their Lord."

Eternity is endless. We had a beginning, but we shall have no end. Unlike the beasts of the field, we will live forever in the eventual unending, unspeakable delight of sharing in the utter fullness of our triune God seen in direct vision (Eph 3:19; 1 Jn 3:2; Jn 17:3), or we shall be endlessly lost in the eternal disaster whose name is hell. There are no long-term alternatives.

If ever there were an indispensable journey, it is our trip through life. All other travels by comparison pale into insignificance. Yet the exquisite care thousands of people every year expend on preparing their holidays to the beach or the mountains or the lake or on an overseas tour and their comparative unconcern regarding the other journey that ultimately matters are folly in the extreme. "What does it profit a man if he gains the whole world and suffers the loss of his soul?" (Mt 16:26).

Why seek spiritual direction? For one thing, "It is a narrow gate and a hard road that leads to life and only a few find it" (Mt 7:13-14). That sentence alone should send shivers up our spines. Why do so few find it? Most do not search and seek, because if they did, they would infallibly find. Truth incarnate has said so (Mt 7:7-8). Mediocre people often have a tinge of religion about them, but it is only a tinge. They take their religion as it comes. They may pray and worship more or less regularly, and they usually stay clear of publicly disgraceful crimes, but they are lukewarm, colorless. Seldom or never do they read a serious book about prayer or study to learn more about God and his plans, to discover how to be humble and chaste and patient. They are always too busy for the one thing necessary.

Why seek spiritual direction? One may respond by asking: why maps? The time is short, and we make the trip only once. There are no repeat performances. We stumble and fall, yes. We stray off the road, yes, but God is always ready to heal, if we are sorry. And through his Church he provides divine truth and human guides to show the way. But the fact remains that we are not forced: we have one life journey to use as we will.

We must dwell for a few moments on our wayfaring image. Along with the characteristic sin of our century, the loss of a sense of sin, is the allied assumption that saving one's soul is comparatively easy and that everyone, or almost everyone, reaches heaven. Funeral homilies now often become unofficial, simplistic canonization ceremonies. If we may believe the polls, the majority of people who bear the honor of the Christian name consider themselves unconcernedly on the road to heaven. They see no great problem, even though divine revelation does.

One of the most sobering thoughts that can enter the human mind is the realization that at this very moment each of us is on one of two paths (there is no alternative third): we are on the way either to the unspeakable and unending ecstasy of glory or the frightful, eternal tortuous despair of hell. The final accounting of our stewardship will not be a mere quantitative tally—it will be the eternal crystallization of what by our free choices we have been making ourselves to be all through our lives: either men and women of authentic love or self-centered egoists.

So it must be for the simple reason that truth and error, good and evil do exist. Furthermore, reality takes its revenge on those who deny it (mistreating the body is one example among many). At each moment we reap the consequences of our actions and omissions, both as individuals and as communities. In a context linking chastity with the common good of society, Patrick Riley observed that in an atmosphere which itself is "libertine and anomic... society will recognize reality only once the mugging begins."[4] Spiritual direction aims at preventing the mugging both in this world and in the next.

Setting a proper context for the work of this volume requires that we consider the current trend to psychologize spiritual direction. While sound psychiatry and psychology have valid contributions to make toward the healing of human woundedness in the forms of neuroses and psychoses, they do not, and cannot, offer adequate treatment for a host of problems rooted in religious apathy and moral aberrations. And it should be obvious that by definition they can lead no one to full sanctity.

Yet, there is reason to think that no small percentage of current 'spiritual direction' is pop psychology: how to feel 'comfortable' with one's person and lifestyle, pursuing liberation from sundry oppressions (real or imagined), raising one's consciousness, being rid of guilt feelings, getting along in a group, managing difficult human relationships. Relevant here are the comments of a friend regarding the proliferation of 'in' books: "They're empty. They're too psychological. The emphasis on the dysfunctional, the addictive, is itself dysfunctional and addictive as I see it. Support groups can end up supporting the dysfunctional, the addictions themselves. Not only that, I see some support groups becoming addictive." Or as another friend put it, spiritual direction "has become little more than an exercise in psychological feel-good."

However, dealing as we must with the whole person, spiritual guides should be aware of, and profit from, valid developments in our understanding of the ways in which we humans operate and of helpful approaches to effective counseling. For example, a director who is exclusively directive (teaching, advising, commanding) needs to appreciate the benefits of the non-directive approach (exploring, supporting, reflecting back what has been said), even though this method is itself limited. In any event, both director and directee must bear in mind that their purpose and means far transcend the horizons of merely natural disciplines. The human person does not, as a merely humanistic approach would suppose, have the native capacity to remedy adequately his inner defects and disorders. Nor can psychology know of itself of the divine plan for human transformation "from one glory to another" (2 Cor 3:18).

In a way this volume is an unplanned sequel to my book *Fire Within*, a recent work synthesizing the thoughts of Saints Teresa of Avila and John of the Cross and the Gospel as they bear on a deepening prayer life.[5] If the response to this latter book proves anything, it is that despite the grave problems of our day, there is within many people a deep hunger for God, for something more than they are receiving in our churches on Sunday morning. Constantly I have been hearing from men and women something like the following: "Where can I find someone to guide me in reaching contemplative prayer, even in grasping what it is? I have tried to find a spiritual director, but cannot. Many of our clergy simply do not understand infused contemplation... or indeed they may wonder why a lay person would even think of something so esoteric." This present work is aimed at answering these needs to whatever extent the written word can answer them. At the very least we shall face the problem and the needs and then offer pointers toward meeting them.

Our contemporaries are weary of weavers of words, of projects and promises, and of programs. They are looking for prophets and saints. Even when they do not articulate it in this way, they are thirsting. They are asking who will speak to them of God from a heart overflowing with the light and love of the Holy Spirit.

# TWO

# The Key Principle
# of Mediation

E VERYTHING IN THE DIVINE PLAN is aimed at the eternal ecstasy of heaven begun on earth: "No eye has seen and no ear has heard, things beyond the mind of man, all that God has prepared for those who love him" (1 Cor 2:9). That there is a self-denying, ascetical element in the Gospel is undoubted, but this hard road and the narrow gate do lead to life (Mt 7:13-14). Speaking of the obedience of faith and love, Hans Urs von Balthasar writes of "the beatific shudder of self-surrender which every believer is basically disposed to experience and which the mystic actually experiences already here on earth. This is the experience of leaving one's own house in a dark night, and of the arrow that burns into the centre of the ego, there to implant the Thou."[1] People who fret about what they call the negative spirituality of authority and obedience, of humility and patience, show clearly that they have only a tenuous and surface idea of what the divine plan encompasses. Their giving or receiving of spiritual direction can hardly escape a flimsy and gossamer character.

Perhaps, in an idealized state devoid of an original catastrophe, a plausible case could be made for an economy of salvation in which God would deal solely and on a day-to-day basis with each individual man and woman: a customized revelation given privately to each person, unique and frequent visions, individualized divine counseling. But in our actual and wounded world such is not the case. For reasons obvious on a few moments' reflection the Lord has decided as a fundamental principle that he will deal with the human race through a select few who will then speak and govern in his name. In other words, we live by divine decision in an obediential economy of salvation. Though there is only one Mediator between God and humankind, the man Christ Jesus (1 Tm 2:5), in both the old and the new dispensations the eternal Father has chosen to lead all of us to an enthralling immersion into the Triune life by the agency of prophets and apostles and their successors. There is no provision in Scripture for a rugged individualism. Mediation is the rule.

Evidence abounds. To make it manageable we shall break it down into two points: all authority originates in God; consequently, human life necessarily has an obediential character to it. We please the Lord and achieve our ultimate fulfillment through styling our lives within the community he established and in obedience to the leaders who govern, teach, and sanctify in the divine name and with a divine commission from the one Mediator. To be realistic, spiritual direction must be seen in this context—or it degenerates into mere human counseling. One may object, of course, that the theme of this book is not primarily a juridical matter, a strictly obediential relationship. To a point there is some validity to the objection. If one views our subject as completely divorced from its ecclesial dimension, it may be difficult to see the point of this chapter, but that is precisely the reason for the chapter. Many of the myopic, indeed sometimes distorted, ideas about spiritual direction stem, not from malice, but from a lack of rootedness in divine revelation. Hence, we cannot answer the question in our next chapter until we have explored the revealed principle of mediation: God has chosen to lead us to himself through our brothers and sisters, that is, in ways that go beyond informal friendships.

First, there is the fundamental function of faith, that is, saying yes to God and to his revelation. There is no other starting point, given the fact that God has spoken his word into the world (Heb 1:1-3).

Without this yes of faith there is no possibility of pleasing God, of taking our first steps toward him (Heb 11:6). We walk "by faith and not by sight" (2 Cor 5:7). Faith, therefore, is the foundational condition for the pursuit of God in his Trinitarian life. In its essence it is an act of obedience to the Lord speaking to his people.

## THE SCRIPTURAL CASE FOR MEDIATION

Throughout Scripture the Lord's speaking is addressed immediately to carefully selected individuals, who then relay the message to his community. Moses is a mediator in both directions: he relays Yahweh's words to the people and returns their response to him. In this work of leading and teaching the people "the way they ought to behave," Moses found that so many came to him for guidance that he sat at his task from morning to evening. Because the work became more than he could handle, he "chose capable men" to aid him in caring for others' needs, in administering justice (Ex 18:13-27). This example can be applied to spiritual direction only in an analogous sense. As the parallel passage in Deuteronomy 1:9-18 makes even more clear, the text directly deals with the administration of justice. Yet because their task included representing the people of God and instructing them in a holy way of life, it can be seen as pertinent to our concern here.

We read further that if the House of Jacob obeys the divine voice, the Lord will make them a kingdom of priests, a consecrated nation, his very own community. These words Moses is directed to speak to the people of Israel. Immediately we then read: "So Moses went and summoned the elders of the people, putting before them all that Yahweh had bidden him. Then all the people answered as one, 'All that Yahweh has said, we will do.' And Moses took the people's reply back to Yahweh" (Ex 19:7-8).[2] As a matter of fact Leviticus 26:46 expressly terms this function "the mediation of Moses."

So seriously does the Lord take this providential arrangement that when the people murmur against their leaders, he considers it a murmuring against himself: "How then have you dared to speak against my servant Moses?" he demands. "The anger of Yahweh blazed out against them" (Nm 12:8-9). Moses was careful to explain to the people that when they complained against him and Aaron, they were complaining against the Lord himself (Ex 16:8; see also Nm 16:11; 21:5).

All the genuine prophets speak as God's representatives. Having been selected, commissioned, and sent by him, they are his mouthpieces. He puts his own words into their mouths (Is 6:6; Ez 3:1-4; Jer 1:9). Hence, as was the case with Moses, so also with the other prophets: to reject them is to reject God himself (1 Sm 15:1-23).

This same mediational principle is operative on the civil and domestic scenes as well as on the religious. Kings are told that their power and sovereignty are gifts from the Lord Most High. If they do not carry out their tasks as God would have them, his judgment will fall on them "swiftly and terribly" (Wis 6:1-4). In the home the Lord honors the father and upholds the rights of the mother over their children, while the latter in dealing well with parents are showing obedience to the Lord himself (Sir 3:2, 6).

The New Testament repeats and focuses on these themes of the old dispensation. All authority, says St. Paul, derives from God (Rom 13:1-2). Jesus admonishes his fellow Jews to obey those who occupy the seat of Moses precisely because of their divinely authorized office, surely not because of their virtue (Mt 23:2-3). In the Church those whom Jesus sends into the world are commissioned and have their office only because he has sent them. They are to go and teach everywhere. In their mission he is with them even to the end of the world by confirming and ratifying their teaching (Mt 28:18-20). They are to proclaim the good news to all of creation with such authority that those who do not accept their proclamation will be condemned (Mk 16:15).

This sense of mission is rooted in the very Trinitarian life, for as the Father has sent the Son into the world, so the Son sends the leaders of the infant Church (Jn 20:21). St. Paul reminds the overseers at Ephesus that it was the Holy Spirit himself who established them to teach, govern, and sanctify the community (Acts 20:28). This is the same Spirit Advocate whom Jesus promised would be with this infant Church forever—to its maturity, up to the time of the *parousia* (Jn 14:16). To the biblical writers in both testaments, for God to be with someone meant that he was there acting together with that person. His "being with" was not an inert presence but a dynamic co-working with his human delegate.

Jesus makes the same point even more strikingly: he identifies himself with those whom he sends. Those who listen to his apostles and their successors are listening to him, no one else. Those who reject these representatives are rejecting Jesus and his Father, nothing less (Lk 10:16). When these men bind members of the Church in their teaching, governing, and sanctifying, their actions are bound in heaven. God himself ratifies their solemn decisions; they cannot err when they use their full apostolic authority (Mt 16:19; 18:18).

The correlative of authority is, of course, obedience. In both the old and the new dispensations the Lord makes it clear that people whom he sends and authorizes to speak in his name are to be obeyed, for he himself is working through them. Mediation requires this response. The abundance of texts mandating submission to human leaders is summarized in Hebrews 13:17: "Obey your leaders and do as they tell you."[3] This divine strategy is strikingly seen in the very Son of the Father. Though he is Wisdom Incarnate, Jesus received 'spiritual direction' in being subject to Mary and Joseph as he grew in "wisdom, stature, and favour with God and men" (Lk 2:51-52).

## THE MORE INFORMAL ROLE OF DIRECTION

While one readily grants that the biblical record makes it clear that in the official operation of the Church the Lord has chosen to work through human instruments, and that he somehow ratifies and affirms what they do in their official capacities, this is not exactly spiritual direction as we envision it in this volume. True enough in part. Thus far we have aimed only to remind ourselves of the fundamental divine plan. God has chosen to bring us to himself through our fellows, not only in a direct and inner relationship with himself alone. But it is also true, as we shall explore in our next chapter, that the relationship of spiritual direction in its fullest sense is thoroughly an ecclesial matter. However, lest we get ahead of ourselves, we presently return to biblical roots.

Both testaments speak, in addition to official mediatorial leadership roles, of more informal roles of direction. But perhaps we should look first at the dark side of this question of pursuing God, namely, those who choose not to accept direction, be it official or unofficial, or who absolutely refuse unwelcome truth. Scripture speaks of the latter when it remarks about the chosen people's past refusal to listen to the word of God spoken through his prophets: they stopped their ears, made their hearts adamant, diamond-hard in resisting truth (Zec 7:11-12). John Henry Newman was not off the mark when he wrote, "There is no truth, however over-poweringly clear, but men may escape from it by shutting their eyes."[4] It is not, of course, likely that the diamond-hard heart would be inclined to read this book, but what all of us need to recall is that until we are thoroughly purified there is some trace of resistance to truth that interferes with our preferences.

Evidence abounds in academia that scientists, philosophers, and theologians (along with their other colleagues and the common man and woman on the street) frequently embrace their worldviews and opinions about religion and morality according to their personal preferences and sympathies, not according to objective evidence. Anyone who has read the history of science, for example, knows full well how often astronomers and biologists (just to mention two groups among many) resist and reject new evidences that run counter to their preferred theories. Indeed, one reads in the daily papers of fraud and deception in reporting scientific research and the hushing up of data that discredit popular theories. Whether one is academic or not, we tend to think what we desire: "Men's opinions are imperceptibly formed by their wishes."[5]

Anyone who is moderately attuned to the things of God knows from experience how we resist personal change for the better. Perhaps we do not set our minds explicitly to a refusal, but we nonetheless cling to what we are and where we are in the spiritual life. If the reader has any doubt about this general trait, a simple question might shed some light: "Am I significantly better right now than I was a year ago? Have I made any concerted effort to improve, to get rid of my faults?" Newman has noted that:

> For many reasons it is very unpleasant to us to change. We cannot change ourselves; this too we know full well, or, at least, a very little experience will teach us. God alone can change us; God alone can give us the desires, affections, principles, views, and tastes which a change implies: this too we know; for I am all along speaking of men who have a sense of religion. What then is it that we who profess religion lack? I repeat it, this: a willingness to *be* changed, a willingness to suffer (if I may use such a word), to suffer Almighty God to change us. We do not like to let go of our old selves.[6]

What has this to do with spiritual direction? People find the path to God only if they really love truth, if they shape their minds and wills to moral rectitude, if they follow the light wherever it leads, if they embrace reality revealing itself, even when the embrace implies hardship, suffering, and unpopularity.

This surely is why Jesus himself laid it down that no one can be his disciple unless one renounces all that one possesses, not just major obstacles (Lk 14:33). Our minds may not be diamond-hard against clear proclamations of revelation, but we are past masters at resisting in subtle ways. We cling to our pet schemes, ambitions, pleasures, vanities. Yet we must "give up everything that does not lead to God" (Ti 2:12). For most of us that is the last thing we are eager or willing to do, even though, if we were consistent theists, we would far prefer to surrender everything in order to be immersed in purest joy, beauty, love, and goodness. Our performance tends to lag behind our protestations. Though one of the aims of spiritual direction is this biblical imperative of self-surrender, our reluctance to change is the reason why some people, even with competent guidance, improve so little.

The other aspect of the dark side is our inability to understand the things of God simply because our being is not attuned to them. An uneducated person cannot appreciate Shakespeare, nor can a materialist grasp divine revelation. The Book of Wisdom has it that the godless because of their malice do not understand the things of God (2:21-22). St. Paul says the same of the "man of the flesh," the worldly-minded individual (1 Cor 2:14; see also 2 Cor 4:4). God does not force himself upon us, either directly through his own inner-action or indirectly through the mediation of his Church. Spiritual direction is effective only if the directee is making a sincere effort to live according to Gospel principles.

We are now prepared to examine our next biblical theme, one-on-one guidance from people schooled in the ways of the Spirit. The sage tells us that we are to seek instruction from our earliest youth even until our hair is white (Sir 6:18). This implies a healthy mistrust of our own views in matters supernatural. We are to put no faith in our own perception: "put no faith in your own perception" (Prv 3:5, also v. 7).[7] Rather we go to virtuous people because their words are "a life-giving fountain" (Prv 10:11; 13:14). Since these holy guides speak wisdom, we come to them for spiritual direction and nourishment (Prv 10:21, 31). St. Paul was of the same mind when he wrote to the Colossians with the advice that they receive instruction and admonition from one another (Col 3:16).

Those who will not attend to the voice of their masters, and will not listen to their teachers are "reduced to the depths of misery" (Prv 5:13-14). On the other hand, competent direction brings joy to the recipient, for the apt reply to one's problem brings satisfaction (Prv 15:23). Hence, the wise do listen and learn, and thus growing in discernment, they themselves learn the art of guiding others (Prv 1:5).

It follows then that a good director is a priceless boon, a friend who becomes a powerful defense, a treasure, a gift beyond price. There is no measure to such a one's worth, says the divine word itself (Sir 6:14-15).


## WHY DID GOD CHOOSE TO USE MEDIATORS?

We may at this point ask some questions. Why does God achieve his purposes through human mediators? Why must we go to and through brothers and sisters? Being all wise and all powerful, why did not God decide to deal directly and individually with each one of us? Would not the unmediated approach of inner enlightenments avoid most, if not all, of our human errors, misjudgments, misapplications, and yes, our stupidities as well?

While it is not for us to gainsay the Lord and demand reasons for his providential plan, we may suggest explanations which cast light on our subject and on the very roots of spiritual direction. If the human race were sinless, perhaps a mediated, obediential economy would not have been necessary, but our actual situation makes clear the wisdom of the divine decision.

For one thing even the objective biblical text is interpreted in endless contradictory ways. Protestant scholars report well over twenty thousand diverse sects (some of them very weird indeed), all of which claim to follow Christ. As elementary logic points out, in a genuine contradiction (one party denying exactly what the other affirms) one of the two must be mistaken. The seriousness of these grievous divisions emerges as soon as we remember that truth is being in touch with reality, while error is being out of touch. In important matters being out of touch with reality can be disastrous.

The problem is compounded when we turn attention to alleged locutions, inner enlightenments supposedly received directly and personally from God. Even though genuine locutions can and do occur, illusions are notoriously frequent.[8] St. John of the Cross pointed out unambiguously that even when one receives an authentic communication from God, there is no assurance that one will understand it rightly and be able to avoid invalid conclusions.[9] Hence, given our woundedness deriving both from original and actual sins, anything but an obediential and mediated economy would be a disaster. This is why Jesus established a Church to teach and discern in his name: "Whoever listens to you listens to me. Whoever rejects you rejects me" (Lk 10:16, NAB). There must be some interpreter who is authorized to correct misunderstandings, of which, we may be sure, there will be an abundance. There must be a visible teacher with divine authority, as St. Paul puts it: "Another reason why we constantly thank God for you is that as soon as you heard the message that we brought you as God's message, you accepted it for what it really is, God's message and not some human thinking" (1 Thes 2:13).

History, past and present, is full of cases of people convinced with no objective reason that God is speaking to them. The messages may be obviously erroneous, even bizarre, but the hearers remain convinced. All too often, they convince others as well. There must be and is in the Catholic Church a leadership that can test these allegations and sift the authentic from the erroneous.

Further, normal and sincere people who do receive divine communications feel a need to submit them to due authority and to receive confirmation. Experienced spiritual directors know well that when God does offer a locution, he builds into it an inner impulse directing the recipient to seek an assurance from a confessor or director. From the theological viewpoint this built-in impulse fits well into the incarnational nature of the Church: inner and outer elements working together and in harmony.[10] It is precisely the mediated approach which offers a protection against our human proclivity to error, misjudgment, and misapplication.

The final reason lies in our need for certitude in important matters. A wife is not satisfied with a probability that her husband is faithful to her, nor is a passenger content that the airliner's fuel supply is possibly sufficient to bring it to a distant destination. People who speak as though religious matters do not require certitude and are content with something less, do not take God, their souls, or eternity seriously.

They have lost sight likewise of the fact that the New Testament always speaks with undoubted assurance. Nowhere does Scripture suggest the idea that God's revelation yields anything less than certitude. Hans Urs von Balthasar notes, for example, that in the Johannine writings faith "is unhesitatingly described as certain knowledge; 'We know that we have been brought out of death into life' (1 Jn 3:14). 'We know that he hears us' (1 Jn 5:14). 'We know that the Son of God has come...' (1 Jn 5:20)."[11]

Why is this so? Even on the merely human level when we entirely trust a person, both his honesty and his knowledge, we have no doubt that he is telling the truth. If, on the other hand, we do not fully trust him, we calculate probabilities of knowledge or reliability. We are doubtful. In the case of Jesus, his overwhelming holiness, his radiant imaging of the Father's glory, left no room for doubt, especially after the resurrection and Pentecost. The apostles were ready to die for what they knew to be the truth. And all through the centuries the martyrs and other saints have been of the same mind. Provided we take God seriously, we too seek certitude in our pursuit of him. Knowing this human need, the Lord mediates his revelation to us through a Church and its ministers: "He who hears you, hears me." He does not in these ultimate matters leave us to our own devices.

In the divine plan, therefore, our salvation and sanctification rest squarely on the obedience of faith, on that founding yes of one's whole person to God revealing himself. It is the yes that everyone in the Church from brilliant thinker to simple laborer, from mature adult to young child, gives to the revelation of the Father in his Son. It is an "obedient surrender to the radiant light," which the disciple offers to the divine Teacher, "The more obediently he thinks, the more accurately will he see."[12] Thus the relationship of spiritual direction is fully immersed in the incarnational nature of the divine plan. The governing principle of director and directee is that they together say this mutual yes, both in thought and in deed.

# What Is Spiritual Direction?

O N THE SURFACE, the subject of this chapter may well seem superfluous. After all, many would assume, the idea of spiritual direction is simple enough. We all know what it is.

Or do we? The longer I engage in the practice of it with thousands of men and women, the more I am persuaded that the reality can be highly complex and ambiguous. Moreover, the wide variety of practices currently called spiritual direction necessitates a careful evaluation of them in the light of divine revelation.

Beginning with an outline sketch we proceed to explore these areas of inquiry:

1. In view of its rootedness in Scripture, exactly what is spiritual direction according to the mind of Christ?
2. What, then, does not qualify as spiritual direction?
3. The question also arises in the biblical framework of supernatural guidance: Who does the guiding? What about the appropriateness of "non-official" spiritual mentors?
4. Finally, given that the purpose of an enterprise tells us a great deal about its nature, what should be happening in the relationship of spiritual direction?

## THE CHRISTIC CONCEPT

Varied indeed are the current ideas about what qualifies as spiritual direction. For example, some view it as a kind of spiritual kindredship, while others see it as structured counseling aimed at psychic development or perhaps the identification of personality types, or even as a means of resolving interpersonal tensions and conflicts. While what is contained in this chapter is not meant to deny the usefulness of some of these activities for some people at a certain period in their lives, it is intended to clarify just what those who follow Christ have in mind when speaking of *spiritual* direction, especially when actually engaging in it. Precisely what is taking place?

In its primary New Testament meaning, 'spiritual' does not exclude the material or bodily aspects of human life. Rather it refers to being guided by the Holy Spirit (Rom 8:14), being the temple of the indwelling Trinity (1 Cor 2:12-13), living under the divine influence (Col 1:19), and receiving one's very prayer from the Spirit (Eph 5:19; Rom 8:26). 'Spiritual' refers to life lived in and through the Third Person of the Trinity (Rom 8:9-11).

Since the all-holy God created everything visible and invisible and pronounced it all good (Gn 1:31), we may not posit an opposition between matter and spirit (spirit understood in the philosophical sense of soul). That is Gnostic, not Christian thinking.[1] Thus Vatican II, speaking of lay participation in the common priesthood, declares that all human activities, religious and secular alike, are to be carried out in the Holy Spirit.[2] This, too, underlies the thought of St. Paul in 1 Corinthians 10:31: "Whether you eat or drink or do anything else, do all for the glory of God." Similarly, Paul signifies by the term 'carnal' not only impurity but also selfishness, pride, ambition, and lovelessness: in other words, whatever is opposed to the divine will and genuine human good.

What, then, is *spiritual* direction? It is the guiding of a person into a life truly under the dominion of the Holy Spirit, who is the primary director. It helps the directee to be more and more docile to the light and promptings of the divine Sanctifier, identifying impediments to this, as well as ways to overcome them, giving instruction and encouragement in living a life of virtue, and assisting the directee to advance on the path of prayer—the road to union with God. Given the sublimity of this task, it is easy to see why in the tradition it has been called the *ars artium*, the art of arts.

## THE ECCLESIAL CHARACTER OF SPIRITUAL DIRECTION

Another word for the biblical principle of mediation, as it is applied to our subject, is ecclesiality. As Pope Leo XIII once pointed out, it is a law of divine providence that God wishes to save and sanctify humankind in and through the agency of men and women. Even the Holy Father receives a priest's instructions when he makes his annual retreat. He reads books and articles written by others, and he receives the Sacrament of Reconciliation kneeling before a simple confessor. Indeed, St. Paul himself, who had encountered the risen Lord in person, was told to get specific instructions, not directly from the risen Master standing before him, but from a designated leader in the Church (Acts 9:6). St. John of the Cross had sound reason, therefore, for insisting upon the ecclesial character of spiritual direction.

What we envision in this volume is not mere counseling, not merely a religiously motivated friendship (though this may be salutary in certain circumstances, as we will note in its place), not mere encouragement that one private person may well offer to another. What we have firmly in mind is the Church herself reaching out to an individual in the form of an individual and serving to enlighten, to confirm, to corroborate, and to heal.

Because Jesus was sent by the Father, and because the episcopal and priestly leaders in the Catholic Church were, in turn, sent by him on the very evening of the resurrection (Jn 20:21), St. John of the Cross stands on solid ground in declaring that the priestly director takes the place of God himself and is not merely a private adviser.[3] To this guide John applies the binding and loosing power committed to the apostles in Matthew 18:18.[4]

Significantly, this ecclesial character of direction supposes the normal situation, namely, that the guide fully accepts the magisterium, the teaching office of the pope and the bishops in communion with him. Otherwise the whole providential principle declared by Leo XIII collapses: human opinions replace guaranteed divine teaching.

From this ecclesiality of spiritual direction a number of conclusions necessarily follow. The first aspect of the director-directee relationship involves an intimate act of faith in the divine word. It fits entirely within the centrality of faith as the fundamental means of attaining divine light, love, and union with the Trinity here on earth and hereafter in the beatific vision.

Second, spiritual direction is one instance among many of the incarnational character of the divine economy of salvation: God works visibly and invisibly. He teaches from within by the indwelling Spirit (Jn 16:13) and from without through human ministers whom he sets up to teach, govern, and sanctify in his name (Acts 20:28).

Third, even when competent non-clerical men and women offer spiritual guidance, their task participates in this ecclesiality insofar as they work from within the Church's immensely rich deposit of faith and apply this wealth to the individual directee. By this means, in accord with Christ's plan, no one operates in the care of souls from mere private opinions, for the divine thoughts and ways tower above human wisdom as the heavens lie far above the earth (Is 55:8-9).

Though St. Teresa did not express herself in theological terms, she took it for granted that individualized guidance has just such roots. She told her sisters that they were to speak to their confessors "plainly and candidly," not only when they received the Sacrament of Penance, but also in sharing with them details of their progress and difficulties in prayer. Her reasoning was that through his priests God is teaching and wants the faithful to speak to them as to him, "candidly and clearly," since the priest is taking his place. This candor, she adds, assures that the directee will come to no harm, even if a given experience does not come from God. The implication is, of course, that without ecclesial confirmation people are liable to stray.[5]

## THE HOLY SPIRIT: OUR PRINCIPAL DIRECTOR

Dwelling in the Church as in his sacred temple (1 Cor 3:16-17; 6:19-20; 2 Cor 6:16), the Holy Spirit is the chief guide both of the official teachers, the magisterium, and of each of the ordinary faithful. Jesus promised the former at the Last Supper that the Father would send the advocate to teach them "everything" and that "the Spirit of truth" would lead them "to the complete truth" (Jn 14:26; 16:13). St. Paul taught the Romans, ordinary men and women, that if they are moved by this same Spirit, they are sons and daughters of the Father (Rom 8:14). Obviously, therefore, the mutual bond, the divine kiss between Father and Son, is the supreme guide for the entire Church and for all her members.

Hans Urs von Balthasar notes that the first few decades after the ascension, as described in the Acts of the Apostles, were not simply a privileged time in which the original witnesses lived, but were in addition "the privileged space in which the Holy Spirit became visible, audible, and palpable; it is the expansion of the explosion that occurred on Pentecost."[6] St. Paul offers this power of the Spirit as proof in its own right of the divine origin of his work and that of the infant Church (1 Cor 2:4).

To readers interested in astrophysics this explosion readily triggers the thought of the Big Bang, that first microsecond of incredible light, heat, and energy-power at the moment of creation. The results still continue in our expanding universe with its enormous marvels. So it is with the divine *Dunamis* (Greek for power), the divine Dynamite in the Church. Without an intimate co-working with the Holy Spirit, there is no spiritual direction in the Christic sense.

## THE ROLE OF THE HUMAN GUIDE

From the primal position of the Paraclete, it follows that human mentors have only a subordinate function, albeit an instrumental one. As docile and faithful members of the Church (we are supposing the normal), moved by the Spirit, directors in turn aid their brothers and sisters in Christ in becoming receptive to the divine light and impulse. What concretely does this mean?

In the directive relationship itself, guides are not primarily teachers in the formal sense. They are not giving a lecture or a course or a homily. Instructing people in general principles, truths, and facts is for the classroom, rostrum, and pulpit. While incidently directors may, and at times must, impart needed information, their main function is to apply general knowledge to a person in a particular set of circumstances according to that person's capacities.

St. John of the Cross rightly saw the role of the human director as teaching an individual how to attain "nudity of spirit," removing all obstacles to the free work of the Spirit. This function makes complete sense once we grant that the Holy Spirit, as principal guide, forces himself on no one. In fact, he is blocked when we place even the smallest of deliberate impediments in his way, however subtle. It becomes evident here why a great deal of knowledge and a keen perception are needed in the director, since detecting the manifold ways we wounded ones resist God is by no means always obvious.

Likewise, the mentor shows the client how to live by faith rather than by mere human norms, and by the divine word rather than by responding to personal preferences. Reluctant as one may be to admit the fact, it does seem that the generality of the human race, the vast majority of whom are theists, are hardly absorbed with the divine will as their supreme norm of decision-making in daily life. "How few there are," notes John Henry Newman, "who live by any other rule than that of their own ease, habit, inclination, as the case may be, on the one hand, and of external circumstances on the other! With how few is the will of God an habitual object of thought, or search, or love, or obedience!"[7]

Since motivation is crucial in the spiritual life as a prime test of authenticity, the individual needs formation in detecting and avoiding self-centered aims. This aspect of spiritual direction involves active purification of the directee, and is part of the role of the director: clearing the way for the divine guide to operate more freely.

In the Christian East, especially in the monastic tradition, spiritual direction involved not only instruction and advice. It was fundamentally a relation of supernatural friendship in which the disciple learned from close observation of the *abba's* way of life. As a Russian text (probably from the eleventh century) put it: having found a holy, God-fearing guide, the directee is admonished to "adhere to him with soul and body; observe his life, his walking, sitting, looking, eating, and examine all his habits; first of all, my son, keep his words, do not let one of them fall to the ground; they are more precious than pearls—the words of the saints."[8]

Participating as it does in the incarnational nature of the Church, spiritual direction also requires that inner experiences be evaluated by an objective guide provided for by the Church's founder. Experience bears out the truth that not only is this sound theology, but also that it corresponds to the felt needs of the faithful. Over and over I have found that people receiving infused prayer and other gifts need a confirming word spoken by an understanding guide. Brilliant and perceptive though she was, even the great Teresa stated her need for the expressed judgment of her confessor to rest at peace that she was not under illusion when she received striking new 'favors' from 'His Majesty.' Inability to find this competent sort of verification is one of the chief frustrations that men and women in our own day point to as an obstacle to growth in a serious prayer life.

From these functions of the director it follows that the holiness being sought is no mere human improvement, no mere psychological achievement. Nor is the path primarily a classification of personality types or analyses of archetypes, Platonic or Jungian. Rather it is a Trinitarian deification (2 Pt 1:4), a transformation from one degree of glory to another into the very image we reflect, a divine image (2 Cor 3:18). This sanctity, and its crowning, is what eye has not seen, nor ear heard (1 Cor 2:9). The directive relationship is a fine tuning of the human harp, that the divine Spirit may play an entirely new and sublime song upon it.

The guidance given, therefore, is no mere private opinion. It must be immersed in the biblical word as that word is understood in the Church that gave birth to the New Testament and for whom the good news was written. It cannot be otherwise, since the same Holy Spirit who inspired the Scriptures is the primary director of the individual soul. Since such guidance is not just one opinion among many, it follows that the directee must weigh it seriously and apply it appropriately.

## THE ROLE OF CHURCH AUTHORITY

If there is anything foreign to the spirit and letter of biblical thinking, it is a rugged individualism based on a secular worldview. What we have intimated in a sketchy way we now explore more thoroughly, namely that spiritual direction is unabashedly other-worldly. It reckons with this world, surely, and it is sensitive to social questions, of course, but it sees everything in a divine light (Ps 36:9), in the light of the Radiant Image of the Father (Heb 1:1-3). And since this Radiant Splendor chose to teach and guide through his Church, spiritual direction after his mind operates only within the magisterium, the church authority which he established.

It has been rightly said that truth is symphonic. Like a symphony orchestra in which one discordant musician disrupts the whole and leads to a musical muddle if not corrected, so also a Christlike care of souls must play according to the Master's score and under his baton. The Lord has chosen to commit both the score and its interpretation into the hands of his teaching Church: "Go into the whole word and teach... as the Father sent me, so I send you... what you bind and loose I bind and loose... he who hears you, hears me... I am with you all days even to the end of the world" (Mt 28:19-20; Jn 20:21; Mt 18:18; Lk 10:16).

This is awesome authority, no doubt about it. So awesome, as a matter of fact, that it is perhaps the chief reason for the world's rejection of the Catholic Church. That mere men would dare to speak as though standing in the place of God himself seems unbelievably brash. But Peter and his colleagues in union with him can claim nothing less—nor can anyone else consistently think otherwise who does not pick and choose among the sayings of the Lord.

Biblical criticism in our century makes clear that often the textual message can be understood in contrary ways. Rare is the text on which the commentators are agreed as to its meaning. If that strikes the reader as an overstatement, I merely invite him or her to read widely among Protestant and Catholic exegetes. One of the former, E. Kasemann, has noted: "It seems to me safer to walk through a minefield blindfolded. Is it possible to forget for a second that we are daily concerned with a flood of doubtful, even abstruse ideas in the fields of exegesis, history, and theology, and that our scholarship has gradually degenerated into a world-wide guerilla warfare?"[9] Joseph Ratzinger adds that "historical research has done away with the Reformation idea that Scripture itself has one clear meaning...."[10]

Those, therefore, are innocent both of history and of biblical scholarship who suppose that they may securely interpret Sacred Scripture by themselves alone. They are wandering into a minefield at midnight. The New Testament is *the* book of the Church. It was written by her first leaders and for her members through all the ages. It can be securely understood only by the teaching office to which the task has been committed by the Lord himself: "I am with you all days even to the end of the world" (Mt 28:20).

The ministry of teaching and guiding in the first-century Church was always carried on in the context of the official proclamation, not aside from it. Vigorously indeed did St. Paul hurl anathemas toward the innovators in Galatia who dared to proclaim a gospel other than what the Church proclaimed (Gal 1:6-9). Timothy was frequently admonished to protect and proclaim "sound doctrine," correcting those who deviated from it. He was forewarned that the time was sure to come when people would be avid for novel ideas and eager to collect for themselves a whole series of teachers according to their own tastes (1 and 2 Tm; especially 2 Tm 4:1-5).

Any candid and informed observer, secular or religious, readily recognizes how prominent this craving for theological, psychological, and social novelty is in our day. And in this field of spiritual direction the abundance of private and conflicting opinions is everywhere to be seen. What is probably most disturbing is that few people are concerned by the welter of contradictory views. If there is anything incompatible with the mind of Jesus and his apostolic circle, it is this relativistic and minimalistic atmosphere in which we live and breathe. For them the indispensable root of instruction and guidance is the sound doctrine so often insisted upon in the pastoral letters to Timothy and Titus.

The Catholic Church is certainly not a democracy. She does not teach according to the latest polls. But she is not a dictatorship either. The first occupant of the papal office (or one of his followers) explicitly ruled out the dictatorial approach to leadership: no one may be forced to accept truth (1 Pt 5:3). Yet, we may still ask why the Church is not democratic in her teaching role—as she is in many practical procedures. The fundamental reason is identical to why no classroom is democratic in the work of instruction. University professors are as dogmatic as the pope and bishops when they claim to be dealing with truth. No chemist would accept the idea that water has no hydrogen in it. No geographer would agree with an assertion that Sydney is a suburb of Singapore. In a grammar school, there are not five correct ways to spell the same word. No teacher takes a poll to resolve disagreements about arithmetic among the pupils.

The poll approach to religion and morality is shot through with a philosophical relativism (which is not Einstein's physical theory) that rejects objective truth. By definition, truth is the conformity of mind with reality. I possess truth when I know that Sydney is on the southeast coast of Australia and that water is made up of hydrogen and oxygen. As soon as one accepts a final, objective divine revelation, one logically accepts an authoritative teacher and guardian of it. No one leaves a treasure uncared for. Thus, there can be no naïve declaration that "I am led by the Spirit" alone. Spiritual direction can flourish only when it is solidly grounded in the ecclesial community to which that revelation has been committed. We approach the guiding task not by promoting our private opinions but through the Father of lights (Jas 1:17), who gave his Spirit to the Church to bring her into all the truth (Jn 14:26; 16:13).

# WHAT SPIRITUAL DIRECTION IS NOT

To say that a grapefruit is not a pineapple and that contemplation is not meditation is not to belittle either the fruit or discursive prayer. To say that Christian spiritual direction is not a number of other enterprises often confused with it is not automatically to downgrade these other efforts to improve the human situation and to solve problems. With this in mind, we now treat more specifically what spiritual direction is not.

**1. Therapy and interpersonal problem resolution.** Experienced spiritual directors know that frequently they meet in their work individual psychological problems and interpersonal tensions, the latter often accompanied with conflicts. Emotional difficulties range from passing but troublesome episodes in a person's life to mild and at times severe neuroses and psychoses, while tensions and conflicts are found in differing degrees in all states of life. Knowing when one may be of some help and when a professional referral is indicated is one of the many skills that make up a director's competency. However, therapy is not strictly to be included in what through the centuries has been called pastoral care or spiritual direction. Hence, we do not envision as within the scope of this volume activities such as attempting to resolve emotional problems through clinical means. A director does not, of course, rule out mention of these sorts of problems when they exist. One may, if competent, even touch upon them. But essentially they are not the director's task.

**2. Psychological paradigms and analyses.** Here we will mention several contemporary approaches sometimes seen as retreat and guidance aids. We refer to, among others, Jungian analyses of 'spirituality,' the Progoff intensive journaling process, the Sufi enneagram system of personality types and their relationships, and dream 'spirituality.' Some people favor one or the other of these enterprises, while others are indifferent or even hostile to them. In any event the Gospel does not suggest anything resembling them. What we can be sure of is that if the counseling is based on little more than humanly conceived paradigms and analyses, it is not Christic spiritual direction.

**3. Oriental programs and techniques.** Eastern asceticism and a reaching out for the transcendent are praiseworthy testimonies to the human spirit's ultimate dissatisfaction with anything that the material world has to offer. Yet, these two factors in the spiritual life of a Buddhist are vastly different from Gospel self-denial and our consequent transformation "into the same image from glory to glory," an immersion into the Triune God himself (2 Cor 3:18, NAB). It follows, therefore, that Zen techniques and instructions for the attainment of *satori* (enlightenment) and enterprises such as *vipassana* meditation have little to do with our formation. The latter concerns aiding people, through instruction and the workings of God's grace, toward a deepening embrace of the living God revealed in the Radiant Image of the Father, the Incarnate Word. Our contemplation is neither an impersonal and neutral awareness nor a vague oneness with the universe, but an utterly interpersonal and loving encounter with Father, Son, and Spirit dwelling in the deep recesses of our being.

**4. Extremist ideologies.** Every error has a kernel of truth hidden within it. The historical problem of heresy is usually not with the kernel but with a ballooning exaggeration that obscures other truths which, if considered, would put the whole picture into proper perspective and clear up erroneous conclusions. The environment is important, for example, and creation is breathtakingly beautiful. But 'creation-centered spirituality' is no more than a superstition, if one takes the three words seriously. A spiritual being who centers on creation is, if consistent, at best a pantheist. But even pantheism is essentially a form of atheism. If followers of this ideology really do not take the three words at face value, one should suggest they choose a different term to represent their views. In any event, Christian spirituality is thoroughly God-centered.

Radical feminism likewise has its kernel of truth. Only too often women have been, and not rarely still are, badly treated by some men. Often, yes, but not always and everywhere—certainly not in the fanciful ways an ideologue imagines lurking behind every bush. No human can live without a god, so it is not surprising that when extremist feminists deny the authority of Scripture and the Church, they may end up venerating instead—how seriously, one can only wonder—the female goddesses within. Hence, programs, conferences, and workshops aimed at 'empowering women' to demand their 'rights' and at exploring almost any issue by 'probing their experiences' are not suitable material for realistic spiritual direction. Especially is this clear to men and women who accept a normative divine revelation and who look to the Virgin Mother of God, the human person's 'solitary boast,' as a model.

**5. First cousins.** We shall detail in a coming chapter a demanding list of qualifications required in a competent spiritual director—one who is able to deal in a professional and wise way with the almost endless number of diverse questions that can and do arise. If, however, we think of men and women who can, in one way or another, be of some help to others on the way to God, but who are not trained adequately to handle the whole range of complex issues that often do come up, we speak of what we may call first cousins to spiritual directors.

Here we envision, for example, priests who are trained to evaluate moral matters in the Sacrament of Reconciliation, but who do not understand well the higher reaches of total Gospel living, including infused contemplation and the conditions requisite for growing to the summit of it. Also included as first cousins are those who direct days of prayer and retreats for individuals on a one-to-one basis. Direction here would mean suggesting biblical texts for meditation and perhaps discussing them afterwards with the retreatant. If such guides do not stray beyond their competence, the relationship can be beneficial, but this is not spiritual direction in the full sense.

A third type of cousin is the 'soul companion,' a friend with whom one shares informally about matters pertaining to journeying with and toward God. It is, of course, difficult in some cases to distinguish a soul companion from a spiritual director. St. Thérèse of Lisieux surely shared frequently and deeply with her sister Pauline while they were both still living in their parents' home. It would appear that the latter at least came very close to being a spiritual director for her little sister.

Nor may we forget holy parents who impart to their children the first instructions in the faith and offer to them their initial bits of spiritual guidance: how to pray; how to overcome selfishness and quarreling and dishonesty; why and how to be just, pure, and patient. Later on these God-fearing mothers and fathers lead their teenage offspring by both example and word to a deepening prayer life. They are spiritual directors in helping sons and daughters to cope with peer pressures, to look at vocational choices with the eyes of God, to relate with the opposite sex in a chaste and respectful manner, to be industrious in work, and universal in their social and mission outlooks.

## WHO DOES THE DIRECTING?

Given the biblical concept of supernatural guidance and its ecclesial character as a development in the New Testament, we now inquire about the appropriateness of non-official mentors. If one must be a priest to participate in the binding and loosing, in the teaching and sanctifying powers committed by Jesus to his Church, what do we make of non-clerics who clearly have engaged in this role in the history of the Catholic Church? What of St. Teresa of Avila who was the spiritual mentor of her married brother Lorenzo and of one or more bishops who came to her for guidance in their spiritual lives? Indeed, what may we say of the direction she gave to her own nuns, and what of the large number of formation personnel up to our own day who are similarly engaged on behalf of candidates for the consecrated life of sisters and brothers?

To be consistent with what we have already noted, and shall further on say about qualifications for this duty, we will now suppose adequate training and competency, even if it is informally acquired.

In this regard, it should be kept in mind that a degree does not guarantee competence nor does lack of a degree imply incompetence. As will be brought out in Chapter Five, a judgment of fitness must be based on other criteria as well.

A brief historical excursus into the practice of 'manifestation of conscience' may be helpful.[11] This was a practice of making known to a superior or director one's inner life: aspirations, motivations, temptations, thoughts and desires, weaknesses and strengths, sins and acts of virtue, and movements of grace. As extrasacramental the manifestation of conscience began as an ascetical practice and was incorporated into early monastic and religious rules, first as a means to personal growth and then also as a benefit to communal life. In the nineteenth century the Catholic Church began to regulate and then finally to abolish the obligatory or elicited manifestation, but she has encouraged the practice in its free, spontaneous form.

The supposition behind this encouragement is that the recipient of the manifestation is competent in moral and spiritual matters. Because of his training the priest is the person primarily envisioned, but history, past and present, makes clear that some lay men and women can and do also possess the required gifts and expertise. In addition to St. Teresa we recall other non-sacerdotal saints like Francis of Assisi and Catherine of Siena who adopted this practice.[12]

The reader may have noticed that in this discussion of non-official spiritual directors we are not distinguishing between male and female. Aside from some matters requiring priestly guidance, neither theology nor history suggests that gender is a factor for exclusion. Nor should we forget that even though non-official directors lack the binding and loosing power of the Church, they do possess an ecclesiality as long as they offer guidance within the faith community and according to the Church's teaching and discipline. The central condition is competence in moral and spiritual matters.

At the same time individual preferences are to be taken into account. Many people, both men and women, prefer a priest-director, if one can be found. Others prefer a woman. In any event, the basic qualification is genuine fitness for the task, whether the mentor is male or female.

## GOALS: WHAT SHOULD BE HAPPENING?

The aims of Christian direction flow first of all from the content of divine revelation, and second, from the instrumental role of the human guide as we explained it at the beginning of this chapter.

The general purpose of spiritual direction is identical with that of the whole economy of salvation, aiding the directee to love God with the whole heart, soul, and mind, and the neighbor as oneself (Lk 10:27). This double love leads one to be filled with the utter fullness of Triune beauty (Eph 3:19-20), a splendor so magnificent that eye has seen nothing like it, nor can we faintly imagine its grandeur (1 Cor 2:9). Ultimately this issues in eternal life, the unending ecstasy of the beatific vision in the risen body (Jn 6:56; 1 Jn 3:2).

In their particular and instrumental role, human directors cooperate with the Holy Spirit in helping directees to live concretely as the saints live. One helps to further the inner order in a disciple's life, for as William of St. Thierry noted, "A man of undisciplined mind is a multitude even when he is alone."[13] One points the way to purification, active and passive, and thus shows the disciple how to break the mesh of selfish clingings, most of which, in a sincere person, are subtle and at first unnoticed. The director helps concretize the Pauline admonition to do everything for the divine glory and thus to avoid making little gods of our needs and preferences. The director explains also the passive purifications resulting from infused prayer as they are experienced by the directee: first to recognize their appearance and then how to respond to their reality.

All of this is simply to say that the Christian director, as distinguished from all other counselors and gurus, is forming the disciple to a total love for God, to an abundant life in him (Jn 10:10). The director applies the biblical purifying word to this unique person (1 Pt 1:22), advising the directee how to give up all one possesses (Lk 14:33), to be content with necessities and to be rid of superfluities (1 Tm 6:7-8), to die like a grain of wheat in the earth (Jn 12:24), to surrender everything that does not lead to God (Ti 2:12). In other words a Christocentric and Gospel-led mentor enables the directee to be led by the primary director, the Holy

Spirit (Rom 8:14), not by egoistic inclinations. This is St. Paul's spiritual revolution (Eph 4:23).

On occasion the director gives counsel about interpersonal problems regarding marriage, the religious life, or the workplace. However, the primary focus is on the directee becoming a "new creation," the setting aside of the old and the putting on of Christ (Eph 4:21-24).

Further, faithful directors are a source of comfort and strength to their charges in the face of the criticisms of the world and the rejection that is sure to come to those who live in devotion to Christ (2 Tm 3:12). Because the world hates the Church as it first hated her founder (Jn 17:14), and whereas it is eager to listen to those who dissent from her teaching (1 Jn 4:5-6), mentors help their disciples discern when the Spirit is and is not speaking. Directors urge fidelity to what is right, not to what is expedient or popular, because it is God's will. That obedience may call for willingness to suffer and even to die for truth and right, as did Maria Goretti and Thomas More.

Directors, therefore, in the spirit of the Gospel householder, draw from the Church's treasure both what is new and what is old (Mt 13:52). They use evangelical wisdom of the centuries, applying it to the new problems and the unique circumstances of the disciples with whom they are working. Always the focus is on the Savior, who "is the same yesterday, today, and forever" (Heb 13:8), who is always the norm, the unsurpassable model, the way, the truth, and the life (Jn 14:6). Hans Urs von Balthasar has remarked that "Jesus' non-inventability, his overwhelming originality... of itself demands assent and effects submission."[14] Being the Radiant Image of the Father's glory, he is himself the prodigious proof of his message and his mission. He is the focal point of all spiritual direction.

We may say that the director aims at furthering progress toward heroic virtues, but according to the present readiness of the directee. Together they prepare to meet the all-holy God face-to-face in the eternal enthrallment of direct vision in risen body.

# FOUR

# Do I Need
# Spiritual Direction?

G IVEN THAT EACH OF US goes to God through the agency of fellow humans, in and through the Church, it would appear that the questioning title of this chapter is clearly to be decided in the affirmative.

Yes, so it seems. However, the matter is not quite that simple. On the one hand both mediation and ecclesiality are mandatory. As we have seen, no one pleases God in attempting a rugged individualism by going it alone without the benefit of available spiritual direction. On the other hand, we have not adequately answered the question of whether one-on-one guidance is necessary or even practical.

We must indeed be taught and sanctified in and by the Church, but may we not—at least some of us—be sufficiently sanctified and taught as one of a group? After all, isn't it enough if we are one parishioner among many at Sunday Mass? Must we have a private mentor as well? Given the sheer number of potential directees and the dearth of competent guides, isn't that a plain impossibility?

If we respond to the necessity question affirmatively, we may further ask what kind of personal guidance is needed. Is an informal chat sufficient? How often is this help to be offered? Once a year? Every month? Is the personal advice occasionally given within the Sacrament of Reconciliation adequate? Do age and spiritual maturity make any difference regarding the need for one-on-one guidance? As we grow in the ways of the Lord, as we imbibe the biblical word and learn more about the outlook of the saints, as our liturgical and contemplative prayer deepen, it would seem that our questions become fewer and our need to consult less frequent.

Is, therefore, spiritual direction truly necessary? An unqualified answer, affirmative or negative, will not do. To respond properly requires that we first consider God's word and then look to the mind of the saints. In that light we will go on to examine some of the specific needs of those who are seriously pursuing God.

## THE IMPORTANCE OF SACRED SCRIPTURE

God's mind is not transparent to us. St. Paul asserts that human wisdom is foolishness to the divine mind (1 Cor 1:20). Even though the Lord is purest light in himself, yet he dwells in light inaccessible, endlessly beyond our intellects (1 Tm 6:16).

Not only is God's inner Triune nature and his plan for our salvation beyond our capacity either to discover before they are revealed to us or to understand fully by revelation, but so are many details of his providential workings in each person's life. Although the visible universe appears completely clear to the casual observer, it encompasses marvels as awesome as tiny atoms and living cells to enormous galaxies and distant quasars hurtling away from us at incomprehensible velocities. The God of nature and of supernature is one and the same, and the latter creation is far more mysterious than the former.

Happily, this Lord has spoken to us, most especially in his Word become incarnate in our flesh. He continues to speak in the Church sent by the Son: "He who hears you, hears me." But in addition to the official proclamations of this Church, Scripture sees as necessary the individualized advice one wise person can offer to another.

Members of the community who are immersed in the word of Christ are to instruct and admonish one another in all wisdom (Col 3:16). How we are to view things and how we are to live in a holy manner are not considered to be obvious. We need wise instruction and counsel. If among the elders we find a perceptive person, we should become attached to him or her and be willing to be taught. If we love to listen, we learn and become insightful and prudent (Sir 6:32-34). So eager should we be for sound counsel that the sage advises us: "If you see a man of understanding, visit him early, let your feet wear out his doorstep" (Sir 6:36). Beautiful and consoling is the reward promised to the teacher of truth and the guide to holiness: "The learned will shine as brightly as the vault of heaven, and those who have instructed many in virtue, as bright as stars for all eternity" (Dn 12:3).

## MIND OF THE SAINTS

The saints exemplify the biblical idea of mediation, of finding lights and inspiration and encouragement from co-pilgrims, especially from those whose wisdom derives from their closeness to God. Perhaps the main problem the desert hermits in the first Christian centuries encountered was the large number of people from towns and cities who sought them out as masters of the spiritual life. Men and women who are earnest about a deep prayer life instinctively know they need enlightenment.

So the saints advise them. St. Francis de Sales told Philothea that finding someone to guide her in the spiritual life was the most important advice he could offer her. He then went on to mention saints who practiced and advised obedience to a wise confessor-director: Saints Catherine of Siena, Elizabeth the princess, Louis of France, and Teresa of Avila. Francis considered a guide for one's soul the biblical "faithful friend," one's treasure who is a powerful defense (Sir 6:14-16).[1]

Fiery St. Bernard was of the view that bishops (not to mention monks and lay people) need advice not only in matters pertaining to their episcopal duties but also in their private lives. An archbishop, recognizing the saint's holiness and genius, asked him to write a book of guidance for bishops. This Bernard did, but at the same time he did not hesitate to offer basic spiritual direction suited to a prelate. We may note in this connection that canon law in our own day requires that major superiors of religious orders as well as bishops seek guidance from a group of advisors. Although this counsel would not usually deal with personal matters, when these leaders submit their personal conduct to a confessor it does concern their own private lives.

The author of the *Imitation of Christ* likewise insisted on the need we have to be guided by another in the ways of God: "Consult with a wise and conscientious man, and seek rather to be instructed by one who is better than to follow thine own inventions."[2] We should not open our hearts to just anyone. But we should treat of our affairs with a wise person who fears God.[3] St. John of the Cross held firmly to the necessity of spiritual direction: "A disciple without a master to lead the way is like a single burning coal—he grows colder rather than hotter."[4] Using another image, John remarks that one without a competent guide is like a blind person: he will take the wrong road and get lost on the way.[5]

Because she was aware of the extravagant errors of the illuminists and also of the aberrations of well-meaning people, St. Teresa made a point of seeking and following direction in all matters pertaining to her relationship with God. Once she had the assurance of her confessor or a theologian about the validity of her prayer experiences, she was at ease. Obtaining their confirmation, she would remark "puts me very much at peace now, although I understand that as long as God leads me by this path I must not trust myself in anything. So I have always consulted others, even though I find it difficult."[6] What she did herself Teresa advised to others. They are to do everything they can to find someone who can give them light. They are to have no secrets from their director in whatever pertains to their spiritual life—no matter how sublime their contemplation may be.[7]

Yet a problem remains. Sincere people well advanced in prayer may tend to feel less need to seek advice. This is not to say that they perceive no need at all, but somewhat less than they previously did. As one religious put it to me: "Personally, I have found that direction was more important and necessary to me in youth. Now that I am older, I have imbibed to a certain extent what is necessary for me to live a life of dedication to God, and it seems to me I only have to get on with it, except for times of unusual occurrences which would lead me to have recourse to more specific direction."

This makes sense, and it has in its support no less an authority than St. Bonaventure, mystic, theologian, and doctor. This saint, notes K.A. Wall, "thought that those who had themselves the gift of discernment of spirits did not need it. However, he was convinced that there were few such souls and that most individuals needed spiritual guidance at least in the initial stages of their advance to perfection."[8]

What should we think, then, of men and women who are easily persuaded that they are doing well and are inclined to coast along, assuming that God alone is their guide? Do these not need accountability as well as advice? Yes, they surely do—and especially they. St. Thérèse remarked that the Lord was her director, but very few people live on her level of self-renouncement and burn with her degree of divine love. Yet even Thérèse received and welcomed a great deal of guidance from her sister Pauline, later Mother Agnes. Nor would she decline to practice what we now take up.

## DISCLOSURE OF THOUGHTS

Manifestation of one's inner life to the superior or to one so appointed was a common requirement in early eastern monasticism, both male and female. St. Theodore the Studite (died 826) argued that just as "God knows everything and nothing is hidden from his sight, but all things are naked and unveiled before him, so must I (your hegumen and father) also know you."[9] This was not principally the confession of sin, which was a matter of priestly absolution, but of humbly making known the inner movements of the heart: inclinations, temptations, promptings, and aspirations. One reason for the practice was psychological, to undo what we would now term the damage deriving from repression. Another was religious, the need for discernment from an older, more experienced guide. Similar stories were told of the blunders and extravagant actions of religious enthusiasts who failed to submit their ideas to a mentor and to welcome instruction, admonition, and healing. Scary tales could be told in our day as well. A third reason for the revelation of thoughts was self-denial—giving up our native insistence on doing what we want to do. The path to this self-abnegation was obedience to one's guide, the submission of one's will to the *abba* or *amma*.

Hence, it was considered extremely unwise to select as director a person who would readily approve of one's own natural inclinations. Irénée Hausherr observes in this connection: "A true zeal for perfection on the contrary, leads one to prefer a spiritual father who is demanding, energetic, and not to be manipulated."[10] He adds that the best director is the one who best succeeds in bringing about this surrender of the directee's will, for it is like a wall between the soul and God. There is no doubt that we do not see ourselves fully as we actually are, that we need someone more objective who can detect what we easily miss, who can teach and heal what is amiss. We must deny ourselves daily to be the Lord's disciples, as he himself insisted (Lk 9:23; 14:33).

If we tacitly cling to doing what we want to do—especially when our desires gravitate toward the easy road leading toward worldly compromise—and yet seek a spiritual director who will not disturb or challenge us, we are under no minor illusion. The individual who has no intention of giving up self-will, remarks Hausherr, "deceives himself into believing that he has been or is searching for a spiritual father. What he seeks is complicity."[11]

## AREAS OF SPECIAL NEED

In many areas of human life, it is one thing to read a manual of instruction and quite another to apply it rightly in concrete circumstances. Hence, tradesmen have apprentices, the military provides boot camps, medical schools have residency programs for interns, and novice teachers practice their new profession under the eye of an experienced instructor. Lecture, study, and examinations are indispensable in the learning process, but they are not enough.

Given the intricacies of human psychology and woundedness, beginners in the spiritual life are likely to have special need of the guiding expertise of a master. Solid homilies in the parish, faithful instruction in school, spiritual reading, and regular retreats are no doubt important aids, but guided application is likewise necessary. It may be useful to suggest with several illustrations how people need personalized applications of what they may have heard in homilies or read in books. In Chapters Eight, Nine, and Ten these matters will be dealt with in greater detail.

**Guidance in spiritual reading.** Occasionally we come across an article or bibliography offering a more or less lengthy list of books recommended as a program of spiritual reading. If the list is confined to the very best, it has undoubted value, but often it is not so limited. Usually the longer the listing, the less is its worth. The inclusion of mediocre works in an extended list, along with possibly damaging ones, exposes the uninitiated to unnecessary reading, if not to positive harm.

Furthermore, one simply cannot wisely suggest a program suitable for everyone. Needs vary according to readiness and growth, and people often unwittingly neglect what they most need. Some choose titles according to advertising claims and a spirit of 'relevance,' while others avoid classics because of disinterest or antipathy.

Then there is the obvious but neglected fact that beginners in the spiritual life—even at times the veterans—simply do not know how to distinguish which among the thousands of 'spiritual books' that appear each decade are excellent or mediocre or harmful. The need for direction in reading is so crucial we shall devote considerable attention to it in Chapter Seven.

**Detecting mediocrity or inner weakness.** Were it a knowing being, lukewarm water would hardly perceive that it is "neither hot nor cold" (Rv 3:15). So also in human affairs progress cannot be ascertained except in terms of some norm of excellence. Whether it be tennis or basketball, scholarship or medicine, music or law, philosophy or theology, performance is evaluated in terms of the best. In matters religious, the Incarnate Word of the Father is the supreme norm.

Yet, there are more than a few people in our churches on Sunday morning who are quite satisfied with their moral and religious behavior. Polls report high percentages of the general population who feel they are clearly on the path to heaven, and few who fear the possibility of hell. These people may be well-mannered and respectable and decent in their conduct. But they regard thirsting after God and the holiness of the saints as visionary, high-flown, romantic, perhaps even fanatic, and certainly not required of themselves. Newman wrote of these men and women, "They have a certain definite and clear view of their duties; they think that the summit of perfection is to be decent and respectable in their calling, to enjoy moderately the pleasures of life, to eat and drink, marry and give in marriage, and buy and sell, and plant and build, and to take care that religion does not *engross* them."[12]

One may say that their standard of concern with God and their own eternal destiny is a refined mediocrity, surely nothing resembling an absorbing pursuit of God as "the one thing necessary." Not realizing what saintliness is, nor having scarcely a clue to the normalcy of deep prayer, not entertaining a serious suspicion that the Gospel calls *them* to heroic virtue and total love, nor that there is any such thing as the universal call to holiness, mediocre people are often unaware of their plight. They desperately need a spiritual director or an alert confessor. Unfortunately, they are among the last to seek the very guidance they need, which is part of their mediocrity.

To those who have no difficulty agreeing with this, it still may come as a surprise that even fervent people profit from an outsider's assessment of the condition of their spiritual lives. The inner workings of our personalities with their strengths and weaknesses, our character traits with their pluses and minuses, our motivations both conscious and unconscious, are to some extent opaque to our own self-perception. Serious people, too, though to a lesser degree, can fail to see where they may be striving beyond their present strength or holding back when they could give more. Competent direction can enlighten them and help them to remain on course.

**Handling periods of difficult, dry prayer.** If there is anything religiously-minded people commonly—indeed almost universally—do not understand on their way to God, it is the dark 'nights' of sense and spirit. Their problem is often not the theoretical explanation, but the practical application: "Does it apply to *me?*" Over and over again in retreat work, I have explained dry, distracted, purifying prayer only to find that most people cannot securely apply the message to themselves. They are intelligent and good-willed. Many grasp what has been said and wish to do whatever is needful to grow. But rarely do they feel confident that they may fit the message to their own situation. They need the guidance of a competent master.

Then there are others who despite what they have heard and read cannot distinguish the healthy and apparent 'emptiness' which is a blessing, from a real emptiness due to selfish clingings which is a cause for alarm. These latter need enlightenment in addition to application.

**Doing penance: types and extent:** A common sign of generosity with God is the desire to make satisfaction for one's own sins and for those of others. Especially in need of guidance are those who have undergone a deep conversion. In their zeal they may tend to be excessive in making reparation for the past. While there are people who need a spur to do even a minimum of penance—and hence need encouragement in that direction—others may attempt a self-denial beyond their strength and present readiness. We can find in a good book the general principles undergirding satisfaction for sin, but a director aids an individual to steer a prudent, yet generous course.

**Carefully moderating enthusiasm for extraordinary phenomena.** While religiously minded people often perceive a need for guidance in their pursuit of God, perhaps the most acutely felt need occurs among those who have been converted from a life of serious sin or from mediocrity. The former are often enough confused as to where to turn and what to do, while the latter need both encouragement and enlightenment. There is a third group that decidedly needs guidance, even if they are unaware of it. I refer to men and women who feed on excitements of various types: outlandish liturgies, for example; or claims that this seer or that one is in contact with heaven, usually in the person of Our Lady. Not only do these 'seers' need direction, but so do those who flock to them, who avidly read everything about alleged locutions or visions, who build their spiritual lives on the latest reports of what the Mother of Jesus is supposed to have said.

Part of the problem here is that many of these people tend either not to seek guidance about the alleged phenomena or to disregard the advice if it runs counter to their personal convictions. Most likely this type of situation is precisely why St. John of the Cross seems to come down so hard on those who think they have supernatural visitations and either make much of them or refuse to let go of them when instructed to do so. They are likely to believe almost any claim to a supernatural intervention, whether it be a message or a cure or some other miracle. What they resist believing is that just possibly they may be mistaken.

There is no doubt that locutions, visions, and miracles have occurred in history and still do occur. There is ample solid evidence through twenty centuries to justify the authentic ones. Yet illusions are also common, as St. John of the Cross stressed. How one can sort out authentic happenings from illusions is not at the moment to our purpose, but what is to the point is that people who are keenly interested in extraordinary happenings clearly need to find a sound guide and follow the counsel given to them.[13] The author of the classic *Cloud of Unknowing* was clear. "I must warn you," he wrote, "that a young novice, unseasoned by experience in contemplation, is liable to great deception unless he is constantly alert and honest enough to seek reliable guidance."[14] Remarking about "treachery according to the different mentalities and dispositions of those deceived," the author goes on to observe that "the devil has his contemplatives as surely as God has his."[15]

**Discerning a vocation.** Given that a divine call is precisely that, a vocation, an invitation from God—not simply a career choice of "what I want to do in life"—and given, further, that the signs of the call are by no means clear to many young men and women, it follows that both recognizing and responding to the call require wisdom and counsel. The Ignatian thirty-day retreat can be especially helpful in discerning the divine vocation in one's life. So is the aid of a competent and prayerful mentor whether within or without a retreat setting.

**Detecting shadings among virtues and vices.** In the common estimation virtues are readily distinguished from vices: honesty from fraud, justice from corruption, chastity from lust, humility from vanity, modesty from arrogance. True as this is, there are also moral excellences that can on the surface bear a close resemblance to opposite faults. A reasonable care for health can easily shade off into pampering the body. Honest recreation is readily extended into idle chatter. Praiseworthy zeal for the apostolate can slowly issue in a neglect of prayer. Evangelical frugality is light years apart from miserliness, just as prayerful and altruistic solitude is 180 degrees different from egoistic isolation. In his biography of John Henry Newman, Ian Ker perceptively notes that "sensitivity may be as much a virtue as insensitivity is a vice—even though it is as hard at times to distinguish it in practice from hypersensitivity, as it is difficult to differentiate in particular cases between courage and recklessness, tolerance and weakness, generosity and extravagance, kindness and indulgence."[16] One can readily recognize here the need for and benefit of skilled counsel in discerning these differences.

**Identifying psychological problems.** While spiritual directors should not dabble at being psychotherapists, in the nature of things they are bound to meet more than a few clients burdened with emotional problems. People more or less severely wounded by a stormy or loveless early home life or by the vicissitudes of adult existence can profit from spiritual direction. From a competent guide, they can receive a reference when the seriousness of the problem warrants professional help. When the difficulty does not require referral, direction itself may serve to alleviate or correct what is amiss. In both cases the client can learn how to be integrated as a whole person, because sound spirituality is sound psychology.

**Assessing progress or the lack of it.** The axiom, "we are not good judges in our own case," applies well to the evaluation of one's own spiritual condition. Beginners especially tend to equate fervor with feelings rather than with unspectacular fidelity to duty. The crucial importance of Jesus' principle, "By their fruits you will know them" (Mt 7:20), often does not register. Theoretically, we can see with a few moments' reflection the validity, indeed the brilliance, of Jesus' norm. But experience shows that many people simply do not see the practical ways of applying it to their own progress in prayer and holiness. A skilled guide supplies realism.

**Providing support and accountability.** To the specific benefits deriving from spiritual direction, we may add one general advantage: its response to our human need for encouragement and prodding along the hard road and through the narrow gate. *The Imitation of Christ,* hardly a book inclined to promote spiritual softness, observes that in more severe temptations we should "often take counsel" and thus find comfort in the trial.[17] In commenting on Galatians 6:2, where St. Paul admonishes us to bear one another's burdens, the author notes, "No man is without his burden; no man sufficient for himself; no man wise enough for himself: but we must support one another, comfort one another, assist, instruct and admonish one another."[18]

While still a teenager and after his conversion experience, John Henry Newman already perceived a need to submit in docile obedience his resolution to give up dances and other worldly amusements. Submitting a resolve to another is a type of accountability which brings with it a stimulation to fidelity, even when the encouragement is unspoken.

A related benefit of direction accrues to the procrastinator who puts off until later what in the depths of the heart he or she knows should be done now: "When I retire I'll attend to contemplative prayer and spiritual reading.... Later on I will search for God in earnest, give up my superfluities, work seriously on my faults. After all, I am healthy and probably will live a good while yet." There may be intent to do good for others, but always it is a project in the nebulous future: "I know I should contribute more to parish activities and help with the RCIA program, but I am so busy. Later I may have more time." Procrastinators in these and other ways need the spur, the stimulus of accountability.

In simple terms the importance of spiritual direction flows from the unspeakable worth, the eternal treasure, that a human person is. Destined to be enthralled without end by gazing on the Father, the Son, and the Spirit and thus transfigured into divine beauty,[19] one individual man, woman, or child is diocese enough—as St. Francis de Sales remarked when someone wondered how a busy bishop could give time to spiritual direction on a one-to-one basis. Newman was of the view that the most useful people in the church are not the leaders but the teachers, and the latter not so much due to their writings as to their instruction.[20] His appreciation of the value of interpersonal influence was clear also in his unpopular insistence that as a tutor at Oxford he be strongly involved in the moral and spiritual formation of his charges.

If God takes the trouble to create us one by one in his own image and likeness (Gn 1:26), and if Jesus died for us as individuals (Gal 2:20), and if in receiving one child we receive him (Mk 9:37), we surely should aid one another on a one-to-one basis insofar as we are able. Pope John Paul II remarked that God in imprinting his own image on the human person thereby confers "on him an incomparable dignity."[21] It is a dignity that deserves individualized, custom-made attention. In his encyclical on evangelization, Pope Paul VI penned what must be one of the most eloquent apprecia-tions of the importance of spiritual direction:

Side-by-side with the collective proclamation of the Gospel, the other form of transmission, the person-to-person one, remains valid and important. The Lord often used it (for example with Nicodemus, Zaccheus, the Samaritan woman, Simon the Pharisee) and so did the Apostles. In the long run, is there any other way of handing on the Gospel than by transmitting to another person one's personal experience of faith? It must not happen that the pressing need to proclaim the Good News to the multitudes should cause us to forget this form of proclamation whereby an individual's personal conscience is reached and touched by an entirely unique word that he receives from someone else. We can never sufficiently praise those priests who through the Sacrament of Penance or through pastoral dialogue show their readiness to guide people in the ways of the Gospel, to support them in their efforts, to raise them up if they have fallen, and always to assist them with discernment and availability.[22]

It would be difficult to put the significance of spiritual direction more pointedly or more gracefully. The individual directee is to be "touched by an entirely unique word" spoken by the mentor as to no other, a word that would not precisely fit another human person at that time with exactly the same nuance of meaning. That observation leads us naturally to our next chapter and suggests its import.

# FIVE

# Spiritual Directors: Ideal and Real

C ENTURIES OLD and seemingly intractable is the problem we take up in this chapter. Theoretically it should be easy to solve if only we make up our minds to do it, but practically it is not. Human beings tend to search and struggle to find ways to satisfy deeply felt needs. That there is among many sincere people a thirst for God and a serious prayer life is scarcely debatable.

Responses to lectures, retreats, and writings received from earnest lay people, religious, and priests, have in recent years made it clear to me that not a few are repeating in their own words the impassioned longing for God expressed by the psalmist: "With all my heart I seek you" (Ps 119:10, NAB). In ordinary parishes and religious convents—as well as in a federal prison where I was asked to speak—I have seen in the faces of these ardent seekers a radiant joy as they hear, some for the first time, about a loving immersion in the living God, and that they too are called to it.

Again and again I find these same men and women asking where they can find the competent individualized guidance they need in realizing what they have heard or read about. They seek to be shown the path to the summit in their own circumstances and states in life.

What these fervent ones need and want are not vague exhortations on Sunday morning but specific, undiluted guidelines according to which they can live the radical Gospel in marriage or in the life of the evangelical counsels. They want better homilies, yes, but they also seek specific help in living as the saints lived.

Individualized help: such is our present problem. The ideal is clear; the reality, murky at best. Vatican II sketched a splendid picture of the ideal spiritual director when in several documents it described what exemplary priests are like. They live in this world but are not conformed to it. They know and love their people but are totally dedicated to the Lord's work. They are sincere, strong, and zealous.[1] Being formed and nourished by personal immersion in Sacred Scripture, priests are presumed to have a profound understanding of theology,[2] even if few have doctoral degrees in it. Their previous philosophical formation should have given them "a solid and coherent understanding of man, of the world, and of God."[3] While priests should "listen to the laity willingly," they are also to be "strenuous defenders of the truth."[4] They have the function of "testing the spirits" and are to give "special attention" to the faithful whom God is drawing "to a deeper spiritual life."[5] What could this mean but that priests, all priests, are pointedly called to be competent, well qualified spiritual directors?

The clergy are to be models of the radical Gospel in pursuing nothing less than perfection according to Jesus' words, "Be perfect just as your heavenly Father is perfect" (Mt 5:48, NAB).[6] They gladly embrace obedience to the mind of the Catholic Church and to the directions of their bishops and superiors.[7] They esteem their charism of celibate chastity as a "surpassing gift" and thus cling more easily to the Lord with undivided heart.[8] Priests are "invited to embrace voluntary poverty," and they are admonished to devote their superfluous income to the good of the Church or to other works of charity.[9] Most of all they are to "abound in contemplation,"[10] and to prize daily visits of personal devotion to their Eucharistic Master.[11] It goes without saying that with the exception of the celibate charism, these sacerdotal traits are requisite in any spiritual director, cleric, religious, or lay.

And so is the final qualification. Seminarians are to master the skills needed in actual direction by receiving careful instruction in the art of guiding souls.[12] After ordination they are to be sure that the faithful committed to their care "are led individually in the

Holy Spirit."[13] The reader may recall that this fits perfectly with our analysis of the theological nature of spiritual direction in Chapter Three.

Yes, the ideal is clear. While achieving an approximation to it in reality is another matter, we ask the reader to notice that the detailed discussion of its concrete realization, which we now undertake, is nothing other than a fleshing out of what Vatican II envisioned. We are not promoting here a private program or trendy ideas.

## ADEQUATE TRAINING AND COMPETENCY

Our main difficulty at this point is an odd one, namely, convincing people that spiritual direction requires, among other things, long and extensive study. It is odd because the same people who insist that their lawyer and physician have advanced degrees and state certification often assume without question that a spiritual guide needs little academic preparation, even though the psychological, moral, and spiritual dimensions of the human person are far more complex than the merely physical. As we have already suggested, a doctoral degree program is not the only way to go in this art of arts, but extensive preparedness and studies (perhaps sometimes not-for-credit) are indispensable.

I am aware that some readers of these words may well judge that my insistence on extensive knowledge is exaggerated, that the pastoral care of souls cannot be as complex and as demanding of expertise as I am supposing. It may be profitable to reflect for a few moments on the view of John Henry Newman, a man possessed of extensive theological learning and extraordinary psychological insight into the intricacies of human nature. In connection with his parish duties, he once remarked how reading patristic literature, which by itself can be a lifetime occupation, had revealed to him "how ignorant we are" when it comes to caring for the spiritual needs of ordinary men and women.[14]

Perhaps the best way to make the point is to share some of what I have learned in several decades of engaging in the spiritual guidance of several thousand men and women, some in a continuing relationship, others by way of one-on-one conversations during retreats and workshops. I have often marveled at the wide variety of questions and problems that come up routinely in this work. While many questions are repeats, as one would expect, there seems to be no end to the problems that arise only once in five or ten years, or indeed once in a lifetime. While a guide should be prepared to deal with the rare questions, or at least to research their solutions, we shall here touch upon the more commonly occurring ones.

**Interpersonal problems.** It will hardly surprise anyone to read that one of the most frequently occurring topics in spiritual direction concerns human relationships and how to react to them, not merely according to human principles but in a genuinely Gospel manner: anger and its expression or repression... impatience... coldness... misunderstandings... quarrels and disagreements... polarizations or divisions in marriage and religious communities... forgiveness or its refusal. Responding to these problems with bland banalities is not sufficient. Competent guidance is needed.

**Ordinary prayer questions.** Also common are queries as to how to pray... the amount of vocal prayer for a given person... distractions... meditation: what is it?... how does one go about it?... what if one cannot "do it?"... time pressure problems with all sorts of varied specifics... the feeling of emptiness at prayer... when is there a real inability to meditate?... how to distinguish it from a passing problem?

**Contemplative prayer.** Among topics for spiritual direction this one is not only frequent, it is one concerning which competent advice seems rarely available. Among questions that often arise: how does infused prayer begin?... what is it like?... how can one tell "empty prayer," which is good, from laziness or passing distractions?... what are St. Teresa's seven mansions like?... how to distinguish them?... how does one grow from one into the other? ... are there fluctuations?... how do we recognize where we are in the development of contemplation?... does it matter if we do not know where we are?... am *I* called to the summit?... what are the two nights, the mystical purifications?... how do they differ from depressions and other sufferings?... how does one discern the dry attention of faith from "doing nothing?"

**Vocational issues.** Young men and women often ask about what course their future lives should take. The guide here needs to understand why and how a vocation is very different from a career, that there is no such thing as a temporary vocation, and why; what the signs of a religious or priestly vocation are. One is then prepared to respond to related questions: what is a vocation to any state in life?... how do I rightly approach my vocation and try to find it?... how do married people live out the universal call to holiness?... what if one's spouse objects to the other's daily prayer time or attendance at Mass?... if I have a religious vocation, how do I discern whether I am called to active or contemplative life?... if to the active apostolate, which one?

**Biblical matters.** Of the thousands of texts in the Bible the director never knows which one he or she may be next asked to explain. The director might also be questioned about inspiration or inerrancy... about who can rightly interpret Scripture... what to think of the myriads of contradictory views people have about the inspired word... how to apply individual texts to one's life and in a manner consonant with sound exegesis.

**Ecclesial questions.** Is an individualistic spirituality acceptable?... why?... must anyone serious about pursuing God accept the Church?... what did Jesus say about this?... may we pick and choose among the Church's teachings?... if not, why not?

**Moral questions.** Confidentiality and secrecy... injustice and the obligation to restitution... differences between willing and feeling... lying and mental reservations... how to be chaste in our sex-saturated world... how to overcome an enslaving habit of sin... how to respond to temptations... what about masturbation, pre-

and extramarital relations, artificial contraception, homosexuality, abortion?

**Doctrinal inquiries.** Meaning of the indwelling of the Trinity... consciousness and self-awareness of Jesus... devotion to the Virgin Mother... relations between the indwelling and the adoration of the Eucharist outside of Mass... what are charisms?... how are they related to the whole Catholic Church and to one's personal life?... what is a vow?... should one make private vows, and if so, under what conditions?... how do they bind?... Sacrament of Reconciliation: how often should one receive it?... how to prepare well for it?

**Psychological wounds and scars.** Especially in our society, a spiritual director can expect to meet all sorts of emotional problems: weak self-image... depressions, situational or chronic... deprivation neuroses... abuse, physical and sexual... alcoholism of a family member... eating disorders... paranoia... interpersonal conflicts, coldness, chronic disagreements, lack of forgiveness, feuding. While the director need not feel it necessary to act the part of the psychotherapist, one should be able to recognize when a referral is needed and to what extent a spiritual mentor may at times be of some help. When appropriate the spiritual mentor should cooperate with a psychiatrist or psychologist in order to more fully aid an individual—for example, a neurotic person who aims to advance in prayer and self-giving to the Lord.

**Types of conscience.** The spiritual director needs to recognize and then to respond rightly to subjective differences in human conscience. It is not likely that a director will often deal with the hardened sinner, since the person with hardly any conscience at all will have little interest in direction. More frequently the director will encounter individuals of tender moral sensibility and those beset with scrupulosity. The differences between these two may be thought slight, but they are, in fact, great. The former is the conscience of a person who loves God with a wholehearted commitment and correctly avoids even the smallest sins, but at the same time does not exaggerate faults or find them where they do not exist. Scrupulous people are sincere, but they are ruled more by fear than by love. Their fear is distorted: small things are seen as large, and unfounded worries about guilt torture the individual from morning until night. The compulsions and obsessions of scrupulosity must be recognized for what they are and treated with skill and care.

**Oriental meditation and practices.** Thoughtful men and women soon find out that this world does not satisfy the longings for the transcendent that lie deep in our being. If religiously minded people do not find ecclesial leadership pointing to the true Fountain (Is 55:1-3), they sometimes stray into illusory paths. The competent spiritual director should know something of Zen Buddhism, for example, and how immensely it differs from Christian contemplation. Alarming is not too strong a word to describe the naïveté of Christian 'directors' who seem to think that Zen *satori* or Transcendental Meditation (the latter being ultimately a Hindu enterprise) are equivalent to what Saints Bernard and Teresa and John of the Cross write about. Not only do these guides fail to point out to their disciples what genuine immersion in the living God is about (Zen says nothing about God), but they do not attract inquirers to authentic prayer. So artless and simpleminded are these mentors that they can hardly appreciate Hans Urs von Balthasar's comment, "No matter how variegated the market display of human world views may be, seen from a bit of distance its stalls and attractions soon come to take on a common air, all equally of human provenance and human proportions."[15]

**Problem of evil and suffering.** Year in and year out, in one form or another, the experienced spiritual director deals with human afflictions and anguish: achings of the heart, throbbing pains in the body, betrayals of spouse or friend, shocking traumas and long lasting burdens, sudden accidents and nameless anxieties. In addition to conveying compassion and understanding, the competent guide needs on occasion and in the right circumstances to explain the whole huge problem of evil and how we in the new dispensation are to look upon it.[16] Pat answers are not enough.

**Evangelical counsels.** Both for young men and women who have not yet chosen their states in life and for religious who have embraced Gospel poverty, celibacy, and obedience, the competent mentor needs to understand both the theology of vocation and the theology and practice of each of the evangelical counsels. What is consecrated chastity? Why is deep prayer its chief purpose? How are the counsels related to apostolate and to witness? Why does vowed poverty entail frugality, dependence, sharing, and avoidance of superfluities? How is obedience to human superiors rooted as a counsel in the New Testament? How is it related to freedom? What are the practical implications of living the counsels in community?

**Extraordinary phenomena: authentic and inauthentic.** Since both types of unusual experiences are more common than many people suspect, the director must have at least a basic capacity to distinguish one from the other. There are genuine visions, locutions, revelations and "spiritual feelings" (as St. John of the Cross calls them), and there are not a few illusions about all these. Hence, a spiritual guide should understand what they are and how to distinguish the valid from the invalid. Likewise important is the proper advice to be given both when they seem to be authentic and when they are not. People are only too easily led off into stray paths by undue attention to what they think are direct communications from God.

**The place of the saints.** The inspired word of Scripture and the heroic holiness of the saints flow from one and the same Holy Spirit of Father and Son. As a consequence each illustrates and illuminates the other. Not only is professional theology immensely enriched by careful attention to these concrete embodiments of the Gospel, but spiritual direction is likewise kept on a guaranteed course to the summit. Once a guide is thoroughly imbued with the mind of these Gospel heroes and heroines he or she far more readily finds answers to questions that are not treated in formal theology books. Knowing their attitudes, understandings, outlooks, and perspectives, both director and directee more easily grasp how men and women are to put on Christ in their own states of life. Without a knowledge of and appreciation for the saints, it is all too likely that the wisdom offered will be mere human wisdom.

**Spiritual reading.** So crucial for solid progress toward God is *lectio divina,* divine reading, that we shall devote to it considerable attention in our chapter on self-direction. For our purposes here the focus is on two points only. One is the mentor's competency in knowing what spiritual reading actually is, along with how it should be done. The other bears on an extensive knowledge of the spiritual classics (at least the chief of them) and the best of contemporary writings. Linked to the latter are audio- and videotape recordings. One of the functions of a capable director is to discuss with directees their selections in spiritual reading and to provide informed discernment regarding what may be of particular worth to read—or of harm—among the thousands of titles issuing from religious presses each decade. While it is true that directors cannot realistically be expected to read everything available, even in one narrow field of specialization, they should through careful choices over the years be able to wisely suggest what an individual directee would find profitable at a given time.

**Putting it all together.** This sketch of what an adequate director should know may strike the reader as overwhelming. Who, taking seriously all we have outlined, would dare accept the office of guiding another human being to God? Youthful and newly ordained John Henry Newman, brilliant and studious though he was, had reason in his first pastoral charge at St. Clemens to be apprehensive about his inexperience in dealing with "immoral souls."[17] Rash would be the budding director who did not feel the same.

It is true that no professional may be expected to have a ready answer to every question that may arise in one's practice. Yet, on a day-by-day basis relying on reference books for solutions is of limited usefulness. A medical doctor or a lawyer may not repeatedly put off dealing with a client's problem on the plea of further study. Nor may a spiritual director. One facet of competency is the knowledge of where to look for answers to new problems. Another is habitual study throughout one's life. A continuing assimilation of information combined with experience and sound judgment in using it are basic requirements for guiding people in the ways of God.

When people are not academically competent, when they have not studied adequately, they tend to do one of two things when asked something beyond their qualifications. Either they simply profess ignorance or they give facile, pat answers which are usually false or misleading. To profess lack of knowledge is honorable, because it is honest. At least it does not lead the inquirer astray. But it is of no help either. The pat answer is not honorable, because it misleads the questioner into thinking a solution has been offered. I will mention three examples of pat answers only too many directors innocently give. To a person beset with time pressures that make opportunities for contemplative prayer difficult: "Well, work is prayer. God understands, so don't worry." To one suffering from clinical depression: "This is just a part of the dark night, so be at peace. We all have troubles, and they can do us good." To one who can no longer meditate, and who wonders what is happening in prayer, and where he or she is in it: "It doesn't matter where you are in St. Teresa's mansions. You need not know that. Just be sincere and keep up your efforts; God understands."

Of course, God understands, but it is clear that guides who say these things understand rather little. Though they may be well convinced of the adequacy of their remarks, they are leading their charges astray. No one who grasps the theology of contemplation and action would say that work is prayer except in the broadest sense (both Scripture and Vatican II contradict the idea). One who understands both the mystical nights and clinical depressions would never equate the two. No one who realizes the normal flow of infused prayer from one mansion to another and the fluctuations among the mansions, together with the very different manner of our operating as we grow from one stage to the other, would dream of saying that it does not matter where one is.

Bearing all this in mind, we concur with St. Teresa in her decided insistence that confessors and directors have outstanding academic credentials. No less than three times in one paragraph of her *Book of Foundations* did she insist that the men who guided her nuns were to be competent, men of learning, as she put it. The nuns were to consult "persons of learning," not anyone who happened along. Superiors were to have "learned men as their confessors," because these would save them from flagrant errors. And the prioresses were to see to it that their nuns had "learned men as confessors."[18]

Among the traits of the director about which the directee was to make a judgment, prominent on the Teresian list was theological knowledge. The saint minced no words as to what she thought of the matter. The guide, she insisted, was not to discuss matters of which he or she was ignorant. We may conclude that when a directee discovers this ignorance, it is wise to avoid consulting the person altogether or at least desist from seeking advice in the area of incompetency. As for the director, the saint observes, "He shouldn't kill himself or think he understands what he doesn't...."[19]

Competency for St. Teresa did not, therefore, mean merely good judgment and skill in the affairs of human life. These gifts she valued, but likewise she sought theological learning to a high degree. It is significant that not only did she regret "timid, half-learned men whose shortcomings cost [her] very dear," but she also was fond of praising those who have "great learning." Even if they lack a lofty degree of prayer themselves, "men of great learning have a certain instinct to prompt them" as they guide others.

She took it for granted, of course, that their academic qualifications were accompanied with humility, a serious prayer life, and fidelity to the mind of the Church.[20] Fidelity to the Church's mind means first of all the "sound doctrine" so often insisted upon in the pastoral letters of Timothy and Titus. Guidance based on dissenting opinions is doomed from the start to sterility, if not to disaster. We need only read ecclesiastical history to be persuaded that this remark is no exaggeration. But learning here means more than soundness and accuracy, crucial though they be. Doctrine and truth are to be enlivened, completed, savored, enjoyed: "You are filled with a joy so great it cannot be described," says the inspired word (1 Pt 1:8). This type of theological, scriptural lore is experienced and relished: "Taste and see how good the Lord is," as the psalmist puts it (Ps 34:8). It is the *fruitio,* the deep drinking of joy, of which St. Augustine speaks.

Few among today's "exact" Biblical scholars, however, make any room at all in their Biblical science for the *fruitio* of the *sensus spiritualis*, to say nothing of assigning to it the place of honour. I say "place of honour" because this act is the central act of theology as a science. According to an unformulated but generally accepted opinion, this act is either banished from "scientific" theology into the realm of unscientific "spirituality," or it must remain suspended until "exact" research has passed its more or less definitive judgment concerning the historical meanings and contexts of the *littera* [letter].[21]

So exacting, so demanding is the task of guiding the souls of immortal beings that the sobering question arises: how could anyone in his right mind undertake it? We have already noted of John Henry Newman that even with his enormous biblical, patristic, and theological knowledge—together with his rare insight into the workings of the human heart and mind—he considered himself on occasion simply to be in no position to give advice to other people.[22] A priest correspondent himself, who was interested in the ministry of spiritual direction but at the same time aware of his own limitations, put it well in a letter to me: "A short course (of further preparation) is not, to my mind, the answer, nor would it appeal to me. There are far too many half-baked experts who seem full of confidence in their ability to direct others, and I have no intention of increasing their number." St. Nilus of Ancyra (died c. 430) had some hard words for these people:

Every art needs time, and great study toward a successful accomplishment. Only the art of arts [spiritual direction] is practiced without having learned it.... Someone utterly unlearned in the work of God will dare to teach it, as if it were easier than the rest; and the thing most difficult to handle is viewed by many as being a snap. Saint Paul says that he by no means understands it, but they declare that they know all about it, who do not ever know that they do not know.[23]

The situation has not changed much in fifteen centuries. A contemporary theologian, de Guibert, adds this practical advice: "The directors who should be avoided most of all are those who have only a little knowledge [of theology and infused prayer] but great self-confidence.[24]

## THE PERSONAL QUALITIES OF A SPIRITUAL DIRECTOR

Academic knowledge is not enough. While a lawyer or a surgeon may excel in legal or medical skills without being a person of lofty behavior, such is not likely to be the case with doctors of the human soul. Some of those who offer advice, says the biblical word, are governed by self-interest. Their counsel coincides with their own egocentric aims. They may tell you that you are on the right road, when clearly you are not. Rather, adds the sage, go for counsel to a devout person, one who keeps the commandments (Sir 37:7-9, 12).

In her own terminology St. Teresa expressed this criterion with two words: spiritual and experienced. By the first term she meant a sincere pursuit of Gospel ideals, a refusal to compromise with worldliness: frivolous amusements (among which she would doubtless include an undiscriminating use of television and other mass media of our day), elegant dining and drinking, extensive wardrobes and pleasure travel. By experience the saint meant a growth into at least the beginnings of infused prayer, together with the holiness it supposes and produces, because even the prayer of quiet is "completely obscure" to those "devoid of experience."[25]

Yet St. Teresa's predilection for theological expertise in her guides comes out even at this point:

Let not the spiritual person be misled by saying that learned men without [advanced] prayer are unsuitable for those who practice it. I have consulted many learned men because for some years now, on account of a greater necessity, I have sought them out more; and I've always been a friend of men of learning. For though some don't have experience, they don't despise the Spirit nor do they ignore it, because in Sacred Scripture, which they study, they always find the truth of the good spirit....

Devils have a tremendous fear of that learning which is accompanied by humility and virtue.[26]

Not surprisingly, of course, what is best of all is a guide who is both theologically informed and well advanced in contemplative prayer: "If you know such a person, it is best to consult one both spiritual and learned."[27] For Teresa one of the surest proofs of holiness is obedience to the Catholic Church and to one's superiors. The saint makes this an explicit criterion for the selection of her own guides. In a letter to Father General in 1575 she writes of two Carmelite priests, "You may be quite sure that, if I found they were disobedient, I would neither see them nor listen to them any more."[28]

Together with sanctity of life, we hope to find in a mentor a genuine interest in and a real understanding of the client's thoughts, feelings, and problems. Interest, however, does not guarantee understanding. Only too often have I heard of sincere directors who for one reason or another do not understand a person's problem. A superior or director may, for example, tell a clinically depressed person to "pull yourself together" or to "snap out of it," none of which the directee is able to do. This sort of inept advice is not only of no help; it probably worsens the situation by putting the person in the hopeless position of being advised to do what cannot be done.

Needless to say, a spiritual director who does not understand a type of infused prayer or one of the two nights of purification is necessarily going to misunderstand the directee in these situations. The lack of grasp solves no problems, of course, and it adds to whatever pain was present in the first place. St. Teresa wrote to the Dominican Banez: "A priest must be more than a confessor to me now. The soul's desire can only be assuaged by the soul which understands it."[29]

This Teresian desire for enlightened sympathy will be found in the guides who love their disciples, who can say with St. Paul, "You have a permanent place in my heart, and God knows how much I miss you all, loving you as Christ Jesus loves you" (Phil 1:8). Of this love will be born also the gift of listening with one's whole being: mind, heart, feelings. As an insightful nun put it to me,

Initially, and indeed all the time, the director must have the ability to listen and individuate the personal stories and problems that are brought to him. No two people are alike, and no two people have exactly the same backgrounds or histories. One of the most off-putting things about a director and one which will ensure that he does not get further patronage is any sign that he is only half-listening, or that he studies the ceiling, the window, or the contents of the room, anything rather than the person he is supposed to be talking to!

The experience often mentioned as needed in spiritual directors includes both the wisdom that should come with advance in age and a feel for the things of God which accompany a deepening prayer life. Scripture combines both aspects in commending the insight found in the virtuous aged: "How fine a thing: sound judgment with grey hairs, and for greybeards to know how to advise! How fine a thing: wisdom in the aged" (Sir 25:4-5). The suppositions are, of course, that those advancing in age have taken time to study in more than a superficial way and that they have matured a great deal through reflection, prayer, and concrete dealings with fellow human beings.

St. John of the Cross is sparing of words when he addresses the positive qualifications of a suitable mentor. One should possess theological competence, soundness of judgment, and the experience of infused prayer: learning, discretion, experience, as the saint puts it.[30] By experience of advancing prayer, John means experience "of what true and pure spirit is." Without being familiar with at least the beginnings of infused prayer, guides cannot lead souls to higher realms, nor can they even understand what their charges are trying to explain.

A final qualification is in order: there must be neither naïve credulity nor closeminded scepticism when one hears of unusual happenings narrated by the directee.We have in mind especially divine enlightenments of sundry types (locutions, visions, revelations) and absorbing and ecstatic prayer. The former are termed theologically "extraordinary," that is, they are not needed for the attainment of sanctity, nor are they necessary components of a life of grace. The latter, infused absorption and ecstatic contemplation, are called "ordinary," that is, they do belong to the usual and normal growth of prayer, leading as they do to the summit to which all men and women are called.

About these phenomena skilled guides are neither gullible nor sceptical. They know that they surely do occur, but they are also aware that illusion is not rare either—especially when there is question of alleged locutions, visions, and revelations. They are open to evidence. They know through both study and experience how to discern the valid from the invalid. St. Teresa sought help in her lofty experiences neither from those who "believed that everything was from God," nor from "those who completely despised these experiences—they did so to try her [Teresa]."[31] In other words the saint wanted help from people whose minds are open to solid evidence, not from those who have a self-confident bias stemming from unexamined premises or from simple misinformation and lack of experience.

We may return for further consideration to the question we raised above: if one takes seriously these exacting requirements on the one hand and the eternal preciousness of a human person on the other, who would dare to guide another immortal soul? Even leaving aside for the moment the need for holiness, who would sensibly claim all the other qualifications? Left to ourselves no one could. But happily we are not left to ourselves: we have the Church Jesus founded and authorized to speak and guide in his name. That brings us back to the ecclesiality of spiritual direction.

One who rejects the Church and her teaching (and grasps what is involved in the rejection) and still presents oneself as a guide to others cannot evade the charge of extreme audacity. How dare I impose my personal ideas (which are often biases) as beacons to eternity, if I have cut myself off from the sole community which enjoys the fullness of the divine promise?

Who then may proceed to offer spiritual direction to others without succumbing to pride and presumption? The humble, the docile, the obedient—all of them rather unpopular virtues in our day. Humble people tend to know what they do not know. If they lack understanding of advanced contemplation, they do not presume to give advice about it.

Even so, they may be able to help beginners. Everything in human life is meant to lead to an immersion in the indwelling Trinity. Patience and purity, duties of state and love for neighbor, work and play, suffering and delight, lead to the "one thing," tasting and seeing how good the Lord is. Humble people learn from the masters, the saints, how to interpret God's word and to live it more fully themselves. Being without arrogance, they grow in prayer themselves and hence in the capacity to guide others in it. Honest and unassuming people typically take to the saints and are eager to learn from them both about prayer and about the style of life that is conducive to prayer. Inspired to heroic virtue by the same Holy Spirit who inspired Scripture, the saints are ideal teachers for directors and directees alike.

Humility leads to docility—that is, openness, teachableness—for the humble listen and "learn before [they] speak" (Sir 18:19). They welcome the Church's proclamation which enjoys Jesus' guiding presence, even to the end of time (Mt 28:18-20). They go to the heroes and heroines of holiness before they attempt to point out to others the way to perfection. They find their doctrine, norms, advice, and insight not in their own inner poverty, their native emptiness (who of us does not begin in utter emptiness?), but in the community of the saints and especially in the ecclesial Mother of the saints.


## MISTAKES SOME DIRECTORS MAKE

Aside from the Petrine promise no one of us, no matter how well qualified, is infallible in our pastoral work (another reason we must keep close to the Catholic Church which cannot err in her binding magisterium). Hence hundreds of possible mistakes in detail can occur in spiritual direction. Our concern at the moment, however, is not with details, but with basic errors that are only too common, bungling that adequate study and thought could readily prevent.

**Overemphasis on methods and techniques.** The first of these fundamental errors is an exaggerated emphasis on methods and techniques at prayer. When someone comes with the desire to live a serious contemplative prayer life, the director's first thought may be mistakenly focused on the way to go about praying. A wise guide, on the other hand, imbued with Scripture and experienced in the ways of the spirit, thinks first of all of the absolutely basic requirement of identifying one's will with the divine will. Even common sense tells us that method and technique are by no means the most important elements in fostering any deep intimacy. Yet only too many contemporaries suppose that the main factor in contemplative "success" and intimacy with God is finding the right approach, be it oriental or occidental.

The saints know better. They understand the Lord himself who said not a word about techniques, but did declare, "Not everyone who says to me, 'Lord, Lord' will enter the kingdom of heaven, but only the one who does the will of my Father in heaven" (Mt 7:21, NAB). Prayer formulas and methodologies without conscientious carrying out of the divine will cannot lead to advancing in prayer.

St. Teresa lays it down, "All that the beginner has to do... is to be resolute and prepare himself with all possible diligence to bring his will into conformity with the will of God.... The more perfectly a person practices it, the more he will receive of the Lord." Then, as if she anticipates our day, Teresa remarks that we ought not to think that "we have to use strange jargon or dabble in things of which we have no knowledge or understanding."[32]

For the inept director, the prosaic practice of humility, patience, obedience, and love of neighbor have little vibrant bearing on contemplation. They seem passé, unappealing. Of interest instead is discourse about mantras, ashrams, yoga, and gurus, and their workshops, along with books about Transcendental Meditation, enneagrams, New Age 'enlightenment.' Unfortunately, there will be devotees who take all this seriously and end up with no prayer life at all.

**Failing to use Gospel norms as the yardstick.** The second elementary mistake is the tendency to guide others according to one's own standards rather than according to Gospel norms. If the master is a saint, there is no problem, for then the norms applied are entirely in accord with Scripture. If the guide is mediocre, retardation and regression, if not disaster, are in the offing. Worldly directors do not, for example, perceive that deepening prayer and self-indulgence do not mix. Being of that mind, such directors are not at all inclined to point out the hard road and the narrow gate that alone lead to life (Mt 7:13-14). Even in her day St. Teresa noted that "so few and so rare" are the "spiritual masters" who do not dilute in this matter that she thought it one of the main reasons "why beginners do not advance more rapidly to high perfection."[33] The saint added that as a young woman she had lofty desires for God and prayer, but at the same time she was beset with "worldly vanities" that impeded her progress. She thought that if she had had "someone to make me fly," she would have turned her desires into deeds much sooner.[34]

**Neglecting to weigh general norms against individual differences.** The third basic error is the failure to see a balance between general norms in the spiritual life, which are applicable to all men and women, and individual differences peculiar to each person. For instance, the seven-fold development in prayer explained by St. Teresa is at the core of her "heavenly teaching" which the Catholic Church in her liturgy presents to all the faithful.[35] Yet, within that overall pattern, God has countless ways of dealing with each soul. Some directors make the mistake of leaving aside most norms and patterns in an exaggerated flexibility, while others apply principles as if there were no individual differences in the capacity and development of their disciples.

"In the interior life we must never take our own experiences [or the lack of them] as the norm for everyone else," said the author of *The Cloud of Unknowing.*[36] Solid mentors should indeed profit from their own experiences in advising others, but since God has numberless ways in which he deals with souls (even if following one general pattern), a mentor should not assume that everyone will travel by a similar path.

**Scant knowledge of infused contemplation.** Our fourth mistake elicits strong language from gentle John of the Cross. Many are the directors, he says, who know only of beginning meditation. Thus they instruct people in it, when often enough these latter should be shown how to respond to the divine infusions. These directors either know little of advancing contemplation in itself, or they do not recognize the signs which indicate that God is beginning to give it. Hence, their advice to work actively at discursive reasoning impedes the very gift the Lord is offering. This bungling advice saddened the saint: "How often is God anointing a contemplative with some very delicate unguent of loving knowledge, serene, peaceful, solitary... when a spiritual director will happen along who, like a blacksmith, knows no more than how to hammer and pound with the faculties...."[37]

The mentor, adds the saint, should not "accommodate souls to his own method and condition, but he should observe the road along which God is leading them, and if he does not recognize it, he should leave them alone and not bother them."[38] Not knowing "what spirit is," these inept guides show disrespect to God "by intruding with a rough hand where He is working."[39] John further on grants that these mentors perhaps err with good will because they know no better, but all the same they may not be excused "for the counsels they give rashly... and for rudely meddling in something they do not understand, instead of leaving the matter to one who does understand."

This "is no light fault," notes the saint, for "the affairs of God must be handled with great tact and with open eyes, especially in so vital and sublime a matter as is that of these souls, where there is at stake almost an infinite gain in being right and almost an infinite loss in being wrong."[40] Mystical theologian John Arintero has even harder words for this elementary mistake. "Many poor directors neither feel nor know nor wish to know the things of the spirit. They have a crass ignorance of the ways of God, a habitual imprudence and rashness, a lack of zeal—or sometimes an excess of zeal—and base and earthly viewpoints." He then cites fellow theologian Godinez to the effect that these shortcomings in directors "are responsible for the failure of the great majority, the ninety-nine percent" who at this juncture in their spiritual lives fail to grow into lofty prayer.[41]

While Arintero's language may strike one as harsh, it does underline the problem we are addressing. One example of it today occurs when psychotherapy is taken as a substitute for spiritual direction. Psychologists may be fine in their field, while being out of their league in things of the spirit—for the reason Arintero gives. Human growth can occur on the psychological level, but growth in prayer and holiness will not be the likely outcome unless the supernatural dimension is being appropriately addressed as well. One would think this obvious, but to some it is not.

**Misinterpreting the dark nights.** A fifth common error is the misinterpretation of the dark nights as depressions or vice versa. This confusion occurs in either one of two ways. A genuine case of clinical depression may be diagnosed by a director as one of the two dark nights, thereby showing that he or she understands neither. Or the mistaken diagnosis occurs in the opposite direction: authentic, dry infused prayer is judged to be an emotional problem—a depression. Of this latter St. John of the Cross speaks: "It will happen that while an individual is being conducted by God along a sublime path of dark contemplation and aridity, in which he feels lost, he will encounter in the midst of the fullness of his darkness, trials, conflicts, and temptations someone who in the style of Job's comforters (Jb 4:8-11), will proclaim that all this is due to melancholia, or depression, or temperament, or to some hidden wickedness...."[42]

One of the more gross mistakes made by directors of weekend workshops as well as by some individual guides is the confusion of oriental states of awareness with Christic contemplation. I have heard one of these speakers actually remark that he saw little difference between Buddhist contemplation and Christian! I use the term, gross, not to cast opprobrium upon Zen awareness, but merely to suggest that while there are points of similarity between the two, the many differences could hardly be more drastic.[43]

For example, Buddhism is agnostic apropos of God, neither affirming nor denying his existence. Its awareness is completely impersonal and thus not a love-communion at all. It is entirely produced by human techniques. Our contemplation is entirely theistic and utterly interpersonal, supremely an immersion in the love of the living Triune God. It is not in the least produced by procedures and methods. A director who sees little difference between these two realities must be remarkably innocent of one or both of them.

In noting these striking differences, I am making no judgment as to what sincere Buddhists, touched by the grace of Christ, may attain in their exercises. The point is simply what Buddhist writers themselves say is their experience. It is vastly different from ours.

**Minimalism.** Then there are guides who counsel people that they should not even think of infused contemplation as meant for them. They are apparently unaware that this view contradicts Scripture and Vatican II, not to mention the saints.[44] With the demise of the two-way theory regarding the call to the summit, one may hope that this particular type of incompetency is disappearing also.

**A clinging, unhealthy relationship.** The final basic mistake we shall notice is the clinging of some directors to their directees, thus hindering them from seeking another's help when necessary. Little need be said of this defect, for it is plain possessiveness, a lack of humility. Sensible guides realize when they are inadequate for a person's continuing growth or when they simply do not understand some problem. Far from clinging to one's charge, the guide should suggest that the directee search for another director either on a permanent basis or for a given question.[45]

## A SCARCITY OF QUALIFIED SPIRITUAL DIRECTORS

We have thus far in this chapter been discussing the ideal, namely what spiritual directors should be like, what the great masters through the ages have been, and the mistakes that qualified mentors today carefully avoid. We now consider the other side of a realistic picture. It would be pleasant and uplifting to report that the ideal and the real for all practical purposes coincide, that with the current renewed interest in spiritual direction and with a multitude of courses and programs styled to prepare directors, we now have an abundance of practitioners who pass muster. While there may be some enthusiasts who think this to be the case, I have seen no evidence to support the idea.

Quite the contrary. Beginning with Scripture, then reading what the saints have to say about the matter, and finally, listening to comments made by contemporaries in search of deep prayer, I conclude that all available indicators point in the direction of insufficiency. Indeed, rarity may not be too strong a word.

The inspired message may serve as our step-off point: "Let your acquaintances be many," says the sage, "but one in a thousand your confidant" (Sir 6:6, NAB). St. Paul was of like mind. He admonished the Corinthians as his "dearest children" and then declared that they may have ten thousand instructors, but not more than one father (1 Cor 4:14). St. Francis de Sales was perhaps echoing Paul when he remarked that a capable director is "one in ten thousand, for those who are fitted for such a task are unimaginably few."[46]

St. Teresa specified the problem when she explained from her own experience how few are the mentors whose advice is not tinged with worldly compromise. In the context, she was discussing prayerful people who remain in the state of grace but are little inclined to reasonable penance and sacrifice. Instead of flying freely to the heights of holiness they advance "with the speed of a hen." Then she recalled her early days when she herself had pursued "worldly vanities" and tried to straddle the fence, "both to practice prayer and to live for my own pleasure."

What was true in Teresa's day seems unfortunately true in ours. Rare is the mentor who does not tone down the Gospel's hard road and narrow gate, the daily carrying of the cross—either by giving the theme little attention or by positively diluting it. Few are the guides who urge their disciples to give up all they possess (Lk 14:33), all egoistic clingings, that they may taste and drink deeply and thus experience the goodness of the Lord (Ps 34:8), and find in him a joy beyond all worded expression (1 Pt 1:8).

In explaining why so few people become "true contemplatives," Arintero remarks that "the chief cause is, as we have already pointed out, the scarcity of spiritual directors who know how to correct self-deception and to encourage souls so that they will resolve to renounce self completely."[47] The current proliferation of popular courses and programs aimed at training people to become spiritual directors implies a recognition of unmet needs among the faithful who desire competent guidance but cannot find it. While the intentions behind these programs are worthy, there seems to be little awareness that a few courses cannot possibly equip a person to fulfill even approximately what we have noted in this chapter.

It would appear that we have in this situation a prime illustration of what Jesus had in mind when he said that those of this world are more astute in their business than the children of light are in theirs (Lk 16:8).

A final comment. Given that we have in the Catholic Church no tests or standards or laws regulating spiritual direction, we may ask whether a private person may offer this service unasked. Hanging out one's shingle of availability would seem to be risky business, indeed rash, if one's training is sketchy and flimsy.

A better sign that a person may be suited to offer guidance is that prayerful people (I do not refer to novelty seekers) spontaneously recognize one's fitness and seek help. Such was the case with St. Teresa: men and women, bishops as well as lay people, knew from her high degree of holiness, insight and sound ecclesial judgment, that she would be an ideal guide to the loftiest reaches of prayer. She had no need to advertise herself. British philosopher and theologian Baron von Hugel considered it a "golden rule" never to "try to begin to help people, or influence them, till they ask, but wait for them."[48] That is always sound advice.

# Part Two

# *Practical Questions and Problems*

# SIX

# Key Concerns in Spiritual Direction

WHEREAS, IN PART ONE, we laid a foundation for understanding spiritual direction, here we take up various practical matters. An informal conversational style is used in order to better present concrete situations and difficulties with which readers might more easily identify. Within this chapter the following topics will be covered:

1. The directee
2. The director
3. Finding a suitable director
4. Approaches and methods
5. The Sacrament of Reconciliation and direction

## THE DIRECTEE

**1. Question:** What kind of person will profit from the directive relationship? Are all those who are seeking spiritual guidance pretty much on an equal footing?

**Comment:** By no means are all people seeking this kind of help equally ready to profit from it. Recall that what is envisioned is a Christic transformation, not a mere naturalistic analysis or psychological enlightenment. Like evangelization itself, spiritual direction supposes receptivity in the directee and thus an openness to conversion. In Jesus' parable of the sower and the word, he taught that the readiness for his message ranges all the way from zero to hundredfold. The same is to be said of receptivity to individualized direction.

**2. Question:** Yes, that makes sense, but your reference to conversion as a needed condition is somewhat startling. Isn't it presumed that a person seeking guidance in living the Gospel is converted to it?

**Comment:** Yes and no. Surely we take it for granted that this individual is basically oriented to God at the very least, but that still leaves open the question of how deep and thorough the conversion is. After all, there are levels of conversion, whether it be intellectual, moral, or religious. A man or woman may have turned from serious sin but not from venial, may love convenient truths, but not the inconvenient, may give God a major place in life but not a total one. Not everyone who attends Sunday Mass and reads religious books has given up all he or she possesses (Lk 14:33), does everything for the glory of God—which is also for one's own good (1 Cor 10:31)—or gives up everything that does not lead to God (Ti 2:12). Saints are disposed for maximal profit from spiritual direction, just as they benefit thoroughly from the Church's proclamation of doctrine and morality.

**3. Question:** Few of us would claim to be saints. Yet, isn't it precisely the purpose of spiritual direction to help imperfect people grow out of their faults and into genuine holiness? I know you agree that this is so. You are not excluding sinners. But then what is the point of speaking of conversion in this context?

**Comment:** The point is the degree of receptivity or readiness. Do I want truth, all of it? Really? Do I want holiness, or will I settle for a refined mediocrity? Do I covertly have my own agenda, rather than the Lord's?

**4. Question:** I think I understand. People, often unwittingly, resist things in the Gospel that run counter to their preferences, things that are unpopular in the world, indeed at times unwelcome in their own families and among their own friends. They have not given God a total yes. Let me then ask what the traits are of a person who is ready to profit from guidance given in the spirit of the Gospel?

**Comment:** My first response to your question is that one should honestly ask oneself: am I really seeking direction? Or am I merely looking for a soul-friend or a sympathetic ear, a sounding board—someone who is likely to affirm me and to agree with my views? There are people who, perhaps without being aware of it, view the mentor as a rubber stamp, that is, with no real desire or intention of following advice unless they agree with it. When disagreement arises, they either ignore the guidance with more or less advertence, or they eventually drop the relationship.

**5. Question:** Wouldn't you agree, though, that there are many sincere people who do not have a personal agenda more or less at odds with the Gospel? They sincerely want to be guided and to follow advice given.

**Comment:** I surely do agree, emphatically so. I find in my experience that these open and receptive ones, these humble and docile ones, do make steady and often remarkable progress. God loves the humble and he gives them rapid growth.

**6. Question:** Then, too, there are people who do love their own opinions beyond merit, but at the same time know they need light. They are probably unaware that they are not fully open to ideas that run counter to their preferences, and yet they are groping for guidance. They may give their director the impression of resisting advice, but at times they may only be presenting difficulties. There must be room for honest questioning not about doctrine, but about practical applications.

**Comment:** True enough, but open people accept solid evidence when it is offered. They are inclined to follow the advice of an expert, even when they do not understand it. This is as true in medicine and law as it should be in the spiritual life. Sincere inquiry and the presentation of difficulties should be welcome, but the arbitrary dismissal of biblical and church witness or solidly based advice does not demonstrate receptivity. People have diverse ways of deflecting direction, perhaps without realizing it. What they may really seek is assurance, someone to talk to. When this becomes sufficiently clear, it needs to be addressed by the mentor.

**7. Question:** Without some sort of obedience isn't it an easy slide into a 'suggestions relationship'—with the director regarded as just one among a number of sources giving 'suggestions' from which one then picks and chooses?

**Comment:** Selecting among various opinions is not direction. Moreover, if the client feels no obligation to follow counsel given, seeing it as one view among others, naturally one is inclined to choose the more appealing, even if it is not of more benefit spiritually. To illustrate, an example of a scrupulous person comes to mind. One can reason with the individual endlessly, but until he or she is disposed to obey wise directives, instead of giving into compulsive thinking and rethinking, the scrupulous behavior will dominate. The director's words have to be seen with a spiritual mind as coming from God and as being for one's good. And they must be heeded accordingly. Through obedience progress can be made, but not otherwise.

**8. Question:** If the directee routinely is seeking simply to talk and be affirmed, that is, with no serious intention to be guided, should the director terminate the relationship?

**Comment:** This, then, is not a directive relationship unless we drain the word of its obvious meaning. Whether it should be discontinued may be decided based on three discerning questions. Does it serve any useful purpose, even though it is not spiritual direction? How aware is the person of using guidance sessions for other than their proper end? Perhaps the director will need to draw the directee's attention to this. Does the director have more important things to do than that which any sympathetic listener may be able to do just as well? A person should not ask for guidance unless it, not a substitute, is the real purpose. Otherwise that person may well be taking up time that could have been given to another who does want to be shown the way to God.

**9. Question:** Whether that is the case or not, do directees often choose to discontinue the relationship? If so, why? Would you offer examples?

**Comment:** Yes, they do… and fairly often. One appropriate reason is that the guide is found to be worldly or lacking in knowledge and judgment, or is not faithful to God's word and the mind of the Church. An improper reason for dropping a director is that, while he or she may be highly competent and prayerful and faithful to Scripture and the Church, the director may contradict what the directee wants to do. For instance, he or she may point out to a married person that artificial contraception is illicit, or to a religious that canon law clearly requires the wearing of a religious habit. Perhaps the quickest way to lose directees is to contradict what they have made up their minds to do.

**10. Question:** What do you think of choosing a mentor who is of one's own cast of mind? At least the two are less likely to disagree or to break the relationship further down the road.

**Comment:** It all depends on the integrity and sanctity of the person choosing. If it is St. Teresa selecting St. John of the Cross, well and good. She could not do better. But if one has a dissenting cast of mind or is already spiritually a corner-cutter, to choose a like-minded mentor is to opt for mediocrity and perhaps for disaster. It is significant that when the author of 2 Timothy warns about novelty seekers who care little about "sound teaching," he remarks that in their caring for change they "collect for themselves a whole series of teachers according to their own tastes… and… turn to myths" (2 Tm 4:3-4). The result of that kind of direction is indeed a running after myths that, if pursued in its logical outcome, will lead to spiritual calamity.

**11. Question:** You are suggesting that the choice of a director is of no little importance, and who could disagree, realizing that the eternal destiny of an immortal soul is involved? Granted also that the first duty of a person seeking this guidance is the selection of a competent, sincere guide. Aside from the universally admitted shortage of such guides, is there any hidden problem for the seeker? By hidden I mean that the seeker does not suspect it.

**Comment:** As we just noted, for saintly people there is no further problem, but for lesser ones the question is often both unrealized and just about as fundamental as it can be: is it truth that I love, or is it my preferences? Do I love religious and moral objective reality or do I pick and choose according to my sympathies? Almost all men and women suppose the former, but in actuality many cling to what they find attractive. If this appears an exaggerated statement, consider the tiny percentage of the population that enters into any serious study in order to find religious and moral truth. And consider likewise that most people, including intellectuals, only too often do not yield to evidence they do not like, as I have noted earlier with certain scientists who will go so far as to concoct fictitious data to get favorable results.

**12. Question:** I have read Newman make the same point brilliantly. All the same, shouldn't we assume that directees are among the number who do love truth?

**Comment:** Once again I must make the distinction: yes, saints love truth and bow to evidence. Martyrs even die for it. But lesser people only too often do not. We have many ways, subtle ways, of 'filtering against truth and evidence' we do not like. I experience this again and again in my conversations and reading. This is why the first condition for fruitful pursuit of God is honesty—intellectual, moral, and religious honesty. Notice that both the Old and the New Testaments insist on truth and love for it. See, for example, Psalm 119 which makes the point over and over, and 1 Peter 1:22 which speaks of our being purified for genuine love by "obedience to the truth." Then there are the Johannine writings: "I am the

Way, the Truth and the Life... [we live a] life of truth and love...
living the life of truth... the Spirit of truth... will lead you to the
complete truth" (Jn 14:6; 2 Jn 2-4; Jn 16:13). God loves reality.
He is the supremely real. Since truth is the conformity of the mind
to reality, we also must love truth, for by it we are in touch with the
way things really are.

**13. Question:** It seems that devotion to truth as you are applying
it to our subject means more than simply an intellectual assent to
revelation. What would some corollaries be?

**Comment:** The disciple must be transparently honest in disclosing
what is relevant. Among the duties St. Francis de Sales mentions is
a complete openness of mind and heart, telling one's guide everything pertinent, good and bad, hiding nothing and pretending
nothing. This candor assures that what is sound in the directee will
be confirmed and strengthened, what is unsound will be healed
and corrected.[1]

**14. Question:** St. Francis' reference to correction raises a touchy
point. Probably it, too, is a corollary of love for truth. I presume
there is sometimes a need, even a duty, to give and receive fraternal
admonition. Most of us find that hard, both to offer candidly and
to receive graciously.

**Comment:** We do indeed, but the wisdom literature of the Old
Testament over and over insists that the wise person welcomes correction and the fool resists it.[2] "The man who lacks intelligence
cannot be taught," says Sirach, but "the wise man's knowledge will
increase like a flood, and his advice is like a living spring" (Sir
21:12-13). We all readily see that there is no point in going to a
medical doctor unless we are willing to follow his diagnosis and
suggested remedy. So also it makes little sense to take the time of a
spiritual mentor if one is merely looking for a confirmation of
one's own view of things. This is as true of the bishop who sought
guidance from St. Teresa as it is true of the pauper who may seek it
from a bishop.

**15. Question:** Then I suppose the next corollary you will mention is obedience to the director. Yet there is a problem here: a spiritual guide ordinarily has no authority of office—no jurisdiction over the disciple. How could one then give an order that requires the response of obedience?

**Comment:** Before I respond to your question perhaps we should recall that through the centuries writers have spoken of a directee's obedience to his or her confessor or director. St. Teresa, for example, held that once a person has chosen a competent guide, the second duty is obedience. More than once the saint speaks of her policy of never going contrary to what her confessor advised or commanded. For her this was to take seriously what the Lord himself said of the Church's representatives: they who listen to those he sends are listening to him.[3] St. Paul added that the Thessalonians were to show respect and affection toward their leaders (1 Thes 5:12-13), and the letter to the Hebrews, 13:17, adds obedience to these duties.

**16. Question:** But that does not fully answer my question: how can there be obedience when there is no jurisdiction? What about when the director is neither a confessor nor a superior in relation to the disciple?

**Comment:** Your correct formulation of the question implies its answer. There is no strict obedience in the sense of conforming to a precept given by a duly constituted authority, civil or ecclesiastical. But there is what we may call an 'obedience' of prudence, following sensible and needed advice. In this latter meaning we 'obey' the directions of a medical doctor or a spiritual guide. We welcome their admonitions as well.

**17. Question:** In this sense, then, we must be speaking of 'obedience to advice,' following the directions and welcoming the admonitions of a wisely chosen mentor.

**Comment:** Well said. And we need to reflect on the biblical idea here once again and how thoroughly the saints live according to it.

With no hidden bluntness the sage declares that fools are confident that their way of doing things is correct, while sensible people listen to advice (Prv 12:15). Blaise Pascal, a physicist and a mathematical genius, was nonetheless humble enough to jot into his notebook, "Total submission to Jesus Christ and to my spiritual director."[4] The saints do likewise, and they assume that anyone serious about sanctity does the same. St. Paul loved the Corinthians so deeply that he wept while having to correct them (he states that his tears were due to his not wanting to hurt them), and yet he also lays down the truth without flinching (2 Cor 2:4-8). St. Teresa loved her nuns dearly, and in an especially tender way Maria de San José. Yet she did not hesitate to point out their faults, and in Maria, even an occasional "silliness." St. Bernard loved his first cousin, Robert, with remarkable tenderness, but when the youth left the austere, rough life of Citeaux for the relaxed, more comfortable monastery of Cluny, the saint did not spare the verbal rod in reproving him.

**18. Question:** Apparently, then, there seems to be no room for a directee to disagree, to contend with his or her guide. Is this so?

**Comment:** Provided one's mentor is competent and remains faithful to the mind of the Church and to prayer, the disciple should ordinarily follow guidance given without disagreeing and objecting. There is a place for questions and representations of difficulties, but they should not be frequent. The directee who often objects to advice is hardly seeking guidance. Such a person is really pursuing a confirmation of self-will. The early Eastern writer, St. Nilus, was strong on this point: "Just as the artist shows his art in the material, and the material does not resist him, so does the teacher apply his knowledge of virtue upon obedient disciples who do not contradict him in anything."[5] The self-willed client by an argumentative attitude is not only avoiding the benefits of obedience, but is dissuading the mentor from speaking his or her mind openly.

**19. Question:** What do you think of a vow of obedience to one's mentor? I personally would be put off by someone who wanted to control my life in such an authoritarian, self-appointed way. So I do not favor a vow of obedience to a spiritual director as this was sometimes practiced in the past. No one is ultimately responsible for my soul before God but myself. I value advice, but in the end it is I who make decisions regarding my life, and I who have to take full responsibility for them, while acting upon the light I have received.

**Comment:** Good people have made this vow. But certainly the director should never propose the vow, or other ones such as never changing directors or never consulting anyone else.[6] People who cut themselves off from the rest of the Church are in grave danger of falling into error. As a matter of fact their very separatism is an error of no small consequence. I personally would be uncomfortable with a vow made to obey me. However, if a director does allow it, "it should be," as de Guibert correctly cautions, "within narrow and well defined limits."[7] Hence, I have no problem with your view. It is clear what you are rejecting: over-control and self-appointed authoritarianism. In some cases a vow may be in order, although ordinarily I would not advise it. An exception, for example, would be that of a canonical hermit who lives in obedience under a bishop's authority and according to an ecclesiastically approved rule of life. Since the bishop may choose to delegate authority to the hermit's director, the hermit would in that case be bound by vow to obey the director according to the rule and not outside of it.

**20. Question:** Is it proper to have more than one spiritual director at a given time? Or if you have only one, would it be wrong to consult someone else on occasion?

**Comment:** Three main points should be borne in mind in response to this question. First of all, given the faith dimension of genuine supernatural guidance and its ecclesial origin, a person should not shop around in an effort to find someone who will agree with his or her own judgment—to find confirmation of one's own self-will. Second, there is sometimes a sound reason to seek advice from someone other than one's usual mentor. This would be the case when one's usual guide, while competent in most matters, may not be such in a given area. Making this point, St. John of the Cross uses a charming example: "Not everyone capable of hewing the wood knows how to carve the statue."[8] There are priests who are suitable in most aspects of the spiritual life, but wisely disqualify themselves in questions of infused contemplation. Likewise, a directee may on occasion seek a second opinion when there is sound reason to think one's mentor may be mistaken. Third, given the judgment of competency one makes in selecting a guide, a person should not have two or more directors. Not only does this waste time for the parties involved, but it also readily leads to confusion in the directee. Once again St. John of the Cross offers wise advice: "A soul should find its support wholly and entirely in its director, for not to do so would amount to no longer wanting a director. And when one director is sufficient and suitable, all the others are useless or a hindrance."[9]

**21. Question:** Is it advisable for a directee to quote the director's advice in handling a domestic problem either in marriage or religious life? For instance, if a husband or wife asks the opinion of the director regarding an in-law problem or a financial difficulty, should the spouse cite him or her as an authority? Should a religious sister or brother cite the confessor's opinion about a community situation?

**Comment:** Ordinarily I think not. The directee may use the information or opinion, but as coming from themselves, not as from the director or confessor. I have three reasons for taking this position. The first is that the director or confessor has no authority to decide the inner runnings of a community or a married household. Second, his or her knowledge is limited, perhaps even partial. After all, the director has heard only one side of a problem. Third, citing the opinion may be resented as an intrusion into the private affairs of the family or religious community.

## THE DIRECTOR

**22. Question:** Even though you have devoted a whole chapter to the matter of competency in a director, I have a number of questions that go beyond professional knowledge. For instance, I would think that people endeavoring to "put on Christ" should be warned about what we might term psychologizing guides, those who view the spiritual life through naturalistic categories. They probably mean well, and do possess some truth, but the emphasis centers on what they learned in psychology courses. The supernatural dimension is mighty thin.

**Comment:** Just as there are retreat masters who give 'retreats' based on temperaments and character types, so we have directors such as you describe. There may be a veneer of spirituality but little substance. Sound psychology can, of course, contribute to the analysis and healing of human wounds and to living happily at home or in the workplace. It can further healthy community in marriage or priesthood or religious life. But there is far more to Gospel living, as you well know.

**23. Question:** Then there are guides who offer advice on the basis of personal preferences or of fads. They may even be trained in theology. They may know what the Catholic Church teaches, but it is not integrated into their own lives or into the guidance they offer to others. No doubt you take a dim view of this approach so at odds with the Gospel.

**Comment:** Yes, I do. The problem is not a new one. It is significant that both Carmelite doctors deal with it in their works. One of the faults St. Teresa writes of more than once is the tendency of directors to discount the importance of small things,[10] or to explain away well-founded guilt. She considered priests who gave her "liberal and permissive" advice as not knowing any better, for "what was venial sin they said was no sin at all, and what was serious mortal sin they said was venial." She wrote of the problem, she noted, to warn others "against so great an evil."[11] The gentle St. John of the Cross reserves his strongest term of condemnation for worldly guides who either positively turn people from the hard road and narrow gate or who simply fail to advise their charges to practice complete generosity in following Gospel holiness. There are men and women in our day as well as in past ages who, inspired to heroic virtue, may meet with sundry rationalizations to cut corners, to lower their aims and aspirations, to seek a soft and easy way, to avoid the cross and ample time for prayer. Counseling mediocrity is, says our saint, "another more pestiferous trait." These mentors "fully clothed in worldliness, since they do not enter by the narrow gate of life... do not let others enter either." They are like "barriers or obstacles at the gate of heaven, hindering those who seek their counsel from entering." They must face the threat of Jesus himself, notes John: "woe to you, for you have taken away the key of knowledge and you neither enter yourselves nor do you allow others to enter."[12]

**24. Question:** In a religious congregation what sort of relationship does the formation director have with those being formed, where matters of conscience are involved? Should the latter receive all 'inner forum' guidance from the former or should the candidates have access to outside consultation?

**Comment:** It goes without saying that the formation director is responsible for ordinary lecture instructions and for the management of routine activities. Usually such a person also handles spiritual direction ('inner forum') as well. In fact, in small communities he or she may be the only one available for it. However, it does seem best to me that those in formation be free to consult, at least on occasion, with some other solid priest or religious. St. Teresa wanted her nuns to have the opportunity to obtain guidance from "learned men," and the Church provides confessors from whom outside help can be sought. It can easily enough happen that an individual may find great difficulty in discussing some particular subject with the formation director.

**25. Question:** But once in a while you find congregations or monasteries that frown upon, if not forbid, a member seeking guidance from someone outside the community. I suppose they feel that this outside director's advice may not be consonant with the 'spirit of the community.' Is this fear justified?

**Comment:** In normal circumstances, no. A sensible mentor does not contradict any sound spirituality, because he and it are in complete accord with the Gospel and the teaching of the Church. I fear for groups that prevent access to outside input, for they are probably narrow and myopic. Indeed, if they are turned in on themselves alone, they can lose the liberating sense of the universal Church, and distortions can develop. Magnanimous St. Teresa knew better. Carmelite herself, she welcomed direction from members of any religious order, provided they were competent and prayerful. I find that her sensible daughters today are of a like mind.

**26. Question:** What about confidentiality? This surely is an obligation of the director? Does theology have anything to say on this point relevant to the directive relationship?

**Comment:** Yes to both questions. Moral theology deals with confidentiality under the label of secrecy, and in this case, professional secrecy. You can find a complete treatment in any solid moral theology manual. For our purpose a few remarks will suffice. Like a medical doctor, a counselor, or a lawyer, a spiritual director is bound to confidentiality by the office. The client need not seek an expressed verbal assurance. Ordinarily what is said within their communications remains there. It is not to be related to others or used in ways that could embarrass or harm the directee. Exceptions are rare and to be admitted only in the grave circumstances spoken of in moral theology. People must have the freedom to discuss their problems with the assurance that no one else will hear of them.

## FINDING A SUITABLE DIRECTOR

**27. Question:** We come to the crucial question of locating a suitable guide, a pivotal concern. When you consider the demanding qualifications competent direction requires and the paucity of programs, in seminary or otherwise, that respond to meeting these qualifications, you conclude that finding a suitable guide seems a formidable task, especially in exploring the higher reaches of contemplative prayer. Would you agree?

**Comment:** Yes, I surely do. The problem is widespread. One of the most difficult and frequent questions I am asked after lectures on advancing prayer and in response to my writings on Saints John of the Cross and Teresa of Avila centers on this practical problem: where and how can I find the kind of guidance your lecture and book suppose? Some add to their question the comment that they have searched but to no avail.

**28. Question:** You don't sound optimistic. Can anything be done? Is there any reason to think that earnest men and women can somewhere and somehow get the help they desire and need?

**Comment:** The answer to both of your questions is affirmative— even though I agree that this is a very complex problem. Surely, if contemplative gazing on the beauty of the Lord is the "one thing" necessary, the highest priority in human life (Ps 27:4), God will provide for those who are determined to grow in it. The present volume represents one modest effort to supply some help both for those who do find competent direction and for those who do not, explaining what can be done in practical terms. Furthermore, going beyond our puny efforts, important though it is to make them, we should expect great things from God's providence. Saints ask for seeming impossibilities and the Lord gives them what they desire. St. Francis de Sales declared that people will find the "loyal friend" if they fear the Lord (Sir 6:16), that is, if they are humble and sincerely desire to grow in holiness. Recommending to Philothea as highly important that she implore the Lord to send her a guide after his own heart, he assures her that he who sent from heaven an angel to show Tobias the way will send her some-one trustworthy and faithful.[13] The biblically wise person exudes the same confidence. After a lengthy section on whom to choose and whom to avoid in seeking guidance, quoting Scripture, St. Francis declares, "Besides all this beg the Most High to guide your steps in the truth" (Sir 37:19).

**29. Question:** I am wondering who judges the suitability of the mentor? As you already noted (Chapter Five), the Church has no test equivalent to state examinations for the practice of law and medicine. Anyone who wishes, competent or incompetent, may offer 'spiritual direction.'

**Comment:** Astonishing as this situation is, it remains a stark reality. One can wonder if Jesus himself had this sort of thing in mind when he said that the children of this world are wiser in their generation than the children of light (Lk 16:8). In any event, for most people the burden of judging suitability falls on the one searching. St. John of the Cross supposes that the directee selects the guide when he remarks that a "person, desiring to advance in recollection and perfection, take care into whose hands he entrusts himself, for the disciple will become like the master."[14] The situation has not changed.

**30. Question:** Would you summarize the main qualifications for which the directee should look?

**Comment:** Because this matter was discussed in the previous chapter, a mere sketch will suffice here. First, the directee should seek a prayerful person, one who is in earnest about a love relationship with God, who takes seriously both liturgical worship and contemplative solitude. Second, the mentor should be distinguished for ecclesial solidity, or as the New Testament puts it in the pastoral epistles, "sound doctrine." As twenty centuries of Church history painfully show, deviating views promote neither deep prayer nor heroic holiness. Third, the director needs adequate theological education, which entails either years of formal study or, in the case of intelligent people, extensive personal reading, study, and reflection. A few courses in 'spirituality' or 'spiritual direction' will not do. Fourth, sound judgment and experience of life are requisite. Fifth, the guide should have a sufficient understanding of psychology, including the ability to recognize human woundedness (for example, neuroses, drug abuse, alcoholism, sexual aberrations) and to know when to make referrals. Finally, the seeker looks for a mentor to whom he or she can readily relate, and be at ease. All these qualifications will enable the director to inspire in the directee a well-founded confidence.

**31. Question:** As you remarked previously, people who measure up to these standards must be rare. Perhaps they should not be rare—if we trained candidates adequately—but they are. How does one go about finding the gem, the "treasured friend" Scripture speaks about?

**Comment:** As St. Francis de Sales put it, sincere prayer comes first. Then one can make tentative judgments regarding fitness from listening to homilies and attending lectures in the locality, or from reading any written works by the individual. Or recommendations may be obtained by phoning the chancery office or a community of cloistered nuns or monks. Or one may ask others, cleric or lay, who have lived in the area for some years and may well know two or three solid choices. I suppose, of course, that all these sources of possible recommendations are themselves reliable, that is, prayerful and of one mind with the Church.

**32. Question:** But are not possible candidates for the office who fit your criteria going to be busy, probably too busy, to take on still another task?

**Comment:** Exactly! In a sense that is the way it should be: competent and generous men and women tend to be in demand. A person that is not busy might not be the one for this job. But let your prospective director make the judgment as to whether he or she can take you on. If you do not ask for too much time with visits or letters, the person in question can probably accommodate you.

**33. Question:** When you actually contact someone, do you ask right off: "Will you be my spiritual director?"

**Comment:** I think not. Until the two of you have actually met and exchanged thoughts, you can hardly be sure that a permanent relationship is desirable. Ordinarily, you might begin by asking simply: "May I see you sometime at your convenience? I'd like to talk with you about prayer (or whatever the question may be)." Then, another meeting may or may not be arranged.

**34. Question:** What is a good reason to change directors?

**Comment:** For sure the reason should not be a flimsy one. Nor should a change be sought because of worldly motivation, such as a reluctance to live the radical Gospel or a disinclination to obey the Church's mind. On the other hand, if the directee finds that the director notably lacks one or other of the qualifications mentioned in Comment Thirty, it may be time to look elsewhere.

## APPROACHES AND METHODS

**35. Question:** What do you think of spiritual direction by mail?

**Comment:** People differ in their reactions to this question. Some feel they can explain themselves better on paper, while others do well in person but poorly in writing. Directors also differ. Some flatly refuse to direct by letter. Others do it and usually experience no special problems. For myself, if I first meet the person, exchanges by mail are satisfactory, even though they usually cannot be as thorough as verbal exchanges. In my view, direction by mail is far preferable to no direction at all. I would add, however, that the directee should be sure to respond to and comment on what the director has written. Many say little or nothing in response to the director's letter, so that the latter can only guess what reaction, if any, took place. Was my advice accepted, ignored, or rejected? What effects have come of it so far? With no response the correspondence becomes more of a monologue. You might be surprised at how common this is. The director responds to the directee, but the following letter fails to comment on what the former has written. Or the reverse can happen. The director leaves unanswered some of the questions or difficulties raised by the directee. For those whose style of writing is overly abbreviated guidance by mail may not suffice.

**36. Question:** How does one go about the direction itself? How does one begin? Is there a set way or procedure? How is one to know what the mentor expects in a conversation or how to write a letter of this type?

**Comment:** Individual guides would probably answer these queries differently. For myself, I know of no set form or format. I would say just be yourself. Write or speak as you are, as things occur to you. Bring up what you wish, what concerns you. We will manage to get to what you need. If the relationship is to be permanent, that is, if it is not confined to one or two conversations about one particular problem, I usually ask the person to write a brief résumé with background information: family and early home life, religion, number of siblings, personal conflicts, educational pluses and minuses, friendships, self-image, personal problems in the past and present, aspirations, vocational history. This résumé, which need not be long, provides the mentor with a context. It also ensures that unnecessary detailing of the directee's past will not waste time during personal sessions or in correspondence.

**37. Question:** Do spiritual directors use interview approaches that are taught to counselors? If they do, should the directee know something about them?

**Comment:** Knowingly or not, a spiritual director is bound to be following one or another of possible approaches, or a combination of them. While this volume does not aim primarily at presenting a guide to directors as such, we think it useful to draw the attention of directees to the fact that there are two fundamentally different approaches that counselors use in their work: directive and non-directive. Some follow the first, others the second. Still others mingle the two according to what is being discussed. In the directive method, as the name suggests, guides positively lead the course of the conversation or contribute to where it goes. While they may on occasion introduce the subject, they surely give information, ask questions, and express their opinion regarding the client's views, reactions, and statements. The non-directive approach likewise corresponds to its name. Such counselors do not positively steer the course of the session nor do they usually offer information.

The directors are reluctant, indeed may positively refuse even if asked, to express their opinion regarding the client's views, problems, actions, or reactions. Directors do not advise the client as to what to think, say, or do. What they do is reflect back to the person what the latter has said: "You feel, then, that your husband (or wife) doesn't understand your limitations," or "It seems to you that your supervisor commonly misinterprets your intentions," or "You usually blame yourself for what goes wrong." The idea in this procedure is that reflecting back draws the client out to further insights and leads to eventual healing.

**38. Question:** What do you think of these techniques? Would you mind saying how you yourself operate?

**Comment:** There is need, it seems to me, for a blending of both approaches. At times I find it helpful to reflect back what a person has said, and at others there is need to ask questions, to give information, or to express opinion. Whatever one may think of an exclusively non-directive method on a merely human level, it alone cannot suffice on the supernatural level. The very name, spiritual direction, suggests as much. The supernatural by definition cannot be drawn out of the natural no matter how skilled or clever the reflecting may be.

**39. Question:** Should guide and disciple chart out a plan for their meetings—a one- or two-year program?

**Comment:** If they judge that plotting out a long-range agenda may be useful, it surely may be tried. In my experience, however, neither I nor my directees have been inclined to pursue that course.

**40. Question:** What topics should be included or excluded in spiritual direction? Is there some necessity to cover certain areas in a more or less systematic way?

**Comment:** I have discovered over the years that almost any topic can come up in spiritual direction. Usually people are not inclined to a systematic choice of subjects, nor do I see any need to adhere to a logical sequence. We are not made that way. However, in my experience, among the questions that surface most frequently are problems in human relationships and inquiries about contemplative prayer. The latter emphasis is why we devote two entire chapters in this volume to prayer and contemplation. To be excluded would be topics that bear little or no relation to one's life with God: political concerns, unneeded excursions into one's past life, detailed narrations of conversations one has had, descriptions of faults of other people. If these subjects do bear on the directee's spiritual life, usually a brief summary is adequate. If more is needed, if something is not clear, the mentor can ask.

**41. Question:** I understand that no list of recommended topics can be exhaustive. But it may be helpful if you would offer a sampling of questions one might consider as a preparation for meetings with one's mentor, whether verbally or by letter.

**Comment:** I hesitate to provide a listing of this type, but if we bear in mind the individuality of the person and the unique slant each one has on his or her questions and problems, a number of suggestions may be useful. Here then are some illustrations:

- Does my way of going about meditative or contemplative prayer seem to be working? Am I profiting from it? Am I making progress? And how do I determine that? Where am I in prayer development? Am I hitting any snags? Do I have problems I don't know how to handle? Am I faithful to giving adequate time to prayerful solitude? Is it my top priority, the "one thing" in my life?

- Am I prayerful during the day—without neglecting others or my work? How can I grow in this recollection?

- Do I waste time? Engage in idle gossip? Indulge in superfluities or in excessive amusements?

- What have I been selecting for spiritual reading? What audio- and videotapes? Am I going about this exercise in the best way for me? Am I growing in and through it? Do I read or listen in a prayerful manner? What books should I read now? What books should I avoid altogether or read with caution?

- Am I improving in humility, patience, love for neighbor, obedience, frugality, indeed, in all the Gospel virtues? What are my weak points that need focused attention?

- In my daily round of duties is my motivation mixed, that is, are unworthy motives mingled with my worthy ones? Am I even aware of this problem? What can I do about it?

- Is my mind in accord with Scripture and the teaching of the Church, which is to say, is it in accord with the mind of Jesus himself?

- How am I using or misusing the mass media? Am I wasting time in my use of them?

- Have I been chaste in thought and reading and speaking and looking (television and actual life) and in my actions? In practical ways am I trying to serve *both* God and mammon?

- Do I suffer daily crosses like a disciple of the crucified Master, with love and in union with him? Do I welcome these opportunities to unite with the Lord on his cross?

- Have I been warm and cordial toward everyone, even toward unattractive people, including those who are cold and indifferent toward me?

- Is my emotional life balanced? Are my responses of joy or sorrow or fear excessive? Am I oversensitive? Do I live more by feelings than by will? Am I insensitive?

- Am I concerned for the poor, both the materially and the spiritually poor? Do I come to their aid? Do I live frugally and share with the needy?

- Am I handling my time pressure problems properly, so that first things come first?

- Where is my center of gravity: earth or heaven (Col 3:1-2)? Do I seek things for themselves or as a means of leading me and others to God?

**42. Question:** If that is a sampling, I rather shudder to think of what a complete list would look like. If anything demonstrates in short order the necessity of spiritual direction, these questions do indeed! And they lead to still another question: you have not yet discussed how often we should consult with our mentors. You must have an opinion.

**Comment:** Yes, I do. No set schedule should be laid down for all people. Frequency of meetings or letters depends on a number of factors: time availability of the director, the needs of the directee, and the individual capacity to absorb what is given. We cannot do everything in one month or even a year. Ordinarily beginners need more attention than those who are mature in living the Gospel. This is why in solid religious novitiates and seminaries the young people confer with their guides every two weeks or on a monthly basis.

**43. Question:** Do some people discuss things to death, constantly returning to the same problem or issue far beyond need?

**Comment:** Yes, at times. Experience suggests that the main reason for repetition in spiritual direction, even to three and four times in one conversation, is deep inner pain. People can hurt so much that they probably do not realize they are going over the same material at great length. Less frequently they may be resisting the mentor's advice or feel that they are not understood. Whatever the cause, in the ancient East the insistence on frequent manifestation of thoughts together with the large number of disciples made lengthy discussions practically impossible. But this was not the only reason for brevity. One did not dispute what the master said. The disciple might ask for a clarification, but docility required that one accept and ponder the concise instruction given. Then, too, there was the fear of idle words, so strongly condemned in the wisdom literature of the Old Testament, and indeed by Jesus himself. "Only rarely," comments Hausherr, "did the master agree to discuss things; if an obstinate disciple did not let himself be convinced, it was better to ask God to change the disciple's heart or to think of a stratagem to make him understand his error indirectly."[15] Letters of direction were usually brief, sometimes astonishingly so. "Many contain only a line or two, even one word, while others [run] to a maximum of two pages."[16] Even though many of us in the modern West would find all this severe, we can hardly deny all basis for it.

## SACRAMENT OF RECONCILIATION AND DIRECTION

**44. Question:** While there is widespread concern about the lack of competent directors, it seems on a moment's reflection that the Church has a divinely provided answer in the Sacrament of Reconciliation. How are the two related, if indeed there is a relation?

**Comment:** Even though most priests are not trained to guide souls into the higher reaches of contemplative prayer and all that is necessarily connected with it, there is a decidedly close relationship in many other areas of the spiritual life. The confessor who functions in this sacrament as he ought is not only an absolver from sin, but also a physician of souls.

**45. Question:** We have spoken of the unique needs of the particular person, and what could be more one-on-one than auricular confession: one priest and one penitent? Would you say more about this?

**Comment:** The Sacrament of Reconciliation answers to one of the deepest needs of the human person: individual, personalized, sympathetic attention to one's woundedness, difficulties, and aspirations, yes, even to one's darknesses and confusions in the pursuit of God. Psychotherapists have discovered what God in his providence long ago committed to his Church. Confession, especially to a regular confessor, is the usual locus, the ordinary place of supernatural guidance for most people. If it is used prayerfully and competently, it becomes an invaluable treasure in the pursuit of God. This is one reason among others why general absolution except in rare circumstances is so wrong: there is no opportunity for addressing individual hurts, needs, obscurities, and entanglements. Just as a medical doctor cannot treat five hundred people with one prescription—he or she is ignorant of each person's problems—neither can the priestly doctor in general absolution.

**46. Question:** Yet spiritual guidance in the confessional does have its limitations in the everyday life of the Church as we find it.

**Comment:** Correct. There is the brevity of time for one thing. When others are waiting in line, neither the confessor nor the penitent feels free to say a whole lot. But if they avoid unnecessary details, the main factors of a problem and its solution can often be addressed. We have already alluded to the limitation of many priests in their ability to guide people in developing intimacy with God. But at the same time, if a confessor is sincere, he can improve his competency in prayer matters and probably be of help in this area as well.

**47. Question:** I would think that having a regular confessor could be a powerful aid to supernatural growth, supposing, of course, that he is both knowledgeable and interested.

**Comment:** Yes, undoubtedly. Through regular reception of the sacrament each partner gets to know the other, and there can be follow-up as they pursue a consistent plan or program. There is likewise the grace of the sacrament and the possibility of checking up on progress. We should value, too, the ecclesial mission ("whose sins you forgive, they are forgiven them.... Whatever you bind... loose..." Jn 20:23; Mt 18:18) which the confessor possesses in this sacred forum. Understanding and respecting this enhances its power and value.

**48. Question:** Are there times when confession should be kept separate from direction? If a priest is suitable for the first, does it follow that he is suitable for the second?

**Comment:** In view of all we have said about competency and the universal call to contemplation the answer to your second question is no—at least if you mean it to cover all cases. However, a good confessor should usually be a fit guide for at least some areas of the spiritual life. The penitent would then limit inquiries to those areas. In response to your first question, yes, confession is frequently kept separate from direction, if the latter refers to the full relationship. But any confessor has the right, and sometimes the duty, to comment on what has been confessed. That is part of his being a physician of souls. However, the penitent also has a right to seek extended and regular direction from his chosen guide, who may not be the confessor.

**49. Question:** Since the primary purpose of the Sacrament of Reconciliation is the forgiveness of sins, does it necessarily include direction?

**Comment:** My immediately preceding comment indicates that the answer to this question is yes, if and when such is needed or useful. Because a confessor is to aid the healing of sin-caused wounds in the penitent and further growth in virtue, he surely ought ordinarily to offer advice and instruction with these aims in view. This sort of guidance can be termed spiritual direction, even if the confessor is not the penitent's regular or permanent guide in the full sense. Bishop Kallistos Ware has remarked, "Confession is like going to a hospital rather than a court of law; the penance is not so much a punishment as a tonic to assist the patient in his recovery."[17] In this sacrament the priest is both a judge and a physician, even though both he and penitent can only too easily lose sight of the second function and be content with the first, the absolution.

**50. Question:** What, then, given what you have just said, of the confessor whose admonition is something very general and probably the same for everyone? This is more akin to a very brief homily than individualized help.

**Comment:** You are right, but if the penitent desires specific help and does not receive it, he or she can ask a specific question—if the confessor seems competent in that area. Hopefully the penitent would then receive individualized advice.

**51. Question:** When a person does not have a spiritual director, is there merit in submitting to a confessor for his blessing such things as one's Lenten program or an important career decision?

**Comment:** In my view the answer to this question turns on the quality of the confessor. If, for example, I know that the priest downplays the role of self-denial, I shall not ask his view of my Lenten resolutions. I am not sure I'd submit a career decision (which, recall, is not a vocation) to a confessor's judgment, unless the decision has tangible supernatural implications.

SEVEN

# Can I Direct Myself?

F ROM CASUAL COMMENTS heard through the years I have
learned that more than a few people do not begin reading a
book at its beginning, which, as a song lyric in *The Sound of Music*
notes, is a very good place to start. It may be especially appropriate
for this volume to suggest that if the reader is beginning with the
present chapter, a mistake is probably being made. The question
mark in the chapter title hints at the misstep.

Without exploring our first six chapters the reader may not be
prepared to appreciate the questions and proposed solutions
offered in the present discussion.[1] Indeed, one may entertain simplistic interpretations of them.

We now tackle a thorny question, a less than ideal situation,
which nonetheless is only too common. What of the person who,
despite earnest efforts, cannot find a suitable guide? Is self-direction
advisable? If not, where does one turn? If yes, what can self-direction
mean, given that Scripture and our whole tradition rule out going
solely on the basis of one's own ideas and preferences? We are supposing here the sort of universal spontaneous initiative that is an
immediate consequence of native human freedom. Endowed as we
are with intellect and will, each of us makes free choices—always, of
course, with the divine concurrence. We are likewise taking for
granted that a healthy spiritual life includes the robust ability to
make practical applications of revealed truths in daily life. We cannot, and need not, run to a guide for our every decision.

Self-direction in this context could mean two things, and we must be clear as to which of the two we have in mind. In its ordinary sense, the expression refers to a spontaneous and this-worldly following of one's own ideas, plans, and reasonings by using one's own resources as guided by common sense and human thinking. This is what St. Paul calls the foolishness of human wisdom (1 Cor 1:20).[2] Hence, for an authentic disciple self-direction cannot mean living according to private principles and a personally-determined agenda. To put the matter in Jesus' terms, this would be the wide and easy road to perdition, to eternal disaster.

What we do have in mind is the man or woman who has sought to find a competent personal guide, but to no avail. Although this individual never lacks the wisdom derived from the light of Christ radiating visibly from the Church he founded,[3] there is a sense in which such a person is self-directed. Even though one follows the Incarnate Word speaking in the liturgy, the magisterium, and the saints, this person applies these resources to his or her own case as much as possible. One of the main purposes of this book is precisely to help people to keep from straying from the path that leads to the summit.[4] The question, therefore, is whether this type of self-direction may be valid, given the circumstance of having nothing else available. And if it is legitimate, what would prevent people from wandering off into erroneous byways and even to the ill-founded conclusions of which history, past and present, is full?

The first answer to this admittedly difficult problem is to evaluate the pat responses that many take for granted: read the Bible and use common sense. God has given both gifts, and he is pleased when we use them to our best ability. He condemns no one who means well. What else can be done?

While this solution may appear plausible, it does not stand up to careful scrutiny. At some length in Chapters Two and Four, we considered the hard view Scripture itself takes of those who trust their own judgment, who do not seek out and follow the counsel of a wise guide. The New Testament demands that the disciples listen to and accept the teaching Church, not their private interpretations: "Whoever listens to you listens to me" (Lk 10:16, NAB).

Scripture itself rules out 'Scripture alone.' Further, we find that the saints are eager to be guided by others whom the Lord provides, and not by their private opinions. Who these others may be we shall consider in the course of this chapter.

Our third reason for rejecting the 'Bible and common sense' view is experience. All through the centuries as well as in our own day, we meet repeated examples of aberrations, both spectacular and prosaic, of people who are confident in their own views and reject any sort of direction. Ronald Knox chronicled in his lengthy tome, *Enthusiasm,* the better known of these extravagant claims, teachings, practices, and movements. And who in our own day can have failed to notice defective ideas—yes, sometimes bizarre ideas—about matters religious that friends and acquaintances commonly entertain?

St. Teresa found it "alarming" how easily some people assume that their imaginings are messages from God. I confess that I share her alarm. A 'visionary' can claim to have received hundreds of visions, and proceed to fill volumes with details on the life of Jesus allegedly received by way of dictation. It seems hardly to occur to many avid readers that they should be critical of claims like these, and that they may thus be distracted from the real Gospel of which we are sure. Self-direction according to 'the pat view' account can lead to a huge waste of time, if not to regression and perhaps to disaster.

## PROBLEMS AND OBSTACLES

We turn our attention, therefore, to the specific difficulties one who has no personal director must face. We shall then be prepared to consider what one may do concretely when no human guide is available.

**1. Question**: We may take it as obvious, I trust, that even though self-direction can have an acceptable meaning, it does lack the immediate and interpersonal ecclesiality that one-on-one guidance enjoys. This you have made clear in earlier comments. What other problems are there?

**Comment:** We may begin with what Frank Sheed called autokiddery, that is, a lack of self-knowledge, our great capacity for rationalizing and self-deception. Unless a person is of saintly caliber, heroic in virtue, and profoundly deep in prayer life, he or she should not underestimate the degree of personal entanglement in the world and its values. "Be quite sure," admonishes Newman, "that every one of us, even the poorest and the most dull and insensible, is far more attached to this world than he can possibly imagine."[5] We readily deceive ourselves in dozens of ways: perhaps as to the amount and quality of dining and drinking, perhaps about the real reasons for buying new clothes, or for engaging in idle conversations and excessive recreation. An alert director can readily notice and point out to the disciple what may well be hidden from the latter. Spiritual direction should be a powerful help to unmasking rationalization as it is likewise a source of objective evaluation on how much progress one is actually making or not making.

**2. Question:** I would like to pursue the last remark. One of my chief problems is that I am constantly thinking of myself: my wishes, my memories, my plans, my ideas. I suspect that my self-evaluation is off the mark.

**Comment:** You are fortunate in having the suspicion. Worse off are those who lack it. Especially beset with ego-absorption are people in pain, physical or psychological. Some hardly think of anything but their own sufferings. Their letters and conversations deal almost entirely with themselves and little with the pains of others. Although we can and should sympathize with their inner hurting, they could profit immensely from a mentor who aids them in being altruistic. Though Jesus was in torture on the cross, he thought of praying for his persecutors, of caring for his mother, of securing the good thief's salvation. Without a director we are in greater danger of getting lost in ourselves, and also of failing to assess realistically our progress.

**3. Question:** In my readings over the years I have noticed that the masters insist on the importance of self-knowledge, the 'know thyself' idea. *The Imitation of Christ,* for example, declares that "the humble knowledge of thyself is a surer way to God than the deepest search after science."[6] I would suppose that a good guide would sensitize directees to their deficiencies as well as give advice on how to overcome them.

**Comment:** Correct. Most of us possess only a dim awareness of the many subtle defects that dampen enthusiasm and maim full generosity. What we have in mind here is not a weak self-image, for that is based on unreality. Rather what we envision is the host of actual defects beginners commonly do not see in themselves: unrealized vanities, inclinations to laziness, idle talking, other useless 'time killers' and distractions, needless indulgences of the palate, cravings for human respect, resistance to correction, love for superfluities, reluctance to obey, a desire for artificial excitements and amusements. Without a living guide it is mighty hard to be aware of these faults, let alone overcome them. Furthermore, self-direction does not readily remedy simple mistakes or lack of information.

**4. Question:** You have already noted how people uncritically assume that alleged visions are to be accepted and promoted. But there are other mistakes. I've heard it said that religious do not need spiritual direction because their rule and superior are guidance enough. Is that true?

**Comment:** No, indeed. Like Scripture itself, a rule needs to be explained and applied. Saints Bernard and Teresa, for example, firmly believed in following their rules, but they had the good sense to reject *'regula sola'* (the rule alone) just as they rejected *'Scriptura sola'* (Scripture alone). What you heard underlines the dangers of self-direction. And further, being a superior does not automatically ensure that one is competent to guide souls in all areas of their inner lives.

**5. Question:** I am rather confident that I know how you will respond to my next question, but let me ask it just to be sure.

122 / *Seeking Spiritual Direction*

What would you say to people who find it sufficient to look up or to research answers to their problems in the spiritual life?

**Comment:** Study can at times yield happy solutions. But unless these people are experienced and considerably advanced, they can readily enough misunderstand or even misapply what they have looked up. Moreover, perhaps without realizing it, they may be relying on sources which are questionable.

**6. Question:** I see something else missing in self-direction, namely, the positive support of a friendly guide. This also Scripture recommends. What do you think?

**Comment:** You make a good point. Even if having to render an accounting of one's spiritual regress or progress is not the loftiest motivation, it does have some value. This accounting is absent in self-direction, as is also the kindly prodding that may at times be called for. Missing likewise is encouragement and example. St. Augustine put it well: "One loving soul sets another on fire."

**7. Question:** Many well-intentioned people look for signs from God pointing to what they should do or avoid. Some open the Bible at random and see the text they come upon as God's answer to them. What do you think of this practice of self-guidance?

**Comment:** I do not recommend it, at least not ordinarily. It is true that the apostles drew lots after prayer to select Matthias as Judas' replacement (Acts 1:26), but God can will something for the apostles that he does not will for the rest of us. If one has a guide, I think God would prefer consultation to searching for a special sign. When some of the scribes and Pharisees asked Jesus for a sign, his answer was not encouraging: "It is an evil and unfaithful generation that asks for a sign" (Mt 12:38-39). To expect that God will steer one's finger to an exact line of Scripture seems much like asking for a divine intervention. This is not to say that God does not give signs. It is to say that we should usually exercise caution in actively seeking them. God is not a puppet on a string.

**8. Question:** One more difficulty with self-direction occurs to me. Our literature on discernment usually speaks of ecclesial confirmation as needed for what one thinks are inner movements of the Holy Spirit. If one has no mentor, from where does confirmation come?

**Comment:** A good question, and I am not sure I have a good answer. If the matter is important, one could seek advice from a wise person on a one-time basis. Or if there is absolutely no one available at the moment confirmation is needed, and if the matter cannot be delayed, a special prayer for enlightenment may suffice. What we now take up may also be of help in this situation.

**9. Question:** Before we proceed to this next area let me ask one more question: would self-direction be preferable to doubtfully competent guidance? Suppose in my efforts to find a suitable mentor to aid me in contemplative prayer, the best I can do is discover one who may be competent, but I am not sure of it.

**Comment:** Theoretically speaking, I think it is better to have no director than a probably unsuitable one. My reason is that the latter may positively lead you astray, whereas, in the former situation you can still search on your own for the correct path to follow, and hopefully find it. But practically I think you would do well to make contact with the doubtfully competent person, and from your conversation you could then decide whether or not to continue seeking direction from that person.

## NO DIRECTOR—WHAT THEN?

**10. Question:** It looks as though we are painted into a corner from which there is no graceful and happy escape. Spiritual direction is important and one is in a precarious predicament without it, yet only too often there is no one available. Can anything at all be done?

**Comment:** The situation is not quite as dreary as it appears. Yes, something can be done, a number of things. Not all is lost. St. Teresa remarked that a person who apparently is left without human guidance should not be unduly discouraged. Referring to such people, she said that "now, in respect to the spirit, another greater Lord governs them; they are not without a Superior."[7] This is part of the saint's habitual mind that God takes care of those who seek him earnestly and do whatever they can to serve him well. They will find the help they need, even if it comes in another form than what they expected or for what they wished. Teresa's conviction is well-rooted in the inspired word: we are to pray for divine guidance in the concrete choices of life. "Dispatch your wisdom," implores the sage, "from the holy heavens, send her forth from your throne of glory to help me and to toil with me and teach me what is pleasing to you since she knows and understands everything. She will guide me prudently in my undertakings" (Wis 9:10-11).

**11. Question:** This divine guidance can, of course, come in the form of inner light. But while this is good, one needs external direction to avoid misinterpretation. You have made this point emphatically—from the standpoint of Scripture and the teaching Church. Surely, you are not now retreating from that position, are you?

**Comment:** No, not at all. Let me be specific. Even if one has not yet found a regular guide, one can often at key stages in life talk with a prayerful visiting priest, a good spiritual friend, or a wise nun—someone who is trustworthy. Even if it is only on a one-time basis, it may provide the needed insight or the verification of one's experiences. A person should be alert to these possibilities.

**12. Question:** What about the Sacrament of Reconciliation? In most sections of the country, surely in metropolitan areas, there is a considerable choice of confessors. Wouldn't a one-time consultation through the sacrament be feasible at times?

**Comment:** Yes, it would. This sacrament is a providentially offered opportunity for spiritual guidance, even if a confessor is not one's regular director. A priest in the confessional is not merely an absolver from sin; he is also meant to be a father and physician to a wounded sister or brother. Most of us can find a conscientious confessor, if we try hard enough. Even if he cannot find time outside the sacrament for extended consultation, he can usually spare a few minutes within it. Hence, prepare your question, and then present it briefly and clearly. Ask advice. Beforehand pray the Lord to enlighten your confessor and give him wisdom—for you and for others as well.

**13. Question:** But as you well know, the Sacrament of Reconciliation is more, much more than an opportunity to seek and receive advice. It renews us from within, makes us over, heals our wounds. Would you say something to this effect, since it clearly relates to spiritual growth?

**Comment:** A recent writer vividly made your point in his own version of Newman's thought on the healing each of us needs:

> If I punch you on the nose, say, which I really should not do, I not only offend you, your nose, God, and our relationship, but I also offend my own being. When I sin, I warp myself, I become bent, kinked, corrupt, twisted. The more I sin, rob, lie, punch noses, and so on, the more corrupt my very being becomes. I need forgiveness. A mere juridical forgiveness is not enough. It is not enough simply to be told that my offenses are no longer held against me, that I have been excused punishment, released from the dock, and given my freedom. I am still bent and kinked and warped and twisted. I cannot come to God in that condition. In that condition the very sight of God would be an unendurable agony, I need the sort of forgiveness from him that will penetrate my very being. I need a medicinal forgiveness that will unbend, unkink, unwarp my being. I need straightening out, cleaning up; the moral quality of my very self needs to be restored to the image and likeness of God.[8]

This is what the sacraments do. While we agree with Newman and his commentator, it remains true that people still need verbal guidance from other human beings. Some find aid in a small group when they cannot find a personal director in the parish. There is the danger of the blind leading the blind, but this type of sharing does offer mutual support and encouragement. It may serve at times as a springboard to competent guidance.

**14. Question:** Is there anything else you would advise? Knowing you rather well, I am confident that somewhere down the line you will be speaking about direction received through spiritual reading and from a study of the saints. But before we get to those points would you have any further preparatory thoughts?

**Comment:** Yes, two points occur to me. One is the need for fidelity to prayer and reflection, an especially acute need for anyone without a director. If you are lost on a journey, you stop, and then take stock to find out where you are and where you ought to be. You do not drift along or follow the crowd. Especially in the spiritual life we should turn to Mary. She whose divinely bestowed destiny was to give birth to the Light of the world and to nurture him is ideally equipped to lead all men and women through the centuries to the Way, the Truth, and the Life. She is such because God the Father in his eternal wisdom chose this spotless maiden for her exalted office. Indeed, as Scripture itself avers, she is "the most blessed" of all women (Lk 1:42), the woman "adorned with the sun, standing on the moon, and with twelve stars on her head for a crown" (Rv 12:1). This text is likewise understood of the Virgin-Mother Church—both are integrally linked and are repositories of divine wisdom. St. Bernard with his rare eloquence immortalized the Mother of Jesus as a sure guide in his homily on Luke 1:27, Mary as star of the sea. One should read the whole discourse, but we must be content with a small excerpt from it:

> When the storms of temptation burst upon you, when you see yourself driven upon the rocks of tribulation: look up at the star, call upon Mary. When buffeted by the billows of pride, or ambition, or hatred, or jealousy: look up at the star, call upon Mary. Should anger, or avarice, or carnal desire violently assail

the little vessel of your soul: look up at the star, call upon Mary. If troubled on account of the heinousness of your sins, confounded at the filthy state of your conscience, and terrified at the thought of the awful judgment to come, you are beginning to sink into the bottomless gulf of sadness and to be swallowed up in the black abyss of despair: Oh, then think of Mary![9]

This centuries-old tradition, rooted as it is in the New Testament, admonishes the faithful who are intent on coming closer to her Son to have a tender devotion to the Virgin, for there is no more sure guide to him.


## DISCERNING GOD'S WILL

**15. Question:** Anyone needs to take stock and to follow the biblical criteria for discovering the divine will. This discernment seems especially needful for people who lack a permanent guide to the summit. Could you offer a brief sketch of what is required for an authentic discovery of God's will?

**Comment:** The rest of what will be said in this chapter, as well as the final chapter on assessing progress, will be aimed in this direction. Here I will try to touch on a few basic conditions for attaining the divine mind, which is always identical with our own genuine good. First, let me mention how most people seem to determine their future course of action. Some, with not the least attention to God's will, simply do what they like—what they find appealing, what brings power, pleasure, or prestige. As the saying goes, "If it feels good, do it." Others are planners and talkers. They are strong on meetings and planning, surveys and techniques, methods and procedures. While there is a place in human life for this sort of thing, it cannot be primary in arriving at the divine mind. Scripture has nothing to say about techniques in this regard. The third group are the wise. They follow the Lord's way of discernment.[10]

**16. Question:** That is what I am after. Would you spell it out?

**Comment:** Yes, briefly. The first condition is simple, but not popular: love truth. Almost everyone assumes they possess this trait, but the evidence is overwhelming that most really love their preferences and pleasures, their own agenda. This is why only a small minority seriously work and study to find religious and moral truth. I am impressed with how passionately and beautifully Scripture teaches us to love and pursue truth and wisdom. The sage, for example, says that we are to court wisdom with all our soul, search out for her, track her down, cling to her, and never let her go. In the end we find rest in her, for she is a mighty defense which brings joy (Sir 6:26-29). The Book of Proverbs tells us that immersion in the divine word is a treasure trove for discovering the mind of God and how one is to serve him well. We are to take the inspired message to heart, keep it deeply lodged there, regard it as the apple of our eye. In it we find life, understanding, and spiritual health (Prv 4:4, 10, 20-21; 7:2). The Master himself has promised that those who seek and search, find. Truth is opened to them. Those who want light—*really* want it—attain light. We need to recall that truth is the conformity of the mind with reality, with the way things actually are. It is not conforming with what is 'in' or fashionable. Wanting truth is not mere wishing or admiring. Loving truth is embracing reality with determination, "searching for her, tracking her down." To will truth is not simply to like it, but to cling to it, to suffer and sacrifice for it, which is what has always motivated the martyrs.

**17. Question:** I would think that there is a cumulative effect, or in popular terms a snowball effect, with this. If one faithfully lives a moral life according to whatever truth one may see, however dim it may be, more truth will be given that person. We see this in sincere people.

**Comment:** We can say that it is a principle of God's providential love that people who are faithful to whatever light they have will be given more light. If they genuinely pursue the moral good, even though they may understand only the dimmest outlines of an ethical life, they will slowly perceive the emerging details of it. If such a person who has rarely heard of God's will nonetheless truly loves truth, beauty, and goodness, he or she will steadily advance toward the Truth, Beauty, and Goodness that is God. Men and women who are unsure of just where the Church Jesus himself established may be found in our modern world, will, if they follow whatever light they have and are eager for more, find the community built on the Petrine rock. So likewise, as St. John of the Cross explicitly teaches, if the seeker is faithful in the first mansion of prayer life, he or she will surely go on to the second; and if faithful in the second, one will advance to the third, and so on to the seventh and loftiest mansion.[11] Or, as Jesus himself put it, "I tell you, to everyone who has will be given more" (Lk 19:26). The same principle applies to the quest for spiritual guidance. If a person prays and strives earnestly to find a competent director, but cannot, at least for a while, find one, all is not lost. If one remains faithful to the light he or she presently has, one will advance in practical wisdom through solid reading, through homilies given by faithful priests, through the pure instruction found in the liturgy, through light given by the indwelling Trinity, and through the support and conversation of a holy friend. As St. Teresa remarked, this person is not without a supreme guide. Just as those who hate light do not come to it because their deeds are evil (Jn 3:19), so also they who live by the truth come out into the light.

This is why growing in prayer and in contemplative intimacy with the indwelling Trinity leads people so readily to moral and religious truth. This is why Jesus declares that if a person is prepared to do the Father's will, he will know that the Son's teaching is from the Father (Jn 7:17). Newman put it well:

> For ourselves, let us but obey God's voice in our hearts, and I will venture to say we shall have no doubts practically formidable about the truth of Scripture. Find out the man who strictly obeys the law within him, and yet is an unbeliever as regards the Bible, and then it will be time enough to consider all the variety of proof by which the truth of the Bible is confirmed to us. This is no practical inquiry for *us*. Our doubts, if we have any, will be

found to arise after *disobedience;* it is sin which quenches the Holy Spirit.[12]

**18. Question:** Hans Urs von Balthasar once neatly said that "sin obscures sight." Would not the opposite be true as well?

**Comment:** Yes, virtue does bestow light. Because goodness itself brings insight, says the divine word, honest men and women find guidance in their very honesty and purity, and the uprightness of the good points out the path to follow (Prv 11:3, 5. See also Sir 1:26). St. Paul is explicit: the only way to discover the good and perfect thing to do, that is, God's will, is to undergo a *metanoia*, a conversion from worldliness to holiness. It is not merely one way among others, it is the only way (Rom 12:2). I might remark, too, that viewing things *sub specie aeternitatis,* under the light of eternity, brings a marvelous perspective—a seeing of things as they actually are. Each of us may ask ourselves how on my deathbed will this slight, this criticism, this indulgence, this vanity, this failure look to me, should I recall it then? The long view will aid me in now deciding how best to act or react now.

**19. Question:** Your discernment method thus far may be encapsulated in four words: love truth, pursue holiness. Are there any other brief guides to the divine will?

**Comment:** There are several, but I would mention three in particular. Loving truth implies loving divine revelation and the way God has chosen to present it, namely, through a teaching Church. Not, therefore, through private ideas or sundry theological currents at odds with the divinely authorized magisterium. We have made this point previously. I must emphasize here that the New Testament is entirely explicit about this condition of attaining the divine mind: "Anyone who listens to you listens to me" (Lk 10:16). Those who listen to the leaders of the Church have the spirit of truth (1 Jn 4:1, 6). Important, too, is our being formed by the liturgy in all its texts and other dimensions. The Church's official worship is a powerful avenue to the divine wisdom.

**20. Question:** Of your two remaining guides to discernment I can, I think, suspect one, but perhaps not the other.

**Comment:** Then let me touch on the one you probably cannot guess: acceptance of the circumstances of life, suffering especially. God's will does, after all, include his permissive will. We correct, of course, what in life can be corrected. But there are many happenings we cannot change. These we embrace with the Savior on his cross. For reasons we cannot enter into here God permits all sorts of evils, even horrendous ones. We can be sure of doing the divine will both in striving to stem the tide of what is wrong and in suffering well what cannot be prevented: *per crucem ad lucem,* as the Latin axiom has it, "through the cross to the light."

**21. Question:** I suspect your final guide must have something to do with prayer—you bring that subject up in almost any context.

**Comment:** Right you are. And I see you understand the point about the centrality of communing with God. In this present discussion I have in mind especially contemplation. As one grows in depth of prayer, divine light arises more and more in one's mind and heart. How could it be otherwise when, as the psalmist expresses it, one "may gaze on the loveliness of the Lord" (Ps 27:4, NAB). The Book of Proverbs explicitly ties in prayer with finding the path to God and thus to happiness. Taking the Lord's word to heart, says the sage, a person turns the ear and heart to wisdom and understanding. He or she pleads for a clear grasp of things and cries out for understanding, searching as for silver and buried treasure. The seeker then attains a knowledge of God, and thus understands uprightness and the path that leads to happiness (Prv 2:1-9).

## SPIRITUAL READING

**22. Question:** I have run out of questions along the line we have been pursuing. It's up to you, I think, to suggest where to go next ... unless, of course, we have considered everything about self-direction that needs to be said.

**Comment:** No, we are a long way from the finish. There remain two aids to 'self-direction' so important that we shall devote a whole section to each of them, and I do think that the mere mention of these two subjects will spark a number of questions in your mind. I refer to spiritual reading and knowing the saints. Suppose we launch out into the first.

**23. Question:** On a moment's thought I see how relevant to a person's guidance spiritual reading is, whether one has a director or not. But in the latter case there is a special pointedness, for one chooses his or her reading and in a way—at least in choice—can adapt it to individual needs. May I ask at the outset if you would include in this discussion listening to audio- and videotapes?

**Comment:** Decidedly yes. Tapes today are a major source of spiritual formation (or deformation at times). Some people may be more influenced by hearing a human voice than in reading the same message in print, and they may bring less of a healthy critical evaluation to the former than to the latter. Directors should, in my view, inquire occasionally not only as to what their disciples are reading but also as to what tapes they are listening to and seeing.

**24. Question:** I'd like then to begin with problems that I and others have regarding spiritual reading and tapes as well. Perhaps more than their elders, the young tend through inexperience to select spiritual reading on the basis of catchy advertisements, on what is popularly talked about, on what is merely new or in vogue. They often tend to have a naïve trust in the printed word. If an idea appears in a book or in the newspaper, it must be true. They need much guidance in developing a healthy critical spirit toward untested reading as well as a sound docility in integrating the very best reading, a balance often unachieved even in people advancing in years.

**Comment:** Right you are. In my teens I just assumed that if something appeared in print it must be true. I should blush at recalling my naïveté, but there it was. Surely no one would publish anything unfounded, still less outright error. As regards spiritual reading, I simply did not imagine that some writers would promote their own private views rather than well-grounded developments of God's word, that they would offer mediocrity rather than the radicality of the saints, that they would embrace fads and 'relevancy' in place of sound doctrine. Even when there was no error in the book or article, I was unaware that only too often it was nothing more than a rehashing of what had been said better elsewhere. I now know better, but there is ample evidence that not a few men and women, young and old, still have not adequately learned this rudimentary lesson. If one has any doubts about this, all he or she need do is browse in a religious book shop and see what is being offered.

**25. Question:** This raises the discovery problem. Among the vast offerings from our presses, how does one find the excellent and avoid the sheer volume of mediocrity, whether old or new? Who makes competent recommendations? Do we believe advertising and book reviews? Do not bibliographies commonly include mediocre entries? Are bestsellers usually reliable?

**Comment:** Let me make a few comments. We must, of course, consider who is recommending a book or writing a review. Not rarely a book review says more about the reviewer than it does about the book. And it goes without saying that advertising often must be taken with a grain of salt. Best-seller status may be indicative of excellence, as in the case of the *Confessions* of St. Augustine and the works of Saints Teresa and John of the Cross, but often books flourish because they are fashionable. I hope our present discussion will, as we go along, help the reader to find worthwhile reading and avoid the flood of mediocrity.

**26. Question:** Then there is the receptivity problem. Basically, it is the centuries-old question of how ready one is for God's message. In this context it is the problem of how capable, indeed how willing, is one to profit from an excellent book or tape. Would you care to comment?

**Comment:** Scripture supposes that we wounded ones have the eyes of our minds at least partially closed to God's marvels and to his words. The psalmist prays that he be opened to appreciate divine wonders (Ps 119:18). St. Paul declares that worldly people are simply incapable of understanding revealed truth (1 Cor 2:14). Jesus himself taught that his word is choked by the hearer's clinging to wealth and pleasure, even to excessive concern with one's work (Lk 8:14). Whether one has a spiritual director or not, one should not readily assume he or she will profit as one ought from even the best input.

**27. Question:** I can't deny that, but all the same wouldn't you grant that most of us who pick up a spiritual book will derive some guidance from it, even if not benefiting as fully as a saint would?

**Comment:** Yes, I'd grant that. But few of us see half of what lies before our eyes. We tend to be dull and dreary in our responses to reality. In an article on the novelist Charles Williams, Thomas Howard wrote of how Williams saw splendor in the most ordinary of everyday realities: "The eye with which he looked at ordinary things was like the eye of a lover looking at his lady. The lover sees this plain woman crowned with the light of heaven. She walks in beauty. Her eyes are windows of Paradise to him. Her body, every inch of it, is an incarnation and epiphany of celestial grace. In her he finds the ecstatic vision that his heart has sought."

For Williams this is no grandiose illusion. Not only is this woman splendid, but so is the rest of reality. "The ecstatic vision of beauty thus vouchsafed to that lover is true, not false. The lady *is* as glorious as he sees her to be. It has been given to him, the man who loves her, to see the truth about her. The rest of us bystanders, mercifully, have not had our eyes thus opened, else we would all go mad. It would be an intolerable burden of glory if we all saw, unveiled, the splendor of all other creatures, all the time. But our eyes are dimmed, as it were, for our own equanimity and protection. We cannot bear very much reality, said T.S. Eliot [Williams' friend].

"For Williams, not just the spectacle of his beloved, but every rag, every moment, every tag end of every situation, every eyelash and event and happenstance, were full of the potentiality of glory.

'Heaven and earth are full of the majesty of Thy glory,' says the *Te Deum*, and Williams thought this was literally true."[13]

Our dullness is especially apparent in our lack of response to the Radiant Image of the Father's glory (Heb 1:1-3). He is the self-evident revelation of truth and beauty, and yet most people do not see. Their deeds of darkness dim their minds.

**28. Question:** A holy mentor no doubt can help open dull eyes, but most of all sanctity of one's own life enables us to see (Jn 3:19; 7:17). How can a book or tape take the place of a person?

**Comment:** Well, it really can't, not fully at least. But it can help. If one chooses available sources well and goes about the reading in the time honored manner of *lectio divina,* the guidance received can be solid and beneficial.

**29. Question:** If you don't mind then, let me ask what this *lectio divina,* this divine reading, actually is. I take it that not just any old religious reading qualifies for what you have in mind as a guide for one lacking a personal director.

**Comment:** Correct. We may begin by ruling out what is not under question. Spiritual reading is not the weird type of literature we might style as fringe musings which clearly depart from God's word as it is understood in the Church. I have in mind, for example, 'creation centered spirituality,' a contradiction in terms. I know of no recognized theologian who takes this idea seriously. Nor do we envision far-fetched theories which lack any serious basis—for example, attempts to integrate Buddhist or Hindu awareness into the Christian contemplation of St. John of the Cross or St. Bernard or St. Teresa, with little admission of how vastly different the latter is from the former. This sort of writing and speaking is far more likely to confuse and distort the Gospel message than to clarify and deepen it.

**30. Question:** I have heard a Catholic priest say on an audiotape that there is no significant difference between Zen mysticism and our own. What would you say to that?

**Comment:** Two words would suffice: incredible incompetence. Zen is impersonal, produced entirely by techniques, and agnostic apropos of God. Our contemplation is utterly interpersonal, not in the least produced by us, and entirely theistic. These are huge differences.

**31. Question:** What else do you rule out as outside our purview here?

**Comment:** I may be brief with three other exclusions, for they are clear. 'Keeping up' with religious and ecclesiastical news and events is not spiritual reading, nor is satisfying one's curiosity: "I wonder what this periodical or book or columnist has to say." Finally, the study of theology, even spiritual theology, is not *lectio divina*, if the purpose is passing an examination or preparing a lecture. This study is closer to professional reading.

**32. Question:** You must be anticipating my next question: what then is spiritual reading, the kind of *lectio divina* that can serve as a powerful aid to anyone intent on reaching God?

**Comment:** Being a 'divine reading' entails three elements which distinguish it from other forms of religious input. It nourishes a person with God's word, even when the content is not expressly biblical (Deut 32:1-3). How this is so we will explain later on. It aids us in growing in faith, hope, and love and in all the concrete details of living our new life in Christ. Second—and most crucial to 'self-direction'—it enlightens the reader with divine truth—a light that enables one to love, praise, delight, and live in the new way that St. Paul calls a spiritual revolution (Ps 19:7-8; Eph 4:23). Finally, *lectio divina* is a prayer experience, a dialogue with the indwelling Lord living within his Church and in each member as his temple.

**33. Question:** These three elements make clear why you ruled out other types of reading about religious matters. But I have a problem with what you just said, namely, that spiritual reading nourishes us with God's word and enlightens us with divine truth. This seems to be stretching it. Most books people read for this purpose are written by ordinary men and women such as you and me. They are not divinely inspired.

**Comment:** Surely not. I am thinking not of mediocre writings and tapes, of which we have a superabundance, or of merely private and human ideas, but of the sort of literature produced by saints such as Augustine, Chrysostom, Thomas, Bonaventure, Catherine, Teresa, John of the Cross, Thérèse. I am also thinking of others who may not be canonized but are full of the same wisdom, a wisdom deeply penetrated with the spirit and thought of the inspired word. Thomas á Kempis and Hans Urs von Balthasar are examples of the latter. These men and women even when they are not quoting or alluding to Scripture are actually expounding and explaining it. They are led by the same Holy Spirit who inspired the sacred texts. In other words, I have in mind either the Bible itself or what I call A-1 *lectio divina.*

**34. Question:** It would be pretty hard to argue with that. Before we get to your A-1 material, I'd like to hear some further thoughts about what has to be the best of all reading, God's inspired word.

**Comment:** While the Bible itself insists that it needs an official herald and interpreter lest we private individuals misunderstand and misapply it, it also presents its teaching as a map of life (2 Tm 3:15-17), as a lamp that lights our darkness, (Ps 18:28; 119:105) as a food that feeds our deepest hunger (Prv 17:1; Mt 4:4). The revealed word solves the puzzles and mysteries of human existence.[14] It liberates us from diverse slaveries (Jn 8:31-36): a domination by things (Lk 12:15), human respect (Rom 8:31), luxuries and conformism in styles (1 Pt 3:3-5), idle chatter (Prv 12:23; Sir 21:16, 26; Mt 12:36), the tyranny of lust (Mt 5:27-30). When read in the ecclesial community which produced it and to which it is entrusted, Scripture corrects our aberrations. It presents ideals of holiness and human beauty of which we would never have thought: forgiving our neighbor without limit, continual and deep prayer, perfect mercy, complete joy, astonishing purity (Mt 18:21-22; Eph 5:18-20; Mt 5:48; Jn 15:11; 1 Jn 3:3). The biblical word comforts us, purifies us to make genuine love possible, and fires our dullness (2 Cor 1:3-4; 1 Pt 1:22-23; Rv 3:1-3). In a word, the inspired message is transformative of the individual and of the community (Is 55:10-11; 2 Cor 3:18).

**35. Question:** But is there not another dimension to the inspired word? In addition to all you have just summarized (and we know that libraries have been written in commentary on biblical content), there is the inner dynamism and attractive power of Scripture that most other writing simply does not have. It is not the all-time bestseller for nothing.

**Comment:** Well said. This, too, is another reason why the Bible is our primary spiritual reading. Inspired by the Holy Spirit himself, it is powerful, alive and active. It cuts like a two-edged sword, and it judges our inner, secret thoughts and emotions (Heb 4:12). Most of all there is the towering figure of Jesus himself as self-evident revelation. He needs no other 'proof' than his person: objective evidence radiates from him. He is convincing proof of compelling love and power, for to see him is to see the Father (Jn 14:19). This reminds me of a young woman—an agnostic or atheist, as I recall—who told me that she came upon the Gospels "read them and fell in love with him." No surprise for one seeking beauty and truth. Jesus' words likewise shine by their own divine origin. As von Balthasar put it, "The Lord's discourses are no less wonderful [than his miracles], indeed for the contemplative they are even more so, and in the Lord's own view, they have precedence as proofs of the truth of his mission over the 'works,' which are intended more as auxiliary evidence for those who find understanding difficult."[15]

**36. Question:** I must admit that I am a little puzzled and much intrigued by your 'A-1 spiritual reading' idea. Let me get to that. Just what do you have in mind? Are there ways of knowing the best reading when you see it, or do you hit it by luck, by just picking up the right book or tape? You cannot seriously mean the latter.

**Comment:** You have asked a great deal in those two questions. What do I have in mind? Let me describe it via several traits. The best reading explains, illustrates, develops, and applies the divine message. Hence, transcending private opinions and ideologies, it shares in the biblical power to clarify and cut like a two-edged sword. Second, it is theologically sound and in accord with the Church's teaching, "the pillar and foundation of the truth" (1 Tm 3:15, NAB). Third, A-1 input often absorbs and sparkles for the simple reason that people hungry for God delight when the truth is presented to them. Then, too, some of the very best religious literature is written by literary masters such as Ignatius of Antioch, Augustine, John of the Cross, John Henry Newman, G.K. Chesterton, Hans Urs von Balthasar. Reading them, when one is ready, is itself a delight. Fourth, excellent writing is not merely repetitive of what has been better said elsewhere and with more depth and clarity. Fifth, because this literature shares in the divine wisdom, it often contradicts popular views, just as Jesus commonly did. To it we may apply the remark in 2 Timothy 3:12: "Anybody who tries to live [write] in devotion to Christ is certain to be attacked" (NAB) or ignored by worldly people. Sixth, the best of spiritual reading is invariably balanced and comprehensive. As someone has said, it is not caught "in the prison of a single idea." This literature does not express an ideology and does not promote the merely fashionable. Nor is it unbalanced by pursuing one thrust to the neglect of others: the horizontal 'fulfillment' or change 'relevance.' The classics possess the beauty of wholeness, for as von Balthasar expressed it, "truth is symphonic." Or as G.K. Chesterton remarked, "You can find all the new ideas in the old books; only there you will find them balanced, kept in their place, and sometimes contradicted and overcome by other and better ideas. The great writers did not neglect a fad because they had not thought of it, but because they had thought of it and of all the answers to it as well."[16]

**37. Question:** We still need an answer to my second question: how can I recognize the best reading when I come upon it, and how can I find what I don't come upon? Is it hit or miss?

**Comment:** As I have already suggested, I would begin by avoiding long bibliographies. They are bound by their very length to include mediocre material. Second, we should consider the source when people recommend a book whether in conversation, in a review, or in an advertisement. That being said, I must grant that you raise a problem not easily solved unless one has considerable experience in the field. But really the situation is much like what we find in other specializations: medicine, law, physics, biology, philosophy, theology. It takes time and study to know who the first-rate writers are and to recognize works of excellence. Until one does know the field well, I would not at all advise 'hit or miss.' Your best bet is to begin by sampling the writings of the saints. You might also follow the recommendation of a person whose knowledge and solidity you can trust. Slowly you will come to know both the classics and the choicest of contemporary authors.

**38. Question:** Would you sketch for us some of the benefits a sound reading program provides for anyone, but in a special way for the person who is looking for individual guidance and cannot find it elsewhere?

**Comment:** This is a large order, and I may have to be somewhat more expansive in reply than usual. First of all, quality books enlighten our minds with divine truth. The liturgy for the Third Sunday of Ordinary Time, Cycle C, includes a lesson from the book of Nehemiah about Ezra the high priest reading from the law to the assembly "from daybreak till midday" and "interpreting it so that all could understand what was read." We are then told that the divine word was so effective that "all the people were weeping as they heard the words of the law" (Neh 8:9). The responsorial psalm beautifully sings that the Lord's Law "is perfect, refreshing the soul.... The precepts of the LORD are right, rejoicing the heart; the command of the LORD is clear, enlightening the eye" (Ps 19:7-8, NAB). The enlightenment sometimes takes the form of admonishing us about both momentous matters (heaven and hell) and what we consider of small account (idle talk or vain display in dress and ornamentation). Of St. Thérèse of Lisieux we read that "at the age of fourteen she was inseparable from the *Imitation of Christ;* no matter where she opened it she could recite to the end of the chapter by heart." She carried the small book with her "at all times." Later she declared that when she could read nothing else, she found in Scripture and in the *Imitation* "a hidden, pure, and strong manna."[17] Further, excellent reading is an antidote to the spirit of the age which assaults our senses day in and day out. It tends to check a gradual drifting into an imperceptible adoption of secular assumptions: "frugality isn't necessary... work is more important than prayer... human opinions are what counts... ready availability of sensory pleasures is a high priority... bodily mortification is passé and sin is almost non-existent." In addition to being an antidote, solid input via books and tapes fits us to heal others wisely (see Col 3:16), and it prepares for and feeds our prayer life. Lastly, we find in this practice motivation. The appreciation a recent writer accorded to worthwhile books in general is pointedly pertinent to spiritual reading: what "intellectual energy is stored in those marvelous storage batteries called books."[18] Extensive experience in spiritual direction readily testifies to the great effect outstanding books have on sincere people seeking ultimate truth. Only God knows how many millions of readers through the centuries have been and still are enlightened and moved by the *Confessions* of St. Augustine and the works of Bernard, Thomas, Catherine of Siena, Teresa of Avila, John of the Cross, Ignatius of Loyola, Francis de Sales, and John Henry Newman—to mention a few. In works of their caliber, immense treasures of instruction and motivation are stored. The guidance they offer is sound and solid, often profound and brilliant, not only because of their insightful penetration and literary gifts, but also because of their fidelity to the revealed word.

**39. Question:** What you say is true, but there is another and darker side to this matter of spiritual reading, namely, the lack of results, the many who don't seem to change much for the better as a result of it. I grant that God's word transforms (Is 55:10-11), that it is a powerful two-edged sword (Heb 4:12), that the man or woman who acts on it so builds on a rock that nothing can destroy him or her (Mt 7:24-27), but all the same we often seem little improved by the hundreds of Scripture readings heard in the liturgy, by the annual retreats made, by the dozens of books read, and the tapes heard. We have to face the fact that reading does not produce automatic effects.

**Comment:** Right you are, and you have put the problem well. It matters a great deal how we do the reading and what kind of follow-up occurs afterwards. In the last text you just cited, Jesus addresses this failure when he speaks of the person who hears even the Lord's words but does nothing about them. He ends up in disaster.

**40. Question:** Since we are of one mind on this point, let me ask about preparations for fruitful reading. Is there anything we do beforehand?

**Comment:** Yes, there is. First comes the choice of books or tapes. You might be astonished at how many people neglect the vastly superior classics in favor of 'what just came out,' and what other people are reading and talking about. Some feed themselves on alleged apparitions or locutions even though there may be little or no evidence that they are genuine and often much evidence that they are not. Others concentrate on a mere psychology dressed in religious terminology and neglectful of the hard road and narrow gate that lead to life (Mt 7:13-14). You may recall what St.Paul thought of this "human wisdom" that shuns the cross (1 Cor 1:20; 2:1-9). Most of us need a keener sensitivity to the myopias of our age. Every century suffers from its limited vision. The Renaissance excessively venerated antiquity, while our milieu worships the new. We tend automatically to assume that what 'just came out' must be superior to what preceded it, blissfully unmindful that this new book or tape will be outdated in a single decade, and perhaps much sooner.

**41. Question:** Though we have touched briefly on recommendations received from others via book reviews and oral advice, I'm not quite satisfied that you said enough. Is there anything you can add? After all, where can we find out what to read if not from advice?

**Comment:** Yes, more can be said. Unless one is sure of the competence and soundness of the one recommending, I'd advise two questions. What is the evaluator's value system and lifestyle? Does this book reviewer subscribe to the radical Gospel and does he or she love the Church's teaching? Is contemplative prayer the reviewer's 'one thing,' the top priority? Second, what experience does this person have of the classics? No one can rightly evaluate the present in a vacuum. In any field one must know the best of the classics and of the present in order to judge well something newly proposed.

**42. Question:** That makes a lot of sense. However, let me suggest a related problem. Suppose a person knows no one who can recommend books or tapes reliably, and suppose some selection must be made. Obviously this individual had better read critically what he or she chooses, and I mean the adverb in its best sense. There is such a thing as a healthy doubt or reservation when one is not confident of the source. I'm sure you agree.

**Comment:** Yes, I do. In this case—only too common if one has no reliable director and no wide knowledge of the field—the book or tape must be evaluated and not immediately accepted as Gospel truth. When the ordinary faithful read or hear a proposal unlike their received instruction, a red flag should be raised. A trustworthy author teaches in accord with divine revelation as it is received in the Church (Gal 1:6-9; 1 Thes 2:13). If the reader is not sure about a statement or about the tenor of the book, I would suggest two discernment questions. One is, "Do the saints live this doctrine?" They are guaranteed models of what the Gospel means. The other question: "Does this article, book, or lecture have the biblical marks of the Spirit: humility (Lk 10:21), self-denial (Mt 7:13-14), genuine love (Jn 13:34-35), obedience to our leaders' teaching (Heb 13:17; 1 Jn 4:1, 6)?" It usually does not take much reading or listening before we find that the signs of authenticity or inauthenticity show themselves, "By their fruits you will know them" (Mt 7:16, NAB).

**43. Question:** We live in an age where 'how-to manuals' are highly popular with people wishing to renovate their homes, to keep a garden, to write more effective letters, to build a telescope. If you were to write a manual on spiritual reading, what would be your salient recommendations?

**Comment:** In the supernatural order the key 'how-to' word is authenticity, the genuineness of one's own person. A wretch of a man or woman may keep a fine garden and chart the heavens with ease, but he or she will make little headway with spiritual reading until there is personal moral reformation. Our mind and heart must be open to God's grace (Ps 119:18; Lk 24:32; Acts 16:14). Hence the more we are uncluttered, detached from selfish clingings, the more readily will the word mature (Lk 8:14). The more humble we are, the more does the Father bestow his light (Ps 25:9; Lk 10:21). The stronger our desires for holiness, the more copious will be the flow of grace: "Open wide your mouth and I will fill it" (Ps 81:11, NAB). The Mother of the Lord declared that he fills the hungry with good things (Lk 1:53; see also Mt 5:6), and this is why the saint derives far more benefit from hearing a homily than a non-saint. The author of *The Cloud of Unknowing,* after invoking the Blessed Trinity in the foreword to his book, charges the reader "with a serious responsibility," namely, that the latter is neither to speak of nor lend the book to any but those who are "deeply committed to follow Christ perfectly." Unless the reader is determined resolutely to follow Jesus in so far as it is humanly possible "into the inmost depths of contemplation," the book is not for him or her. Worldly, material-minded people, busybodies, and the hypocritical will not grasp its spiritual message. The author had "no intention of writing for them and [he prefers] that they do not meddle with it."[19]

**44. Question:** Supposing authenticity, what would you say about the actual reading? Does *lectio divina* in itself differ from other serious reading?

**Comment:** Yes, it does. We should read for spiritual profit, not for mere curiosity or to 'get through with it' or to be delighted with the wit or brilliance of the author—though these latter are fine byproducts. We choose a suitable time and a quiet place, so that the message may more readily settle in. We read slowly, mingling prayer and pondering into the reading itself. "Have the book of this Law always on your lips; meditate on it day and night" (Jos 1:8; see also Ps 1:1-2). We avoid craving it, a spiritual gluttony that dissipates rather than deepens our inner life. The theologian Sertillanges wisely pointed out that "the mind is dulled, not fed, by inordinate reading, it is made gradually incapable of reflection and concentration, and therefore of production; it grows inwardly extroverted, if one can so express oneself.... This uncontrolled delight is an escape from self; it ousts the intelligence from its function and allows it merely to follow point for point the thoughts of others, to be carried along in the stream of words, developments, chapters, volumes."[20] Better to read a few books prayerfully than many superficially.

**45. Question:** What would be a sound spiritual reading program? Would you have a list of books to recommend?

**Comment:** We have already noticed the weaknesses and disadvantages of long lists of books, so let me say at this point that I tend to shun recommending specific works unless I know the person to whom I am speaking or writing. Yes, I could put down fifty titles of A-1 reading, but what a given individual should now read depends so much on what has been read and what his or her present needs are that a particular suggestion, excellent though it may be in itself, may well be off target for that person. That being said, I may offer a few general observations. Input on contemplative prayer is essential. Ordinarily, one begins with one or two sound introductory works and proceeds on to the masters. At the head of a short list of masters would be Saints Teresa of Jesus and John of the Cross, probably in that order. Somewhere early in one's serious pursuit of God should be read the *Imitation of Christ* and the major classics written by other saints: for example, Augustine's *Confessions,* Francis de Sales' *Introduction to the Devout Life* and *Treatise on the Love of God,*

Thérèse of Lisieux's *The Story of a Soul,* Newman's sermons, and French spiritual writer Dom Chautard's *Soul of the Apostolate.* Periodically one should intersperse among didactic works the lives of the saints for all the reasons we shall now consider.

**46. Question:** But before we leave our present topic let me ask one quick question: should directors occasionally ask their directees what they are reading? Or, perhaps better, should directees periodically offer an account of their reading to their mentors?

**Comment:** Yes, and I would prefer the latter, namely, that the directee spontaneously keep the guide informed regarding his or her reading and listening materials. The main reason for this is that it easily happens that in all innocence a person will pick highly questionable material, quite unaware of the harm it can do. On the other hand, one may fail to select what is decidedly needed.

## KNOWING THE SAINTS

**47. Question:** We come now to what I know is one of your favorite topics, but I confess that I do not quite know what question to ask first, or second for that matter. Perhaps you could get the ball rolling?

**Comment:** Gladly. The saints are the heroes and heroines of the human race, greater by far than the political and military names with which history books are replete. Why this is so has been eloquently proclaimed by men and women more capable than I. Nonetheless I may add a few words aimed at explaining why these men and women are, after Scripture and the Holy Spirit, the best of directors. Loving the saints does not make one a saint, but it is a step in the right direction. Nor does reading the lives of the saints prove heroic virtue, but it is a sign that the reader is on the right track, the one that leads to the King of all sanctity. As Newman put it:

It is very certain that a really holy man, a true saint, though he looks like other men, still has a sort of secret power in him to attract others to him who are like-minded, and to influence all who have any thing in them like him. And thus it often becomes a test, whether we are like-minded with the Saints of God, whether they have influence over us.... The holier a man is, the less he is understood by men of the world. All who have any spark of living faith will understand him in a measure, and the holier he is, they will, for the most part, be attracted the more; but those who serve the world will be blind to him, or scorn and dislike him, the holier he is. This, I say, happened to our Lord. He was the All-holy "the light shined in darkness, and the darkness comprehended it not."[21]

This is why unspoiled children are fascinated by stories of the saints and why adults earnest about living the Gospel fully are ignited with the fire of God's love by Gregory, Catherine, Xavier, Neri, John Vianney, and hosts of others.

**48. Question:** Now that the ball is rolling I feel ready to pursue our subject. Could you explain in more detail why you so value the saints both in their lives and in their writings? Some of our contemporaries, even those who consider themselves religiously minded, disagree with you on this. They tend to look on the saints as more or less irrelevant in our day.

**Comment:** Let me begin with complete candor. A chief reason, probably the very first reason, saints are not popular with a particular mind set is that they embrace the Gospel and the Catholic Church completely. They are not selective. And you know that the full Gospel has never been popular, especially with the dissenting mind. It is not popular today. However, some of the people to whom you refer are often rejecting a caricature. They do not know the saints as they actually are. Poorly written biographies and sentimental art have contributed to this unrealistic view.

**49. Question:** So also have remarks we sometimes hear. Perhaps the most common negative one is the definition, "a martyr is a person who lives with a saint."

**Comment:** I'm glad you brought this up—that statement ranks high on my list of pet peeves. Though there is a kernel of truth in it, on the whole it is utterly false. A saint is indeed a rebuke to our coldness and laxity and selfishness. It is precisely a mediocre, lukewarm man or woman who would make this complaint. Jesus himself said that we must die to ourselves as a condition of producing fruits of holiness (Jn 12:24). That is a type of martyrdom, and saints are perfect examples of it. But I doubt the complainer has this understanding in mind. He or she usually means that a saint is hard to live with and unpleasant. This I totally reject. The saints I have read about (and the people of heroic virtue whom I personally know) are gentle, kind, loving, altruistic, and generous. I would far prefer to live with a saint than with the person who makes this complaint. I'd have both a luminous example and a most pleasant companion.

**50. Question:** Now that we have dealt with objections, I should like to inquire into your fundamental reasons for valuing the saints as highly as you do.

**Comment:** A book could be written in answer to your question, but for our purposes a mere sketch will have to suffice. Anyone can fill in the outline simply by reading well-documented lives of these heroic men and women. My first reason is theological: it is the same Holy Spirit who first inspired the biblical word and then through the centuries inspires these people who incarnate that word with entire fidelity. It necessarily follows that the saints are the best exegetes we have of what Scripture means, the best explainers by their lives and their words of what God intends in his revealed message. While noting this is not to belittle professional exegetes, it is to recognize that the scholars commonly, not rarely, contradict one another in their explanations of one and the same text. Logic points out that in a contradiction one of the two parties is necessarily wrong—which is to say that biblical scholars frequently err. There is instead with the saints an enriching complementary diversity where, for example, Gospel frugality is concretized in one way in a married saint and in other ways by religious and priestly saints. My second reason for valuing the saints is the wholeness of their outlook. We lesser ones tend to be partial, seeing and emphasizing one or other aspect of reality and losing sight of the whole picture. The ideologies and 'isms' of our day are eloquent examples of this human narrowness. St. Catherine of Siena, for example, was an activist in the best sense of the term, but she avoided the stifling confinement of mere activism. Yet she was primarily a mystic—a woman of burning love for God and neighbor, which was the main reason she did so much on the human level. Third, the saints are utterly ecclesial. They love the Church because they love its founder who gave it its inner charisms and its outer structure. They teach us in action and word how to distinguish the human from the divine, how to look beyond human sins and stupidities and see the Holy Spirit achieving his ends despite our faults. Our fourth fundamental reason is that the saints are dauntless in the faith. Though of themselves they are as fragile and weak as the rest of us, God has made them strong, as the preface of the Mass for martyrs declares. Some of them radiate divine splendor in their martyrdoms characterized by miraculous fortitude, while all of them do so in their daily heroic fidelity in living the Gospel which the world loves to ignore or attack. Finally, the saints speak like emissaries from heaven itself. Their words are often fire and light to us weary wayfarers.

It is no wonder that the saints are our best theologians. Augustine, Thomas, and Bellarmine were intellectual geniuses of the first order. Even better, their minds marvelously penetrated into truth because their wills were on fire. Medard Kehl recently wrote that "for von Balthasar good theology is contemplation brought to conceptualization."[22] This the saints do.

**51. Question:** I trust that your additional reasons for pointing to the saints as superlative spiritual directors may be briefer?

**Comment:** Hopefully, yes, though I think you will grant that they are not peripheral.

- The words and deeds of the saints express untainted faith and doctrine. On the feast of St. Bernard the liturgy sings at morning prayer, "Blessed Bernard, your life, flooded by the splendor of the divine Word, illumines the Church with the light of true faith and doctrine."[23]

- The saints have an extraordinary knack for getting things right in matters which perplex the lesser of us: integrating action and contemplation with the neglect of neither... how to be caring and warm and yet correcting what is amiss... how to exult in creation and yet not cling to it possessively... how to love one's family while not joining them in wasting time.

- They are sensitive to and point out faults that lesser guides do not notice: eagerness for idle news... preoccupation with the faults of others... subtle ways of being vain... clinging to earthly trifles.[24]

- The saints teach in action how the Gospel is to be applied in daily life for each age group and state in life. Boys and girls: Dominic Savio and Maria Goretti... married men and women: Thomas More, Margaret Clitherow, and Elizabeth Seton... religious: Benedict, Francis, Dominic, Teresa, Thérèse... bishops and priests: Chrysostom, Borromeo, Pius X, John Vianney.

- From them we learn how to repent, even indeed to realize vividly that we are sinners. One could say that the saints are men and women who know that they are sinners. How well they know it! They have met the living God deeply and are therefore acutely aware of his purity and love together with their own lack of response.

- They teach us likewise how to live in troubled times, how to see, hear, and experience scandals both in civil and ecclesial spheres and yet keep our inner peace and love for the Church. We also learn from them how to avoid cynicism and to do something positive about what is wrong (Rom 12:14, 17, 21). In other words, we learn that the best way to change the world is to become saints ourselves.

**52. Question:** I notice you are speaking of the lives of saints, of their actions, not as much of their writings. Wouldn't you want to say more of the latter?

**Comment:** What you note is correct and intended. Yes, I would like to add a few words about the writings of the saints, though we actually covered much of that in our discussion about spiritual reading. My one modest additional point here can be summarized and illustrated by two brief sentences written by Christopher Dawson before his conversion to the Catholic Church:

> To me at least the art of the Counter Reformation was a pure joy, and I loved the churches of Bernini and Borromini no less than the ancient basilicas. And this in turn led me to the literature of the Counter Reformation, and I came to know St. Teresa and St. John of the Cross, compared to whom even the greatest non-Catholic religious writers seem pale and unreal.[25]

The writings of the saints have a purity and power, a light and fire, a holiness and a realism, matched and surpassed only by the inspired word.

**53. Question:** You have said elsewhere that the saints are walking theology books. I am pretty sure you mean more than that they teach sound doctrine in life and word. Could you amplify your idea?

**Comment:** Saints surely do exemplify what the Catholic Church is and what she stands for. They are the best and the most authentic advertisements we have. What I'd like to add is that the details of their lives *are* a rich source of spiritual direction—not simply in their concrete responses to concrete situations but especially in our acquiring their *minds*, their ways of seeing things, their evaluations of reality. One of the most important results of reading the lives of the saints is that one thereby slowly acquires their outlooks and attitudes. Once we possess a lively and habitual sense of the way in which they viewed reality—people, problems, priorities, trials, and most of all God himself—we automatically attain a mindset that enables us to see how we ought to act in our own circumstances. Would saints watch this televison program or engage in this conversation or dine in this restaurant or buy these clothes? Would they eat as much as I do or be as fussy regarding exact preparations, dressings, and condiments? Would they choose my recreations and friends? How would they deal with this annoying companion or troublesome relative?

**54. Question:** This pretty well exhausts my questions about what one can do when no competent guide can be found. And I see, too, that most of this chapter can benefit those also who do have such a mentor.

**Comment:** I have one more observation. We can now say that for people who engage in the very best of spiritual reading and who are immersed in the saints, 'self-direction' is not really *self* direction. They are being guided by the masters themselves, even if they lack the blessing of a living voice.

EIGHT

# The Role of Prayer in the Spiritual Life

EXPERIENCE IN SPIRITUAL DIRECTION, both at home and abroad, has made clear to the present writer that the central concern of most people seeking guidance in their pursuit of God is contemplative prayer. While a thirst for the divine has never been dead in the Church, it seems to be characterized in our day by a renewed intensity in the lay, religious, and clerical states. This *sensus fidelium*, this perception of the truly faithful, is so much on target that it coincides with the biblical "one thing," the top priority in any human life: "to gaze on the loveliness of the Lord" (Ps 27:4; see also Lk 10:38-42, NAB).

It is not for nothing that the very incarnation itself took place deep in the flesh of the contemplative woman *par excellence*, in her whose personal spiritual life was twice characterized by St. Luke as pondering the word in her heart (Lk 2:19, 51). As von Balthasar put it, "Because she was a virgin, which means a pure, exclusive hearer of the Word, she became mother, the place of the incarnation of the Word."[1]

Each of us is an incarnated puzzle, and each of us has an insatiable thirst for the infinite. Never content with the limited nibbles and tastes offered by created realities, we find buried in our depths a dynamic that is restless and voracious. Even the self-avowed atheist is, in his or her endless desires, a witness to this basic need for

*153*

the divine. Though Jesus shared in none of our wounded sinfulness, his actions as well as his words pointed to the primacy of
immersion in the Father: "In the morning, long before dawn... he
went off to a lonely place and prayed there.... He went off into the
hills to pray.... He would always go off to some place where he
could be alone and pray.... He went out into the hills to pray....
He was praying alone.... He would spend the night on the hill..."
(Mk 1:35; 6:46; Lk 5:16; 6:12; 9:18; 21:37).

In this chapter questions basic to an understanding of prayer in
the spiritual life are addressed. The next deals with practicalities in
our efforts to commune deeply with God.

## THE EXPERIENCE OF GOD

**1. Question:** Perhaps we may begin with a subject that is widely
popular among certain religiously minded people today. I refer to
the experience of God and to its substitutes such as Transcendental
Meditation and Zen *satori*. Oriental phenomena and their striking
differences from Christic contemplation have already been discussed. Here I would like to inquire about our own experience of
God. This will necessarily lead to reflection on some basic questions regarding advanced prayer.

**Comment:** You might be surprised at the large number of our contemporaries who claim to experience God in one way or another.
One study, done by a psychologist at the University of Cincinnati,
reports that almost all of the more than two hundred interviewees
"affirm God's presence to be a reality.... They reported that God
being present to them was more real than any sensible reality. Many
said that they experienced God closer to them than any other person in their sensible world. His being present was not an imaginary
experience born of fantasy. In fact, they contrasted God being real
to them with the products of their creative activities."[2] I by no
means wish to vouch for the authenticity of all these accounts, but
on the other hand one may not responsibly dismiss all of them out
of hand as illusions. Real encounters with the living God do occur.

**2. Question:** How can you be so sure, so confident, that not all these allegations are illusory? After all, St. John of the Cross himself maintained that illusions about divine communications are not rare.

**Comment:** Indeed they are not rare. I fully agree with him. But the fact remains that genuine experiences of the divine are also not rare. How can I be so confident? Since this is not the place to discuss the authenticity question at length, let me be content with offering three reasons, in addition to the primary witnesses of Sacred Scripture and the teaching Church. The first reason is the universal testimony of our sainted mystics. These marvelous men and women speak with one voice, even though independently of one another, about their meetings with the divine. For example, anyone, knowing the no-nonsense kind of woman St. Teresa was and reading with an unbiased mind her accounts of advanced prayer and other communications from God, should be struck with the sheer realism of what she reports from her own life. This woman hated deceit and was acutely sensitive to the possibilities of self-deception and fanciful imagination. Yet she reports experiences such that they could not have been manufactured by anyone, and still less by a person of her integrity.[3] My second reason for being confident in the reality of at least some experiences of God is extensive work in spiritual direction. I have dealt with not a few men and women of unquestioned mental soundness and moral integrity whose narrations of what God has done in them bear all the marks of authenticity.[4] Then there is the capping witness of heroic virtue: "By their fruits you will know them." Genuine encounters with pure goodness and matchless beauty leave one, as St. Paul put it, "transformed into the same image from glory to glory" (2 Cor 3:18, NAB). Heroism in holiness is itself a moral miracle, impossible to unaided human nature. This is apparent to anyone who knows well both himself or herself and heroic virtue.

**3. Question:** Given then that genuine experiences of God can be distinguished from counterfeits, how is it that people are so eager for reports of new visions and revelations, even when the Catholic

Church frowns on many of them? There are sincere people more interested in crossing an ocean to visit the place of an alleged apparition than in visiting the Blessed Sacrament in their parish church.

**Comment:** Because we have talked about this attitude elsewhere, I will only observe that while we value a genuine communication from God—as St. Teresa did her own—we build our spiritual life on God's public word in Scripture and on the public teaching of the Church he authorized to speak in his name. Yes, this Church does value divine interventions in the lives of ordinary men and women, for she spoke in Vatican Council II of the faithful experiencing divine realities,[5] tasting fully of the paschal mysteries, and of burning with love during the Eucharistic Sacrifice.[6] Yet these intimate encounters with the Lord are inseparable from humility, obedience, chastity, justice, and love for neighbor. While the Catholic Church often insists on these everyday virtues, she never requires that we visit the place of an alleged apparition. Hausherr speaks of "the eternal tendency toward pseudo-mystical empiricism."[7] People would do themselves a favor if they followed the sober decisions of the Church in these matters and the teaching of Saints Teresa of Avila and John of the Cross.

**4. Question:** Leaving aside, then, extraordinary phenomena, I would like to ask about ordinary perceptions of the divine. Just what do people experience in advancing infused prayer? How is it known to be more than mere emotion?

**Comment:** Two general comments first, and then some particulars. God originates the awareness, not we ourselves. We may trigger an emotion by reading something, by hearing, or by thinking. In contemplative prayer a divine awareness is given. It simply is there, brought on by nothing we have done. Second, there is a wide variety of ways in which God communicates himself. There is a sense of the divine indwelling presence (Jn 14:15-17; 1 Jn 3:24). Or sometimes one perceives a spiritual 'touch' or 'tasting' (Ps 34:8; Eph 5:2; Jer 20:9), a given desire and yearning for God (Ps 42:1-2; Ps 63:1; Is 26:8-9), a perception of peace and being comforted (2 Cor 1:3-4; Phil 4:7), or a new imageless and thus dark knowing of God (Jn 14:21; 2 Cor 4:6). The soul experiences an enkindling, an outpouring of love from and for the Lord (Rom 5:5; 2 Cor 5:14), which brings its own refreshment (Ps 19:7-8; Jer 31:25-26).

**5. Question:** May I interrupt for a moment? Does anyone in the wide world receive all these variations in prayer? Or do individuals as it were specialize in one or the other of them?

**Comment:** The type of experience is not the choice of the recipient. The Lord decides who needs what and when and with what degree of intensity. Remember that the divine infusions range all the way from gentle and delicate to strong and intense. If one grows normally to the fullness of the transforming union, I would think most, if not all, of these variations would be experienced at differing times.

**6. Question:** I have other questions about all this, but perhaps I'd better let you finish what you are describing. It is fascinating.

**Comment:** Yes, it is. To continue, at times the contemplative has the vivid experience of being engulfed in God, surrounded by him, or immersed in him. Augustine described it thus: "On every side I was encompassed by you."[8] This is an awareness of the interindwelling spoken of in the New Testament: God dwelling in us and we dwelling in him (1 Jn 4:16). Not surprisingly, this interabiding is sometimes perceived—a weak word for the mighty reality—as being embraced by the Lord. St. Angela of Folingo somewhere declares that it surpasses any parental hugging of a child. St. John of the Cross remarks, "The soul could not bear so close an embrace, if it were not already very strong."[9] This union-embrace is what St. Paul must have had in mind when he remarked that he who clings to the Lord becomes one spirit with him (1 Cor 6:17). It is what the mystics mean when they speak of starlight being united with sunlight or of the flames of two candles becoming one flame.[10]

**7. Question:** It's hard to imagine anything more than this. You must be finished?

**Comment:** We are getting close, but you must remember that this is only a sketch. Read the mystics if you want to fill all this out. At times, says John, the Lord reveals "some deep glimpses of his divinity and beauty by which He greatly increases [the soul's] fervor and desire to see Him.... God communicates to her some semi-clear glimpses of His divine beauty."[11] In a well known exclamation that has echoed through the centuries St. Augustine declared, "Too late have I loved you, O Beauty so ancient and so new, too late have I loved you!"[12] One of the aspects of this divine encounter most frequently mentioned both in Scripture and in the saints is the burning of love accompanied by radiant joy. Again and again the inspired word talks about exulting and dancing in sheer delight and about burning with a love that is received, not produced.[13] Once again we listen to Augustine: "Sometimes you admit me in my innermost being into a most extraordinary affection, mounting within me to an indescribable delight. If this is perfected in me, it will be something, I know not what, that will not belong to this life."[14] Elsewhere he writes of the divinely given fire, which John of the Cross terms, "burning with love": "How I was set on fire for you by [the psalms] and how did I burn to repeat them.... By your gift we are enkindled, and we are borne upwards. We glow with inward fire, and we go on. We ascend steps within the heart, and we sing a gradual psalm. By your fire, by your good fire, we glow with inward fire."[15]

Finally, we add the elements of power, strength, and freedom given along with the new knowing, love, and delight. This inner might and vitality develop into the heroic virtues of the transforming union.[16] We find here the explanation of why martyrs can so spontaneously, freely, and fearlessly go to torture and death: "Where the Spirit of the Lord is, there is freedom" (2 Cor 3:17, NAB). Genuine experience of God is, therefore, the new life, the new creation. It is a revolution (Jn 10:10; Gal 6:15; Eph 4:22-24). All other mysticisms in comparison pale into insignificance.

**8. Question:** I think I half know how you will answer my next question, but let me ask it anyway. How can we distinguish the experience of God from mere emotions, especially when it is delicate, not over-powering?

**Comment:** The last chapter of this book on assessing our progress is relevant here. We do not evaluate our growth in the spiritual life by our subjective feelings. That being understood, let me mention several differences:

- Emotions are humanly produced and, to a large extent, can be controlled. Experiences of God are neither.
- Affective and humanly produced experiences do not become continual. In the transforming union the divine awareness on one's deepest level is continuous.
- Feelings are heavily of sense, while divine perceptions are of spirit, though they may overflow into our sense life.
- Sense affections do not produce new knowledge of God or insight into divine mysteries, while infused prayer does both.
- Even deep emotions are not necessarily accompanied by growth in goodness; authentic contemplative encounters with God always bring holiness with them.

**9. Question:** One of the thoughts that struck me as you were speaking of the wide and immensely rich variations in genuine experiences of the Trinity is how vastly superior this Christic contemplation is to what Buddhists and Hindus write about. I do not wish to belittle these fellow sojourners, but the fact is that there is no real comparison. Am I being arrogant?

**Comment:** I would not consider the modest recognition of plain truth to be objectionable or arrogant. Facts are facts, whatever label is put on them. God is the origin of our contemplation, not we ourselves. And so we have nothing to be vain about. It's a pity how, because we do not proclaim all this loudly and clearly from our pulpits, some of the faithful stray from what we have to pale imitations and to the garish—empty 'highs' of unbridled eroticism, drug use, and worldly amusements.

**10. Question:** I have several practical questions. The variations you speak about in the experience of the indwelling Trinity sound rather advanced. I know you explicitly mentioned among them a yearning for God, which, I suppose, can feel dry and empty. What if a person has only, or at least mostly, that dry desire for God, a desire not deduced from an idea but that is 'just there'? Suppose one seldom, if ever, experiences those delightful variations? Is all lost?

**Comment:** No, nothing essential is lost—provided the dryness is not due to mediocrity, to willed corner-cutting, or to freely chosen self-centeredness. When the Catholic Church examines the lives of candidates for canonization, she does not explore their inner delights or lack of them. She looks for heroic virtues, the concrete living of the Gospel. This we spell out in our last chapter. Hence, if a person is generously giving God everything and with no reservations, he or she need not worry about dry, empty-feeling periods at prayer. Most probably they are purifications which prepare one for still deeper immersion in the Triune God.

**11. Question:** At times I notice that when I am trying to express myself in word or writing about something religious and do not know exactly what to say or write, apt ideas begin to flow readily. Later I may be surprised at how correct and suitable they are, because at first I didn't know what I was going to say. What is this?

**Comment:** What you describe sounds identical to what St. John of the Cross calls successive locutions. This is nothing extraordinary. God is simply assisting our thoughts when we are in a prayerful mode. I notice something like this in writing letters of spiritual direction. I may have a difficult question which at first I don't know how to answer. Then as I go on the ideas easily flow. Afterwards it surprises me how apt the response turns out to be.

**12. Question:** I'd like to turn our attention to problematic aspects of spiritual experiences and how direction is related to them. The dangers of illusion should be obvious to everyone by this point in our discussion, so I would like to focus on authentic encounters with God. Genuine though these may be, they are by definition subjective because they occur within the realm of someone's mind, will, and feelings. Consequently, they can be subject to all sorts of mistaken conclusions. Am I not right?

**Comment:** Indeed, you are. History, past and present, bears you out. This is why I have accented more times than once the crucial objective basis for spiritual direction, especially in our earlier discussions of mediation and ecclesiality. We spelled out the divine intention in detail. Catholicism has always insisted on discernible facts and hard objective evidence. She has likewise looked with a wary eye on emotionalism, alleged private revelations, and subjective persuasions. History is replete with examples of the wayward and even weird ideas to which private judgment leads. In his classic, *Now I See*, Arnold Lunn spoke of Fif, a "funny internal feeling," which for many people, including not a few academics, serves as a basis for what they hold about religion and morality.[17] This sort of person seldom, if ever, tries to prove his or her position with facts and logically argued evidence. One has this bias based on subjective experience and that is enough.

**13. Question:** I see your point. Atheists I have met in print and in person do not reason to their conclusion, as John Courtney Murray in *The Problem of God* clearly shows. They speak of evil, but cannot logically show that it leads to their conclusion of not believing in God. But we are talking here about theists of a certain type who also can be highly subjective and mistaken regarding what they consider to be experiences of God. How should they relate on this score with their mentors?

**Comment:** When we explained the nature of spiritual direction, you will recall my pointing out that in our ecclesial economy the Holy Spirit is the chief guide, while the human mentor is secondary and instrumental. Thus the latter's main function is to help free the directee from all impediments to being led by the Spirit (Rom 8:14). And one of the principal hindrances to the divine action is our inner clingings, our private persuasions, and misguided desires.

**14. Question:** But you have not yet answered my question: how should a directee relate to his or her director regarding inner experiences?

**Comment:** I am getting to the answer, but we needed some preliminaries first. The directee should faithfully and simply share with the mentor what happens—and does not happen—at prayer. Likewise anything that appears to be out of the ordinary should be shared. One then follows the advice given and, in the latter case, drops the matter. If a locution or vision is from God, the good is achieved with no need to focus on the favor. If it is not from God, the harm from pursuing it is precluded. One should never act based on what he or she thinks has been heard or seen without getting approval from one's guide. I trust I need not again insist that I am here supposing the mentor is competent.

**15. Question:** How important are these religious experiences in the spiritual life? I refer to those found in the charismatic renewal, to extraordinary phenomena such as visions and locutions, and to the contemplation referred to in the works of Saints Augustine, Bernard, Catherine, Teresa, and John of the Cross. Many of us go for months or years without feeling much of anything during prayer.

**Comment:** There is no one answer to your question, for it deals with what are, or may be, very diverse realities. If the experience is solely emotional, it can be healthy or unhealthy. If it is the overflow from genuine and spiritual contemplative light and love sensibly perceived, it is of great value. If it is merely or mostly a natural reaction to music or group enthusiasm, it needs to be evaluated. Does it lead to authentic living of Gospel virtues and to solid doctrine? If the experiences are theologically extraordinary and not needed for the flowering of a life of grace, they are far less important than love and its manifestations. Visions and revelations, even the best of them, are, says St. John of the Cross, of less value before God than "an inclination to aridity and suffering for love of Him."[18] St. Paul was of like mind: miracles, even the moving of mountains, or the gifts of prophecy and profound knowledge of God are all worthless without love (1 Cor 13: 1-3). If by "religious experiences" you refer to genuine infused prayer, the answer to your question must be that they are of immense value. However, we must remember that these contemplative experiences include not only delightful meetings with the indwelling Lord but the dry yearnings and thirstings he infuses as well.

**16. Question:** Some people propose experience as a source of theological truth, a type of divine revelation. What do you think?

**Comment:** If I may be permitted a blunt expression, I consider this view to be a prime example of theological incompetence. I do not ever recall hearing or reading this opinion qualified by absolutely indispensable conditions. For one thing mere private experiences never rank with the public revelation committed to the apostles and the Church. For another, private experiences are worth no more than the quality of holiness in those who claim them. Experience is notoriously ambiguous, for it all depends on whose experience we are talking about. The marital experiences of St. Thomas More and the celibate life of St. John Vianney are immeasurably more valuable than those of lukewarm husbands and of playboys. The history of comparative religions is full of movements noted for extravagant 'experiences,' many of which we now see as aberrant and damaging. Theologians who propose undifferentiated experience as a theological source cannot be taken seriously.

**17. Question:** Would you say a few words about contemplation? What is it?

**Comment:** Because this is not a book on prayer as such, my words will be few.[19] But we should be clear first of all as to what Christian contemplation is *not:* an oriental state of impersonal awareness produced by exercises and techniques, an inner colloquy, an introspection or, as Thomas Merton put it, a "consecrated narcissism," sterile intellectualism, academic ponderings, a withdrawal from material reality, an escape from the business of life, a mere exulting in nature (good as that is), strong emotional feelings about God and religious matters, discursive meditation, thinking things over, visions and revelations. This being noted, we can define infused contemplation—which normally follows on meditation when one is ready for it—as a new divinely given, general, non-conceptual, loving awareness of God. Sometimes it is a delightful attention. At other times it is a dry desire, or even on occasion a strong thirsting for God. He takes the initiative. He leads: we simply follow and receive. The Lord determines the kind of contemplation we need at a given moment, either the delightful type, which encourages and draws us on, or an arid reaching-out that purifies us for still deeper prayer. The contemplative enterprise "is nothing else but a naked intent toward God for his own sake."[20] It is a deepening communion with the indwelling Father, Son, and Spirit. As von Balthasar put it, "Man is the being created as hearer of the Word, and only in responding to the Word rises to his full dignity. He was conceived in the mind of God as the partner in a dialogue."[21] We readily conclude that the dignity of the spiritual director is a lofty one, a companion-guide in the directee's journey to the endless bosom of the Trinity.

## IMPLICATIONS FOR SPIRITUAL DIRECTION

**18. Question:** Weighty offices imply weighty duties: "To whom much is given much will be required." I would imagine from these fundamental realities highly practical and crucial consequences follow in daily life. How do they affect spiritual direction?

**Comment:** You imagine correctly. From the Lord's own words it follows, first of all, that a deep prayer life is indeed the "one thing," the top priority in anyone's life. The director aids the directee to see this clearly and then to get all else in order. Further, while work is justified by something else, prayer, like love, needs no justification other than its own indispensable excellence. The businessman and the mother, as well as the nun and the monk and the priest, orient their sundry duties as fitting into and deriving from their communion with God. Everything else they do is aimed at providing the circumstances and means so that they and those close to them can be immersed in God: "Action is directed and subordinated to contemplation," as Vatican II stated. Because most people do not find this principle obvious, the spiritual guide clarifies it by examples when he or she and the directee wrestle with the practicalities of daily duties.

**19. Question:** It is true that these fundamentals have to be intellectually grasped before most people will concretize them in their particular choices. This is another reason why well thought out homilies and spiritual reading are so important. Direction is neither pulpit nor classroom. But I wonder if you have any further basic issues before we go on to our next area of concern.

**Comment:** Yes, there are a few. A person at prayer is a question listening to the only answer. As Peter put it, "Master, to whom shall we go? You have the words of eternal life" (Jn 6:68, NAB). No one else does. God is the sole solution to the human puzzle. Second, contemplation is the soul of all of our prayer—vocal and liturgical. It is the inner, deeper, more important element. Third, because the divine inflowing is gentle—God respects our freedom by never forcing himself on us—to mature in prayer requires no selfish clingings, no division of the heart, no attempts to serve God and mammon (Lk 8:14). Lastly, after the example of Jesus and the saints, each of us needs ample time and a suitable place for prayer. This "ample time" adds to the efficacy of work. It does not subtract from it, as is commonly believed. These conclusions, too, are proper subjects for scrutiny in a program of spiritual direction.

**20. Question:** Your final conclusion leads nicely to what I'd like to discuss next: namely, the integration of prayer and work and how spiritual direction can further it.

**Comment:** Yes, I did intend to lead you on with the "ample time" idea as contributing to work and especially to one's apostolate. Contemplative love informs and energizes all the Church's activities, just as St. Paul declared that the love of Christ drove him on (2 Cor 5:14). As von Balthasar expressed it, contemplation is "the first impulse in all [healthy] change. This is the sense in which contemplation is more active than action, if the latter is taken to mean external deeds... Just as a watch will stop if the spring is broken, so the whole action of the Church would come to a standstill if the contemplative love at the heart of it all were to cease."[22] This is why the greatest doers in the history of the Church have been the mystics: Augustine, Gregory the Great, Thomas, Bonaventure, Dominic, Catherine, Francis, Teresa of Avila, John of the Cross, Ignatius, and John Vianney. A spiritual director should not allow the disciple to forget this truth in all the pressures of daily life.

**21. Question:** How does an alert guide keep this ideal before the mind of his or her charge?

**Comment:** The first requirement is for the guide to be convinced of the truth and to live it. Then when the occasion presents itself, the director can point out the underlying reasons why deep prayer is the soul of effective action. Let me mention several of them. Lasting enthusiasm is born in contemplative communion, for it is in this love that energy is found to overcome our natural inertia, laziness, drifting, apathy, and dullness. One who loves much, does much. So also a person's activity is committed, stable and steady. Mediocrity and contemplative prayer do not coexist for long. "Woe to faint hearts and listless hands," declares the sage, "and to the sinner who treads two paths" (Sir 2:12). Motivation is pure. Our human tendency toward mixed motivation in our good deeds and our tendency to rationalize our faults both are diminished as our prayer life grows. Further, the man and woman of prayer are strong and fearless. The gospel proclamation requires daring (Phil 1:14; 2 Tm 4:1-2), and it is not to be diluted (2 Cor 4:1-2). The apostle accepts unpopularity, even "insult, derision all day long" (Jer 20:8), and is undeterred at the opposition of the worldly (2 Tm 3:12; Col 1:24). Mystics, invariably happy persons even in suffering, lead by example as well as by word, because they radiate God whom they have tasted in prayer (Ps 34:5, 8; 1 Pt 1:8; 5:14). Not surprisingly, mystics are warm and loving in their human relations, since love of God and neighbor grow together, given that there is only one virtue of charity. They also see more beauty in their sisters and brothers, because God puts "his own light in their hearts to show them the magnificence of his works" (Sir 17:7-8).

**22. Question:** Once in a while someone will ask about being what is called an active contemplative. What do you answer when you meet this question?

**Comment:** It depends on what the questioner means, for the expression can be understood in several ways. Let me comment on a neat medieval formulation of it: *"ex plenitudine contemplationis activus"*—"activity arising from a fullness of contemplation."[23] In view of all we have said I can think of one answer only to this idea: strong encouragement. There is no other theologically sound and complete way to operate in human life except from love, and the deeper, the more burning the love, the more fruitful the work. What von Balthasar said of the priestly apostolate may be applied in varying ways to anyone's endeavors to influence others toward God. "The clergy, whether old or young, should make no mistake about it: no matter how far the sermon has been prepared by the standards of modern exegesis and of pastoral sociology [in case they still find time for this], if it has not been achieved in personal prayer the congregation is fed stones instead of bread. And the faithful have a very fine sense for whether the preacher's words come from the depths of personal prayer or ultimately are as flat and as vain as anything they might read in a newspaper."[24]

**23. Question:** Sometimes people expect that a growing prayer life should further the healing of psychological wounds such as a weak self-image or clinical depression. They tend to suppose that contemplative prayer and spiritual direction may render ordinary counseling superfluous. How do you react to this supposition?

**Comment:** C.G. Jung is reported to have said that in the second half of his life he had met no mentally ill person whose problem was not fundamentally a religious one. He meant the problem was due to lacking some basic need religion normally supplies. While this may well be true, I would add that contemplative prayer and competent spiritual direction do not render superfluous any and all psychiatric aid. Human healing is often more complex than an easy answer would suggest.

**24. Question:** Apparently then, my question requires some distinctions and some extended discussion. What do you see as valid in what Jung seems to have meant?

**Comment:** The deepest wound—indeed, it is death—we humans can sustain is alienation from God, being cut off from our origin and destiny. We cannot function normally without an anchor and a goal. If this is what Jung had in mind, I agree with him. If we have a purpose in life and a consuming love, we can endure almost any suffering. Because they are head over heels in love, saints are invariably happy people. But saints are not born such. There are boys and girls, men and women, so badly wounded by early home life that they find it difficult to relate to God in an intimate way. These people usually are missing much that religion supplies, but they often need psychological help together with a serious pursuit of God. Just as it would be wrong to refuse to seek medical aid in setting a broken leg on the plea that God can heal it, so one is mistaken in expecting contemplative prayer by itself to restore a poor self-image or lift a clinical depression.

**25. Question:** That makes sense. But if you say that contemplation may not be expected to heal psychological wounds by itself, are you not suggesting that it does have some therapeutic value? And does not competent direction in prayer thereby contribute to a person's healing?

**Comment:** Yes to both questions. Contemplation heals anyone at the deepest levels where the person is most radically fractured. Sin is *the* illness. Serious sin is a basic split from God, an alienation from truth, beauty, love. Venial sin is a distancing of oneself from one's *raison d'être*—it is an illness but not unto death. Moral sickness often creates inner havoc, even when it does not beget neurosis or psychosis. Always it aggravates these latter problems. Contemplation and the Gospel virtues which are a condition for its flourishing definitely have a healing effect, even when they are not the sole remedy.

**26. Question:** I follow you to some extent, but I don't fully see just how it heals. Could you offer a bit more detail?

**Comment:** You will notice on a moment's reflection that people who are not pursuing God in a serious way are invariably running after replacements, licit or illicit: multiplying material things; chasing after amusements, vanity, and prestige; dining and drinking elegantly; taking drugs and engaging in sexually aberrant behavior. Everyone has a god, if not the real God. Created as we are for unending truth, beauty, delight, and love, if we reject the genuine source, we ache inside. Pursuing things as little gods, one finds that they serve as narcotics that partially and momentarily deaden the inner aching. Contemplation not only exposes the sham in all this, but it begins to heal by putting one on the right track: seeking happiness where it actually can be found. Reality heals. We begin to drink of the supreme reality, the one who has defined himself as pure Love (1 Jn 4:16). Our emptiness is finally being filled. Love is the health of the soul, especially divine love.

**27. Question:** It is a pity that millions of people do not see and understand that simple reality. I'd like to ask if there are other angles to it.

**Comment:** Yes, there are, and alert spiritual directors will steer their disciples to the reading that will further their grasp of the basic solution to the human puzzle. By putting us in vital touch with our origin and destiny, contemplation tends to heal our inner fragmentation, both individual and communal. Feeding our deepest hunger for truth, joy, celebration, beauty and love, contemplation sensitizes us to these universal human needs and 'puts us together' as individuals. To love, one must linger with the beloved, and contemplation is precisely that, lingering with the supreme Beloved. In unifying and integrating the individual, this divine communion likewise heals communal divisions among normal people. If the prayer is genuine, it brings humility and therefore shared vision, an acceptance of the revealed word and the Church authorized to teach it. Experience as well as Scripture make it clear that without shared vision there can be no close community.[25] Raissa Maritain, herself a mystic, put this in philosophical terms when she wrote in her journal that human beings do not really communicate with each other except through the medium of *being* or one of its properties. If someone touches the true, like St. Thomas Aquinas, the contact is made. If someone touches the beautiful, like Beethoven or Bloy or Dostoyevsky, the contact is made. If someone touches the good and Love, like the saints—the contact is made and souls communicate with each other. One exposes oneself to not being understood when one expresses oneself without first having touched these depths—then the contact is not made because being is not reached.[26]

The author of *The Cloud of Unknowing* remarked that contemplation somehow bestows personal attractiveness, an idea that accords with Ezekiel 16:13-14 and is suggested by 2 Corinthians 3:18. "When grace draws a man to contemplation it seems to transfigure him even physically so that, though he may be ill-favored by nature, he now appears changed and lovely to behold. His whole personality becomes so attractive that good people are honored and delighted to be in his company, strengthened by the sense of God he radiates."[27]

## PRAYER STYLES

**28. Question:** If you don't mind, perhaps we can shift our gears at the moment. I would like to discuss styles of prayer, an idea that is presently popular and taken for granted in some quarters. I am thinking of Zen Buddhist awareness and its techniques, of centering prayer and whether indiscriminately proposing it for all sorts of people is wise, of charismatic prayer. Are these forms in competition with one another or in any way opposed? Are they a problem for Christic contemplation? Which should one choose? Does it matter? Are oriental methods worth trying? I see here many questions relevant to spiritual direction.

**Comment:** I do too. We will have to take one thing at a time, and perhaps it will be best to begin with what is most unlike our contemplation. Like most of our contemporaries, you include in your question Buddhist awareness among prayer styles. While I understand why you do—many people take for granted that *satori* is contemplation, prayer—I must be clear from the outset that Buddhism is not a religion. Buddhists themselves insist that it is not. If religion is a relating with a supreme being and not merely a moral code or a this-worldly awareness, then Buddhism cannot be a religion. Its articulators are openly agnostic apropos of God. They neither affirm nor deny him. Hence, whatever *satori* enlightenment may be, it is not prayer. Spiritual directors should make this clear when they are asked about it.

**29. Question:** You have written about this elsewhere, I know, but would you summarize briefly what spiritual guides should point out when they discuss the matter with their charges.

**Comment:** They note the commendable similarities, of course, between Christianity and Buddhism: a realization of the inadequacy of this world, a stretching out for transcendence, an attempt to solve the problem of suffering, a concern for a moral pathway. But what is often not realized are the huge differences, indeed the radical contradictions. In addition to what I said in my previous comment, directors should point out that Zen awareness is impersonal and produced entirely by techniques, while our contemplation is utterly interpersonal and received from God, not produced by us at all. Buddhist writers I have read deny that they are dealing with prayer. They do not relate *satori* with divine love, while we say time and again that our contemplation is prayer which grows in depth and its heart is love for the three divine persons. People who suggest or imply that Buddhist and Christian contemplations are similar are either incompetent or lacking in candor. Whatever else Zen may be, it is not a style of prayer.

**30. Question:** We have heard and read a great deal about centering prayer in the past few years, and I think you would agree that it is a style of prayer. Should spiritual directors promote it?

**Comment:** Centering prayer, properly conceived, is nothing new. Without using the term, St. Teresa speaks of it, but she was wiser in her advice than are many contemporary proponents of the method. She did not propose the simple practice as generally or commonly suitable, but only for certain people at a certain time in their journey to God. Many people are not ready for the approach, while others are beyond it and would be hindered were they to try it as a daily practice. In addition, one finds a prominent 'salesman' for centering prayer declaring what appears contradictory and adapting it in an oriental manner: "though we are not God, God and our true Self are the same thing." Oriental methods are cited favorably. I get the impression that proponents of centering prayer offer Christians, even beginners, an easy access to contemplation. By this method one is supposed to have a speedy way of finding God in advanced prayer. As it is now presented, I find it difficult to imagine centering prayer as anything but a passing fad. Far better for a spiritual mentor to guide his or her disciples to Saints Teresa and John. They are sure and solid.

**31. Question:** There has been considerable controversy about charismatic prayer. When a directee asks about it, what do you say? Do you advise people to join prayer groups which pray in this style?

**Comment:** From personal participation in charismatic meetings and in many contacts with men and women devoted to the movement, my overall impressions are favorable. Yes, there have been excesses and aberrations here and there, but one may not condemn a movement because of the faults of individuals in it. If a given group has strayed, we need not be alarmed as long as they welcome correction and stay close to the teaching Church. I think the charismatic movement has done and is doing a great deal of good for individual people and for the benefit of the Church. Joining a particular prayer group is not mandated by the Church, but it can be a strong spur and support for those who are comfortable with spontaneous shared prayer. One bit of advice I would offer a charismatic directee is that he or she should be sure to provide ample time for contemplative solitude with the Lord. Jesus' example is mandatory for all of us: "He would always go off to some place where he could be alone and pray" (Lk 5:16).

## SOLITUDE AND COMMUNITY

**32. Question:** I should like to take up your last remark about contemplative solitude. Is it realistic to suggest in our century that busy lay men and women in an extremely complex and driven society habitually "go off to some place where [they] can be alone and pray"? Not a few people would accuse you of trying to monasticize lay life.

**Comment:** Yes, I am well aware of the criticism, but it is superficial and off target. The crucial question is not what I am or am not trying to promote, but what the Lord and his saints, married as well as religious, have done and what he and his Church teach. The monasticizing objection probably stems from a subconscious tendency we wounded humans have to dilute the radical call of the Gospel. People given to one-step thinking love to put labels on what they do not like, and then think they have disposed of the matter. Mediocrity has deep roots. Lay men and women today who are serious about prayer—and this I know from personal experience with them—completely reject this criticism. Yet, you ask whether contemplative solitude is realistic in our day and in all states of life. The answer to your question is an emphatic affirmative. Especially in our complex and driven society, as you put it, do we need healthy solitude with God. Solitude is a time for unwinding, for *be*-ing. Modern men and women are over-stimulated, over-worked, over-met, over-talked, over-amused. That is one reason so many are superficial and trivial. There is no chance for them to grow and develop beyond where they are. In solitude we begin to possess what we already have. Seeds can begin to grow. In Christ we already have everything, but over-activity and over-stimulation smother it. As he himself said, we don't give ourselves a chance to mature (Lk 8:14). Further, prayerful solitudes enable us to see, as Henri de Lubac somewhere notes, into the "mysterious other side of the universe," the side of infinite depth that explains the surface side.

**33. Question:** Perhaps we should define terms. Many a disagreement stems from people using the same words but with different meanings.

**Comment:** Right you are. Solitude is not isolation. Solitude is a turning to the other person, in this case the supreme Other, with undivided attention. Isolation is a cutting of oneself off from all others, and thus it is an illness, while solitude is a radical healthiness. Much to the point is von Balthasar when he remarks, "Nowhere in the Christian life is the believer more an individual than in contemplative prayer.... In contemplation he is intent on hearing an utterance of God never given before."[28] Over the years I have marveled how the Lord treats each person as new and unique, for there is no end to the various ways in which he communicates himself. Directees all have their own ways of describing their experiences of divine favors, but they never cease to come up with new accounts which I have never heard before. But if this is to happen, we must be available to the Lord. He does not force himself on people who really want their pressures and take no means to attain the calm and composure any healthy person needs. Vatican II urged a healthy silence and solitude for all the faithful, including lay people who must pray in secret and without ceasing.[29] Seminarians and priests are to live in intimate and constant companionship with the Trinity with their lives permeated with reverence and silence.[30] Liturgical prayer should "continue in prayerfulness and sharing."[31] Cloistered religious give themselves "to God alone in solitude and silence" and "constant prayer."[32]

**34. Question:** What would you say to the objection that a person praying in solitude is cut off from the community, is in a way antisocial, and that communal prayer is therefore quite enough?

**Comment:** First of all, this view contradicts Jesus himself both in his practice of solitary prayer and in his teaching that all of us are to go to our rooms, close the door, and pray to the Father in secret

(Mt 6:6). Second, there is a confusion between solitude and isolation. Chatting with one's beloved alone is a solitude that goes out to another, whereas isolation is avoiding all persons for negative reasons. As we have noted, the former is healthy, the latter is unhealthy. Third, communal prayer, if it is to be rich for all concerned, needs the deepening that comes only from contemplative communion with the Lord in solitude. Moreover, "the individual contemplating in his room is not separated from the choir of the Church at prayer, but as we shall show later, celebrates the liturgy in a different form, no less real and effective."[33]

**35. Question:** I gladly grant what you are saying. Yet all the same, it seems to me that a spiritual director should be alert to the directee perhaps abusing solitude by making it an excuse for the neglect of duty and work to be done.

**Comment:** There is no doubt that such is possible. As a matter of fact some people use noise as a means of isolating their deeper selves from others. One of the benefits of spiritual direction is precisely that an objective guide can more readily detect and point out self-deceptions of this type.

**36. Question:** This seems an appropriate place to bring up communal prayer, for that is as much a New Testament reality as is prayer in solitude (See Mt 18:19-20; Acts 2:42, 46; 20:36; Eph 5:19-20; 1 Tm 2:1-8). Yet communal prayer in some places has fallen on hard days. It would help directees to point out why group prayer remains important, and most of all liturgical prayer: Mass and the Liturgy of the Hours.

**Comment:** I find that most directees in my experience are convinced of the significance of communal prayer, but nonetheless they do not always adequately understand why it is crucial. The infant Church readily grasped that it was a community of prayer, a *"societas orationis,"* as Pope Paul VI once phrased it, before it was anything else. Peter declared that the faithful were called out of darkness into the light in order to sing the praises of God (1 Pt 2:9), and so the laity joined their shepherds for daily communal prayer (Acts 2:42, 47). God speaks his word first to the Church he founded. She is the infallible listener to the word who hears it without twisting its meaning, and then prays and proclaims it. She is, notes von Balthasar, "the original contemplative who sits at the Lord's feet and listens to him, and as virgin and mother opens her heart to receive and bear the seed of the word." When that word comes to the individual person "praying as part of the Church, [it] comes attended, as it were, with an innumerable host of others praying with him."[34] Not only is this group worship due to God, but it is also a mutual support to the members of the community. We do not need support to do evil, but we surely do need example and solidarity to persevere in good. People who love one another enjoy doing things together. If a family or other community does not desire to pray as a group, they had better examine whether they actually are of one heart and one mind (Acts 4:32). Finally, we pray together because co-celebration is a joy and a fulfillment. St. Bernard remarks somewhere that "nothing on earth resembles heaven as closely as a choir singing the praises of God" (Rv. 8:2-4; 19:5-9; 22:17). Hereafter, however, the enthrallment shall be ecstatic, eternally ecstatic, because we shall enjoy a clear vision of the Lord, to whom we are singing.

**37. Question:** Granted that liturgical celebration needs the enrichment that derives from contemplation, would it not also be true that liturgical worship furthers contemplative depth?

**Comment:** Surely. You will notice that religious orders exclusively given to contemplation lay great emphasis on the celebration of Mass and the Liturgy of the Hours. For all the faithful, the homily, for example, "seeds" the assembly with the word of God. Or as von Balthasar remarks, it "transforms the assembled community into a Church which hears the word: the Church contemplative."[35]

## CALLED TO THE SUMMIT

**38. Question:** I know that over the years you have often spoken and written about the universal call to the fullness of contemplation, a call addressed by God to all men and women in every state of life. And I understand that this is not the place to develop all the evidences from Scripture, the magisterium, and the saints—especially Saints John of the Cross and Teresa of Avila.[36] But would you explain briefly how spiritual direction can further our climb to the summit?

**Comment:** I shall assume what should be obvious to anyone engaged in guiding others to holiness, but often is not: namely, that the director be of the mind of Scripture and the Church, and thus himself or herself convinced that there are not two tiers of holiness, but only one. The director needs to know how to guide married people to the highest mansions along a path compatible with their state, while not diluting Gospel teaching, just as the married saints do not dilute it. The practicalities of the wedded path to mystical prayer can be learned to a large extent from common sense and from one's married directees, if the director is single. Genuinely holy people in any vocation have a remarkable gift for discovering how the radical message of the New Testament (and the Old as well) is to be adapted to their concrete circumstances. I have often in conversations with my own directees admired their ingenuity in managing to have ample prayerful solitude even in the pressures of daily life. They are illustrations of the adage, "where there is a will, there is a way."

**39. Question:** You will grant, I know, that this is easier said than done. All the same, I must grant on my part that it can be done—as soon as one is determined to do it. What else should the mentor do to lead his or her disciples to the summit?

**Comment:** The mentor wants to check at some point early in the relationship to be sure the directee is not aiming at a refined mediocrity, at a whittled down version of holiness. I find that people, especially thoroughly sincere men and women in any state of life, are both surprised and enthralled to learn that the heights are for them as well as for monks and nuns. While the mentor should not nag, he or she should periodically remind the directee that the goal is total, four times insisted upon in the greatest commandment by

Jesus himself (Lk 10:27). That this is the common testimony of the great mystics we may illustrate from the witness of *The Book of Privy Counseling*:

> Believe me, if a contemplative had the tongue and the language to express what he experiences, all the scholars of Christendom would be struck dumb before his wisdom.... Whatever we may say of it is not it, but only about it.... [Our] highest destiny is union with God in consummate love, a destiny so high, so pure in itself, and so far beyond human thought that it cannot be known or imagined as it really is.[37]

# Practical Problems
# and Questions
# about Contemplation

N O ONE WHO HAS LONG WORKED at a serious prayer life needs
to be persuaded that problems and pitfalls along the path are
not rare. On the one hand, intimacy between Creator and creature
makes any merely human intimacy pale by comparison—such is the
case with the saints. On the other hand, prayerful people run into
all sorts of snags as they strive to grow in greater intimacy, demon-
strating the usefulness of this chapter. Anyone who has read thus far
is well convinced of its need, just as beginning cooks need no proofs
that they require recipes and practical advice from master chefs. We
now consider some of the practical problems and questions regarding contemplative prayer which may arise in spiritual direction.

**1. Question:** Books on contemplation, and indeed parts of this volume as well, deal with such lofty reaches of spirituality that they
seem at times closed off to me, too high above me. Many ordinary
men and women are inclined to think upon hearing of the universal
call to the contemplative summit: "That is beautiful indeed and I
wish it were for me, but you don't know to what depths I have fallen
and how weak I presently am. It can't be meant for me." Wouldn't
you agree that discouragement is a common obstacle to growth?

**Comment:** Yes, I would, but when God forgives sin he does not simply cover over one's corruption as a new snowfall covers a refuse heap. He renews, restores, and beautifies from within. The sinner is made new: "Though your sins are like scarlet, they shall be as white as snow" (Is 1:18). The saints are of the same mind, as are all solid spiritual writers. "No matter how grievously a man has sinned, he can repent and amend his life," declares *The Cloud of Unknowing.* "Let no one dare call him presumptuous for reaching out to God in the darkness of that cloud of unknowing with the humble desire of his love. For did not our Lord say to Mary [Magdalene], who represents all repentant sinners called to contemplation: 'Your sins are forgiven.'"[1]

**2. Question:** Prayer is not only a duty, says Scripture, but also a delight. Yet many of us ordinary people also experience it as a burden. We get restless and watch the clock. Is this oppressiveness normal? Does it suggest that when I have to force myself to pray that actually I am trying something beyond my strength or readiness? Would it be better to say a few vocal prayers and be done with the matter?

**Comment:** The experiences to which you refer are common, but they do not indicate that you are beyond your depth or readiness. Burdensomeness at prayer is not due to the nature of communing with God but to our imperfection. It is our sinfulness, our woundedness which needs purification, that causes the dark fire of contemplation to be perceived as dry and difficult. When the two mystical purifications (St. John of the Cross' two nights of sense and spirit) are completed, the person is very well aware of God's presence and ordinarily enjoys him. Even on the merely human level when two people relate with a deep and pure love, they enjoy being in each other's company. A man loving in this way finds nothing dull or burdensome in visiting his beloved—just being with her is a delight. Keeping one's eye on God continually, as Psalm 25:15 tells us to do, should be the most normal of all human actions. But we must be patient. Spiritual mediocrity is not the work of a day or a year. It dies hard. One of the surest signs of lukewarmness, perhaps impending disaster, is to be content with "a few vocal prayers and be done with the matter," as you aptly put it.

## MEDITATION AND METHODS

**3. Question:** While meditation is not contemplation, it is usually the normal path into deepening prayer. How do we Christians plunge into meditation? Granted that methods and techniques are not the primary factors in developing an interpersonal relationship with anyone, and even less with God, nonetheless some advice about what you do and do not do seems needed. Where and when does one begin?

**Comment:** As for methods, we should view them as means to an end, not as the end itself. Properly speaking, discursive pondering is not prayer. It is a preparation for prayer. Reflecting on what we have read or seen or heard leads into communing with the Lord. How we do this reflecting is an aid, not a fixed mold. Like scaffolding, it is used only to the extent that it is helpful. Further, we should see that methods in prayer are not the most important factor in success at it. Living the Gospel fully is the number one priority.

**4. Question:** Should we view meditation or other techniques as a lifelong enterprise? Some instructors give the impression that what they advise is the way to go, and there is no other. You can find seventy-year-old people still struggling with techniques and procedures they learned in their youth, and they seem to get nowhere.

**Comment:** Right you are. And wrong is the advice you have heard. Meditation is by no means meant to be terminal. It is but a beginning. By its nature it slowly becomes more affective and simple, less intellectual and multiple. It gradually leads one into being ready for the first delicate infusions of contemplative communion.[2]

**5. Question:** Now the tips. We cannot manipulate God, of course. But all the same there probably are right and wrong ways in going about our human contribution to discursive meditation.

**Comment:** Yes, there are.

- Meditative prayer should be calm and unhurried. There is no set amount of material to be covered. One sentence or paragraph may at times serve for an hour or a week of reflection and inner dialogue with the Lord.

- Beginners may overemphasize thinking at prayer. Imagination and reasoning have their places, especially in the early stages, but at any stage of development love is the core of communion.

- Dialoguing with the indwelling Trinity includes other types of affectivity which are naturally sparked by diverse reflections: praising, sorrowing, yearning, thanking, petitioning.

- Simplicity is in order. One should not be bewildered by an excessive concern with techniques, steps, and procedures.

- One should pay comparatively little attention to the method itself. Such a preoccupation can obstruct the Holy Spirit during the actual time of prayer.

- Prolonged difficulty with a given procedure might suggest another approach... or a combination of other approaches. Consultation with one's guide at this point would be appropriate.

- When one finds oneself united to God in a simple loving attention or yearning, the methods should be left aside. One has what they are meant to bring about.

**6. Question:** Christ has said, "Without me you can do nothing." How does he fit into this picture of beginning meditation?

**Comment:** I am pleased that you raise this point. It is crucial in all of the seven mansions. There can be no prayer at all without him, the winner and giver of all graces. Furthermore, he is in the flesh the visible picture of the invisible Father.[3] He who looks on him sees the Father (Jn 14:9). Or as von Balthasar puts it: "Each concrete episode of Christ's human life... tells us something of the inner life of God."[4] He is therefore the supreme exemplar of what prayer should be in itself and how it is to be integrated into the daily activities of ordinary living. "This is my Son, the Beloved... Listen to him" (Mt 17:5). There is no better pattern.

**7. Question:** Since Jesus is inseparable from his Mother, could you say a few words in a practical vein about her relationship to contemplative prayer?

**Comment:** After her Son and always in view of him, Mary is presented in the New Testament as the exemplar of prayer, the contemplative woman *par excellence*.[5] She is at center stage in the divine economy, for as Vatican II expressed it, the Mother of the Lord shines forth to all the faithful as "the model of virtues." She "unites in her person" the central doctrines of faith.[6] In addition to her being the Mediatrix of all graces given by her Son, she is also exemplar as well as object of meditation. She is the perfect model of Mother Church at prayer, the model of singleminded fidelity and burning love. She is the object of meditation because every virtue, theological and moral, flowers in her in sheer radiance and consummate perfection.


DIFFICULT PRAYER

**8. Question:** Popular paintings of the saints sometimes portray them in ecstatic delight at prayer. Although there is such a thing, and granting that it is normal, anyone who has persevered in a serious prayer life knows well enough that dryness and distraction are part of the package as well. Leaving aside for the moment advanced communion with God, I should like to begin by asking about the alleged inability to meditate discursively that we sometimes hear about. Is this inability real?

**Comment:** Yes, it is, and I meet it fairly often, especially among women. St. Teresa was one of these and she wrote about it. Yet we should be careful about coming to that conclusion in a given case. We are not at the moment considering the common inability to engage in discursive reflection when God begins to offer infused communion, but of those who from the outset of their spiritual lives find that they cannot meditate. They mean that they cannot proceed from point to point, idea to idea, without doing considerable violence to their prayerful inclinations. The director should check to be sure that this inability is genuine. There are people who hear or read about centering prayer and are not ready for it, or who dabble in oriental techniques that simply cannot yield Christic communion. Speaking of the ordinary need which most beginners have to meditate on the mysteries of salvation as the approach leading to advanced prayer, the author of *The Book of Privy Counseling* remarks "Some will refuse to enter through this door [of meditation], thinking to reach perfection by other ways. They will try to get past the door with all sorts of clever speculations, indulging their unbridled and undisciplined faculties in strange, exotic fantasies, scorning the common, open entry I spoke of before and the reliable guidance of a spiritual father as well."[7]

**9. Question:** You are suggesting, then, that there is an inability to meditate at prayer which is due neither to willed mediocrity, nor to the beginnings of infused contemplation?

**Comment:** Yes, I am, and you are probably wondering what one should do in this predicament. Often the answer is a greater emphasis on affectivity, on a simple abiding with God somehow sparked by an uncomplicated pausing over a psalm verse or a divine mystery such as a scene from the passion or the Eucharist. The focus is not on reasoning, but a recollecting, an active gazing. The *Imitation of Christ* puts it well: "If thou knowest not how to meditate on high and heavenly things, rest on the passion of Christ, and willingly dwell on His sacred wounds."[8]

**10. Question:** Perhaps the most troublesome stage of growth in prayer is the gradual transition from active to passive prayer, from discursive meditation to the incipient bits of dry, infused contemplation.

**Comment:** This passage is indeed both common with generous people and most discouraging—unless they are well informed and guided. Without adequate instruction and direction some people give up a serious prayer life because they think they are getting nowhere. If they read of the three classical signs of the transition taking place, the signs given by St. John of the Cross, they often seem unable to confidently apply them to their own situation.

**11. Question:** Since you explained the transition and its signs in *Fire Within*, those details need not be repeated here. But would you refresh our minds with a brief sketch?

**Comment:** A person can recognize the beginnings of infused prayer when three signs are found together (one or another by itself is not enough—it could be due to something on a merely natural plane):

- One experiences a disinclination to meditate discursively, an inability to profit from active reflecting. This disinclination and inability are not due to laxity, but rather to being drawn toward God in a simple, idealess way. Even though distractions may abound, the Lord is infusing a dark longing for himself. This yearning is usually dry, delicate, and brief.

- An inner perception of emptiness replaces the ideas and pleasures of former discursive thinking. The person is giving up worldly pleasures and is not yet purified sufficiently to enjoy God with any depth. Hence, there is a lack of comfort and closeness. The Lord seems distant and finite things do not satisfy.

- There is a marked earnestness in serving God better. This sign shows that the first two do not proceed from mediocrity, but from a new and better form of prayer.

**12. Question:** You speak of God drawing, giving, or infusing this dark awareness of himself. Do we experience this infusion, this pouring-in? And if we do, how is it perceived or given?

**Comment:** I wonder if you are not equating infusion with absorption or something close to it. The latter, the absorption in God of St. Teresa's fifth mansion, is surely infused, but there is also a delicate awareness which is infused. In other words, I suspect that you are implying that one pretty clearly perceives the receiving, an experience of receiving. Initial dry prayer, St. John of the Cross' first night, is often 'simply there' without our noticing any pouring-in. If you perceive that your being is in a wordless way reaching out for God, and if this reaching out is not a result of your reasoning to the conclusion that you should want him, it is hard to imagine that it could be other than given.

**13. Question:** The desire for God, and at times a loving attention to him, come and go. Distractions abound. Yet what is given is brief and delicate in this transitional stage. Does it follow then, that we read and stop, read and stop?

**Comment:** If I may borrow St. Teresa's phrase, we read and reflect until the Lord gives "something better" than meditating in an active way. So if you notice that you are wanting God either dryly or delightfully—even if distractions come and go—then you do not read or meditate at that time. We do not try to rise to passive prayer. We do not try to empty our mind as a Buddhist would do through techniques. What we do is gather ourselves together, think of the Lord in one of his mysteries, but with no need to ponder discursively if and when the Lord gives the dry desire for himself or a delightful awareness. If nothing is there, then, yes, read and ponder. But do remain sensitive to the presence or awareness of him, dry or not, when it is given. Let him take over when he chooses.

**14. Question:** It is difficult for some people to apply to themselves the three signs of being in the first purification. How can one know if the beginnings of arid contemplation are actually taking place?

**Comment:** Long experience in spiritual direction has taught me over and over that people commonly have great difficulty in making this application. Hence, the aid of a competent guide is of immense help in assuring them in one way or the other. We must suppose that the questioner is trying to give God everything. There may be a slip or fall here and there, but not due to deliberate neglect or will. If one is knowingly mediocre, there is no question that the beginnings of contemplation will not be given. For the lukewarm person the question is practically answered: John's signs do not apply. We may further note that, since we do not actively try to empty the mind in an oriental manner, we wait quietly for the Lord and gently direct our attention to him.

**15. Question:** Your last remark could use more development, I think. Just what is this waiting quietly for the Lord? How does it differ from a plain blank, from mere idleness?

**Comment:** A good question. Most of us are so inveterately accustomed to being active in prayer—reasoning, imagining, conversing—that we mistake for nothing the divinely given desiring or attending or loving. Dark, imageless, unreasoned, loving attention is not nothing. What God infuses in a wordless way is incomparably superior to what we can produce with all our multiplicities. Further, a calm awareness of the Lord, even if it is dry, is not a blank. The mind and heart are focused on God, not suspended in a blank oblivion.

**16. Question:** But how can we tell a healthy "emptiness" from a hollow vacuum due to laxity? How do we know we are being purified in the void?

**Comment:** The two questions answer themselves: willed laxity is the chief distinguishing factor. People who are trying to give God everything, and who experience what we have been describing, have no reason to suspect a misapplication to themselves. They will also notice a decided reluctance to reason at prayer, together with an inner strength developing, and a genuine progress in humility, patience, and love for others. Raissa Maritain noted in her journal that "reading or meditation do violence to my feelings and tire me greatly; whereas arid silence with God sustains me, rests me, and I would not give it up for anything."[9]

**17. Question:** People are often surprised and invariably disturbed when periods of satisfying contemplation alternate with periods of arid emptiness. They worry about their 'infidelity' when a deeply perceived communion, or even an absorption in God suddenly disappears. Quite automatically they assume or fear they've done something wrong.

**Comment:** What you remark is completely correct. It would be hard to exaggerate what we may call the law of fluctuation in prayer. In every stage, from discursive meditation through the transforming union, prayer comes and goes, flows and ebbs, increases and decreases in intensity, changes from one type to another. I know from experience that it is difficult to convince people that they should expect these in their own lives, even when they have advanced far.

One of the reasons we should not only understand but welcome these alternations is that we need them: delight to draw us on, dryness to detach us. As von Balthasar put it: "The alternation of consolation and desolation, of rapture and seeming rejection, is God's great educative process by which he seeks to detach us from our desire to hold on to what we have."[10] This reminds us that feeling cozy at prayer is one of the possessions we must renounce if we are to be faithful disciples of the Master (Lk 14:33).

**18. Question:** May we conclude then that what we have just been speaking about, "difficult prayer," is likewise beneficial prayer, nothing at all to be concerned about?

**Comment:** Yes, that does follow. St. John of the Cross salutes this arid, infused contemplation with the words, "Oh happy night!" And the author of *The Cloud of Unknowing* noted that the single-minded person is strengthened and purified in this detachment, while others "are marvelously enriched" even though they do not know how. The resulting inner void brought about both by one's efforts and the beginnings of infused yearning for God is highly beneficial and normal. He rightly concludes of this darkness:

> Diligently persevere until you feel joy in it. For in the beginning it is usual to feel nothing but a kind of darkness about your mind, or as it were, a *cloud of unknowing*. You will seem to know nothing and to feel nothing except a naked intent toward

God in the depths of your being. Try as you might, this darkness and this cloud will remain between you and your God. You will feel frustrated, for your mind will be unable to grasp him, and your heart will not relish the delight of his love. But learn to be at home in this darkness. Return to it as often as you can, letting your spirit cry out to him whom you love. For, if in this life, you hope to feel and see God as he is in himself it must be within this darkness and this cloud. But if you strive to fix your love on him, forgetting all else, which is the work of contemplation I have urged you to begin, I am confident that God in his goodness will bring you to a deep experience of himself.[11]

**19. Question:** If we grant that the dark nights together with all their benefits are effected by the fire of infused contemplation, how do we view other sufferings that sometimes accompany the nights? I refer to illnesses, contradictions, misunderstandings, failures, and blame. These too, can be purifying, can they not?

**Comment:** Yes, any suffering borne generously and with love for the Savior purifies us from defects, but of themselves human experiences are not mystical interventions of God. An old-fashioned scrubbing board and a contemporary automated washing machine may conceivably be found in the same home, but the one "purifier" is not the other. The mystical nights are not any sort of trial, although other types (illnesses, contradictions, failures) may accompany the passive purifications. Yet in a practical vein what we do regarding any hardship, mystical or not, is to embrace it willingly with the Lord on his cross. We do what we can, of course, to right what is wrong. We thus enter on the hard road and through the narrow gate that lead to life (Mt 7:13-14).

**20. Question:** Sooner or later most of us get ill, sometimes very ill. And it is commonly said that when pain becomes intense, one simply cannot pray. Is this true?

**Comment:** Yes, if we take prayer in the sense of an infused peaceful awareness of the divine presence or an intense yearning for God, then piercing pain can so focus our attention on itself that we may be unable to perceive the divine infusions. But, if we include as prayer the simple offering of our suffering with a glance of the will, then prayer in severe illness is both possible and profitable. As *The Cloud of Unknowing* expresses it, "Your patience in sickness and affliction may often be more pleasing to God than tender feelings of devotion in times of health."[12] My expression, a "glance of the will," is not perhaps the best, for a glance stems from a cognitive faculty, not a seeking one. But all the same, the will cannot operate except as following the intellect. Hence, in this sense we may speak of a willed glance at the Savior and an intention to be in union with and for him.

## CONDITIONS FOR GROWING

**21. Question:** I would suppose that anyone who has worked earnestly at living a solid prayer life sooner or later wonders why growth into the higher reaches is so slow. We read on the one hand of St. Teresa declaring that 'His Majesty' can do great things in a short while. On the other, we are vividly aware of our snail-like trip up the mountain. God wants us to be utterly filled with himself, as St. Paul remarked, far more than we do. Why does he not just brush aside all our defects and impediments in one fell swoop and give us what we want so badly?

**Comment:** The key to answering this question is hidden in your three words, "want so badly." The Lord's policy is that he respects the freedom he gave us. Without it there could be no human race, and consequently no love in visible creation. The English word, want, is ambiguous. In this context it can mean either wish or will, velleity or determination. When you say "what we want so badly," you can mean one or other of two things. You may be referring to the determination of a saint who has decided in no uncertain terms to live the Gospel with total generosity, or to the lesser of us who admire heroic virtue and would like to have it, but have not yet been thoroughly converted to it. If God gave the transforming union to people of divided hearts, to people who still, even if only in minor matters, were seeking created things for themselves, he would be forcing our freedom. He would be imposing incompatibles. Men and women who seek finite things for themselves may admire advanced prayer and wish it to some extent (a velleity), but they do not will it (a determined decision). They 'want' in the first sense but not in the second. Hence, there must be conditions for growing in prayer, conditions that are clearly marked out in the New Testament.

**22. Question:** This is not the place to spell all this out in detail. But perhaps you could sketch in schematic form how total determination makes prayer development possible. Obviously we must be free of mortal sin, but what else is required?

**Comment:** Voluntary venial sins of any kind, willed 'little things' contrary to the divine will, all hinder progress in prayer. Indeed, if these small faults are clung to, there can be no growth. Some instances: gossiping about people's faults; idle words; useless talking; excessive indulgences in food, drink, and amusements; disobedience to one's superiors and to the Church's teaching and discipline; deliberate coldness toward others; corner-cutting in prayer; neglecting to share one's resources with the needy; petty lies and injustices; failing to provide sufficient time for contemplation. (Some of these sins could be mortal, of course.) Even on the human level, two people cannot be intimate with each other in a genuine sense, if one is willingly offending the other. The final chapter of this volume, on assessing our progress, may be used as a further answer to your question.

**23. Question:** Do you think personality or temperament types are either helps or hindrances to growth in prayer? For example, would a sanguine person be more or less apt for mystical communion with God than the choleric?

**Comment:** I cannot cite any chapter and verse of Scripture that answers this question, but it seems to me that temperament of itself has little if anything to do with one's journey into God. The great condition is what we have already insisted upon: doing the will of the Father perfectly. Jesus himself has made this point more times than once. But let me respond to something you have not exactly asked: namely, does human vivacity, a person's aliveness, have anything to do with responding to God and thus to the gifts he wants to give? My answer to this question is affirmative.

**24. Question:** I don't quite catch the drift of what you have in mind.

**Comment:** Hans Urs von Balthasar once made a remark that suggests what I mean. "Man only needs to know, in some degree, what he really is, to break spontaneously into prayer."[13] But in order to break spontaneously into prayer one has to be alive, responsive to reality. The more we are vibrantly living, the more we are enthusiastically aware of what and who we are, the more we become enfleshed glories to the Father in the Son, who is himself the radiance of the Father's splendor (Heb 1:1-3). A vibrant awareness of what we are should trigger all sorts of different types of prayer. Let me mention several examples of what I have in mind. You yourself could add to the list.

- An appreciation of our greatness should prompt incessant praise and thanksgiving directed to the origin of our human existence. Contemporary science with its anthropic principle now asserts what St. Thomas said centuries ago, namely, that man is the pinnacle of visible creation. Psalm 8 expressed the idea in singing that we are little less than gods.

- An awareness of our utter dependence on God both for our existence, our talents, and for the least blinking of an eye should spark profound professions of genuine humility.

- The recollection that we are beings unspeakably loved by the Father[14] requires the response of continual loving communion with a whole heart, whole mind, whole soul, and entire strength (Lk 10:27).

- The remembrance that we are sinners suggests the calm but abiding expression of sorrow and a plea for mercy so eloquently found in the psalms and on the lips of the publican in the temple (Lk 18:13).

We may draw two conclusions from these recollections, these prayer-sparkers. One is that those who are vividly aware of the splendid gifts of nature and grace with which the Lord has endowed us will find prayer the most natural thing to do. Even more, it will be like the atmosphere in which the bird flies and the water in which the fish swims. What could be more normal than to burst into praise and love and thanksgiving? The second conclusion points to the need we have to be recollected in the midst of our daily activities. The more we are inwardly dissipated, the more we lose touch with our indwelling guests, the less are we prompted to praiseful prayer.

**25. Question:** Dialogue with God requires a wondering response. It seems to me that this one word, wondering, itself calls for further unfolding. I find that, beginning with my own personal *mea culpa*, most of us humans are anything but alive with awe and astonishment. The least atom is awesome, and a single living cell is immeasurably more so, yet how many of us are impressed? It cannot be surprising that we pray so little and so dully. We are not responsive to reality. We are not alive to the supreme wonder of all, the Lord and Source of wonders.

**Comment:** You could not be more on target. As you rightly note, God is the supreme wonder from whom all created marvels, amazing as they are, derive their tiny participations in the totally awesome one. How many of us marvel at ourselves? Do any of us pause to examine the splendid constructive texture of a carrot or a cherry or a piece of celery? Even the most commonplace of things loses its commonness when seen for what it truly is. The eyes of our minds are closed. As the psalmist prays to God to "open my eyes that I may consider the wonders of your law" (Ps 119:18, NAB), so should we. We are not in awe of God because we are not alive to the reality right before our eyes.

**26. Question:** Though I have run out of questions dealing with conditions for growing in prayer, perhaps you have something to add of which I have not thought?

**Comment:** Yes, there is the biblical idea of quiet and calm. Turmoil and noise, both inner and outer, are obviously destructive of communion with God. They obstruct any serious conversation. This is one reason among others why we must tame unreasonable anger, why we need purification from a thousand illusory desires, why we should do our part in the building up of harmonious community life (marriage, rectory, convent), why we must foster humility and seek to be freed from vain worries and idle concerns.

## IMPEDIMENTS TO PRAYER

**27. Question:** Your observation leads nicely to our present focus of attention. Noise and turbulent emotions are not the only obstacles to growth in prayer. I should like to ask about a poor self-image. There is no doubt that humility promotes prayer, but while granting that a diminished self-regard lacks the realism of humility, I wonder if it may not produce much the same results.

**Comment:** Unrealism is by definition unhealthy, and thus of itself a weak or poor self-image impedes growth at least to some extent. The fundamental reason is that we tend to project on God what we think of ourselves. "Since I am next to worthless and unlovable," one may conclude, "how could God (indeed, how could anyone) love me tenderly? He must find me drab and unattractive, perhaps even repulsive. How can I possibly be intimate with him?" Even if one does not reason explicitly in this fashion, he or she assumes the situation to be as the quotation describes it. Hence, all such a person reads and hears about in evidence of the universal call to the summit of contemplation, all the examples of ecstatic saints profoundly immersed in God, may just add to discouragement and a sense of futility.

**28. Question:** That sounds like a huge impediment to me. What can be done for this person?

**Comment:** There is good news and bad news on this point. The good news is that the woundedness of a poor self-image can be healed, at least considerably so. The bad news is that the healing is neither automatic nor rapid. Even though professional psychological analysis lies outside the immediate scope of this volume, experience with this problem suggests four observations. The first is that with the aid of a competent counselor one's growing insight into the origins of the dim self-assessment (usually found in early home life) has a healing effect, moderate though it may be. Second, as these persons slowly learn how to give and receive warm love, it slowly dawns upon them that they are indeed lovable and therefore worthwhile. Third, they should try not to give in to discouragement and a sense of futility at the slow pace of the healing process. Lastly, genuine growth in prayer is possible, even if felt intimacy is absent. God, after all, bestows his grace on his wounded children as well as on the healthy. And we are all wounded in one way or another.

**29. Question:** Perhaps the most persistent and frequently cited impediment to a contemplative prayer life is what you often refer to as a lack of time or time pressure. I would not expect you to repeat here what you have written elsewhere (in *Pilgrims Pray*), but perhaps you could offer a few pertinent pointers to aid the many people who are convinced that they cannot fit contemplative communion into their busy daily schedule.

**Comment:** In order to keep my answer brief, let me suggest a bare outline, each item of which might be pondered in prayer.

- We cannot do better than begin with Jesus' answer to this complaint in the Martha and Mary account in Luke 10:38-42: "One thing is necessary"—an immersion in the Lord.

- The first and greatest commandment, a total embrace of God through love, ever remains the first and the greatest.

- Action is a means, temporary and provisional; contemplation is our end, eternal and permanent. The former is therefore to be subordinated to the latter, not the other way around, as Vatican II explicitly pointed out for everyone in the Church, not simply for monks and nuns.[15]

- Jesus, who was immeasurably more needed by his contemporaries than we are by ours, never used that obvious fact as a rationalization for cutting down or omitting his long and habitual times of prayer. See, for example, Mark 1:35; 6:46-48; Luke 5:16; 6:12; 9:28-29.

- People simply do get to their priorities. They do what they really want to do: sports, TV viewing, entertainments, chatting on the phone, traveling.

- A deeply prayerful husband or wife, priest or religious, teacher or nurse, is far more valuable to others than a merely competent worker of little personal qualitative depth.

- People in love take it for granted that being with their beloved is the high point of the day. They do not habitually allow lesser activities to crowd out this favored time.

**30. Question:** It would be fair to conclude that a genuinely contemplative person has to be a determined man or woman. The life is not for the mediocre. But the fact is that many of us, even the fervent, live in an atmosphere of religious indifference. A few of us contend with a hostility to the very idea of an earnest prayer life. What counsel would you have regarding this obstacle?

**Comment:** A milieu of mediocrity not only fails to provide a support and stimulation to one's pursuit of God, it can be a positive hurdle. Although lukewarm priests and religious may not verbally try to dissuade a fellow community member from spending ample time in prayer, the undermining of prayerfulness readily takes other forms. In marriage it can happen that one spouse shows hostility toward, or a decided displeasure with the other who devotes time to contemplation. This situation recalls the remark in 2 Timothy 3:12: "Anybody who tries to live in devotion to Christ is certain to be attacked." Since this is a matter of principle, not one of compromise, the fervent husband or wife is called upon to join firmness with gentleness. The specifics of just how this may be done in concrete circumstances and with diverse personalities will call for the virtue of prudence and perhaps advice from one's spiritual mentor.

EXPECTATIONS IN PRAYER

**31. Question:** I do not know if I am typical or not, but I have found that often what I have taken for granted about contemplation is just not so. How often Saints Teresa and John of the Cross surprise me in what they say! My ideas are usually not totally wrong, but often they are a mixture of valid and invalid. Are others like me in this?

**Comment:** You have lots of company. Many people have unreal expectations about what their prayer is or should be. St. John of the Cross touched on this when he remarked, "Many individuals think they are not praying, when, indeed, their prayer is intense. Others place high value on their prayer, while it is little more than nonexistent."[16] These are two grave misunderstandings, not slight errors. Yet we should not be surprised at them because communion with God is mysterious (Rom 8:26-27), even if it appears clear and obvious.

**32. Question:** What would some of these erroneous expectations actually be?

**Comment:** Before I answer your question, let me remark on what you yourself just suggested, namely, that in each expectation there is usually something valid mixed in with something invalid. We humans often see only part of a picture and then draw erroneous conclusions. For example, some people infer from the necessity of methods for many beginners that procedures and techniques are prayer itself. They confuse means with ends. I think one reason methods, occidental and oriental (for example, centering prayer and Zen), are so popular is the mistaken expectation that techniques offer something more than a scaffolding. People often do not realize that what may be helpful at one time can be a hindrance at another. They who place undue stock in procedures need to recall that Scripture says not a word about techniques for communing with God.

**33. Question:** It seems to me that some people view Christic meditation (I am not referring to oriental awareness exercises) as a mine for new ideas, insights, intuitions—as a kind of refined theological reflection on divine revelation. They may even assume that they should develop new and splendid things to say to God.

**Comment:** Once again we have a typical admixture of truth and error. Yes, in our liturgical celebrations and in discursive meditation we do receive new and enriching insights, but as we grow into infused contemplation clear ideas and specific thoughts give way to a more simple and wordless immersion in God, even to the point where one in no way is able to express in words the intimacy experienced with the indwelling Lord. In contemplative prayer we are not seeking brilliant ideas or well-articulated expressions but rather a deepening love and commitment.

**34. Question:** Distractions are a problem for almost everyone. Is it right for us to be disturbed by them to the extent that most of us are? Or are we making mountains out of molehills? Is it real to expect our prayer to be free of mental wanderings?

**Comment:** We are taking it for granted that our minds should be uncluttered by deliberate, willed distractions. That being assumed, we may add that, given our human woundedness, thoughts foreign to our prayer are to be expected. We should not be discouraged by either their frequency or their persistence. Unless we are drinking of the absorbing or ecstatic infusions described in St. Teresa's fifth and sixth mansions, which so focus our inner powers on God that distractions cease at those times, we can expect to wander off, at least occasionally. Unwilled meanderings are no proof that our prayer is either bad or without profit.

**35. Question:** I have on occasion heard a person seem to downplay what you have often termed "ample time for prayer" by remarking that quality of prayer is more important than the quantity of it. This sort of person comes across to me as a minimalist, an individual given to corner-cutting. Is this a rationalization, or am I expecting too much in thinking that the amount of time we spend in contemplation is important?

**Comment:** We can agree that advanced communion with God is more important in itself that discursive meditation, but to conclude that therefore one needs little time for it is both shortsighted and illusory. For one thing the speaker assumes, and probably gratuitously, that his or her prayer is qualitatively advanced. Why else would one make the statement? Further, people who *de facto* do enjoy lofty prayer are precisely those who want and seek and do provide more time for it. The shallow assertion is itself an indication of a deficient prayer life. Saints are never grudging in the time they spend with God. Still more important is the example of Jesus. He who had the very deepest, the unmatchably most profound communion with his Father, habitually, says Luke, went out for those prolonged and frequent periods of solitary prayer. His conclusion was the exact opposite of our minimalist.

**36. Question:** It seems to me that perhaps the most frequent misconception about meditative and contemplative prayer is implied in the avid pursuit of experiences, usually enthusiastic and pleasurable experiences. Despite the repeated cautions of spiritual writers that feelings are not primary in our communion with God, I find that most people assume without question that progress in prayer is measured by the delight we find in it. If you agree that this is so, what do you think of it?

**Comment:** I surely do agree with you that this is a common assumption. Almost everyone takes for granted that when we feel a delightful divine presence during prayer, we are doing well. When on the other hand our time is spent in dryness and darkness, emptiness and restlessness, things are assumed to be going badly. The kernel of truth in this expectation is that there is such a thing as a delightful experience of the living God, and that this experience can be an indicator of progress (Ps 34:5, 8; 84:2; 1 Pt 1:8; 2:3). The error arises when people forget that the pleasurable feelings themselves need to be tested. They may arise from sources other than God. Genuine prayer will yield the biblical signs of authentic love of neighbor, humility, glad acceptance of the cross, obedience to the Church's teaching and discipline, and a frugal lifestyle. Jesus himself declared that it is not those who shout buoyantly, "Lord, Lord" who enter the kingdom but rather they who do the will of the Father (Mt 7:21). The pursuit of experiences leads to illusion and can prevent solid growth. An authentic spiritual life is not a "progress from one mountain-top experience to another. Quite the contrary, the Christian life is lived mostly in the valleys. Indeed, often in the desert. Openness to experience is one thing. The passion for spiritual elevations is another. The pursuit of religious experience is the shortest path to illusion."[17]

**37. Question:** Closely allied to a yearning for feelings at prayer, so it seems to me, would be our expectation that advancing into a loftier communion should entail a progressive growth in light-filled clarity. If beginning meditation is characterized by definite images and ideas, why wouldn't a superior communion include a still more brilliant intellectual content?

**Comment:** Once again there is a kernel of truth in this expectation, but also an invalid conclusion. The kernel is that the final contemplation of the beatific vision includes the marvelous clarity of consummation when we shall see God "as he really is" (1 Jn 3:2). This brilliance is due to the light of glory, an enabling and divinely given power, which we do not enjoy in this life. However, it does not follow that infused prayer in our pilgrim state should likewise be light-filled in the same way. No created mind of itself can see God directly, for he is endlessly beyond our best and most brilliant ideas. He necessarily is hidden (Is 45:15), and though he is purest light, he must dwell in "light inaccessible" to us (1 Tm 6:16).

**38. Question:** Discouragement in one's prayer life is obviously a huge stumbling block to men and women who begin to pursue God with enthusiasm. After seeming to get nowhere despite all their efforts, many slowly give up the enterprise as not meant for them. Their hours at prayer seemed futile, dry, and empty. Their conclusion: "empty prayer is bad prayer—why keep at it?"

**Comment:** This misunderstanding returns us partially, but only partially, to the expectation of pleasurable experiences which we were discussing a bit ago. Operative here is the assumption that successful prayer should feel good, that if one perceives an inner emptiness while communing with God, something must be wrong. A distinction is in order. If our void is due to conscious mediocrity in living the Gospel, to a willed lukewarmness, then of course an inability to pray is a natural but unfortunate consequence. How can we be in a vibrant contact with the Lord when knowingly we are holding back with him? The solution to empty prayer caused by mediocrity is simple: change, repentance.

**39. Question:** Yes, this makes sense. But the fact is that fervent people also experience the inner void. Contemplation seems at times futile and frustrating even to them.

**Comment:** True. They represent the other group in the distinction I mentioned a moment ago. Generous men and women sooner or later will meet dry, empty-feeling prayer. But in their case the news is optimistic. Their aridity is due to purifying contemplation. They are making progress, and if they understand the benefits of their dark night, they should not feel frustrated. Their difficult situation is fruitful and beneficial.[18]

## NEW PRAYER MOVEMENTS

**40. Question:** Human nature being what it is, many of us gravitate toward novelties and shortcuts. We have dealt with some of this already, but I would like to ask a few more specific questions.

**Comment:** First, I would like to offer a few thoughts about the question of newness and novelty. I assume neither of us is opposed to new ideas as such. After all, most old and solid practices were once new and probably then considered by some people to be novel. What concerns me is the person who embraces a new proposal without discernment, study, or evaluation. Likewise, you find people who, with little knowledge of the history of theology, will enthusiastically embrace an idea as new which is actually centuries old—something which long ago was proposed, tried, found lacking, and then discarded by minds far superior to those of present day promoters.

**41. Question:** My first specific question bears on general outlook. How should we who know comparatively little about advanced communion with God react to the welter of new ideas about it: oriental techniques, ecumenical spirituality, centering prayer, journaling as an aid to prayer, shared prayer, and charismatic prayer meetings?

**Comment:** No one can sensibly evaluate proposals in any field (medicine, law, plumbing, architecture, theology) without first being in possession of a competent mastery of that field. Neophytes enthusiastically embrace novel ideas because they have no solid vantage point from which to assess their worth or lack of the same. I do not see how anyone can reasonably judge any of the movements you name without first understanding in a somewhat thorough way what the masters have written. When you have grasped the works of people like Bernard of Clairvaux and Catherine of Siena, Teresa of Jesus and John of the Cross, you are fitted to recognize a genuine development or to reject what actually is a foreign body. Without a background in the classical tradition of the masters, the beginner should seek out and depend upon the advice of a guide who does possess this firm grasp. Led by one's own uninformed enthusiasms, one will most likely end up embracing what might be fashionable today but will fade tomorrow. In the process worthwhile contemporary developments may be passed over.

**42. Question:** What do you think of recommending a positive emptying of the mind, a freeing of it from all thoughts, whether the techniques for doing this are oriental or occidental? This seems to be a popular approach to attain an awareness of the transcendent.

**Comment:** First of all, the idea of an empty mind seems impossible, whether as an ideal or as a practical enterprise. Second, it is not Christian. We are told in the very first verses of the inspired book of prayer, the Psalter, about pondering the divine word day and night (Ps 1:1-2). The model of contemplation, Mary Immaculate, is presented by St. Luke as a woman who ponders the divine mysteries (Lk 2:19, 51). Nowhere do we read of emptying the mind as a procedure for encountering God. When the Lord gives a loftier, non-conceptual communion, well and good—and he surely gave it to his Mother. But even then the mind is not empty. The spiritual writer Thomas Green saw this point when he remarked of beginners in meditation that St. John of the Cross "values the meditative ways by which beginners come to know God. He would have little sympathy with the advice, sometimes heard today, that even beginners can simply 'center' on a God they do not yet know. We humans can only love what we know."[19] In our biblical and Catholic tradition, we actively meditate until God takes the initiative and gives us something better on which to focus our attention, that is, the beginnings of infused prayer. For St. Teresa to sit before the Lord with an empty mind is to be a 'ninny,' not exactly a desirable state! It is difficult to see the contrary teaching as anything more than another among many fads.

**43. Question:** I grant that an empty mind is an abnormality, but suppose that centering prayer aims at reducing or slowing down one's thought processes, at dislodging the mind from its usual ways of thinking? Do you have objections to this?

**Comment:** Achieving an inner calm is beneficial, of course, but I am not at ease about your formulation, "dislodging the mind from its usual ways of thinking." The Teresian and Sanjuanist advice seems more in touch with reality: operate in the human manner until God begins to give in his divine manner. In other words, meditate discursively until God infuses the dark knowing and loving we call contemplation. I find somewhat unreal the promise that by a centering method one has a quick access to God, a contemplative experience of his presence. Perhaps an oriental emptying approach may yield some sort of impersonal awareness, but this is not Christic communion—an impersonal awareness is not a contact with the living, Triune God.

**44. Question:** Do you have any other reservations about centering prayer?

**Comment:** Yes, I do, and I have spoken of them elsewhere, so let me be brief here. I think it is a mistake to teach centering approaches to a general group whether via book or lecture. For many people they are a hindrance, not a help. People who should be meditating discursively (and that includes most beginners) can be impeded by the emptying or slowing down advice. Even the advanced, who habitually receive infused light and love, can also be impeded since an active centering procedure interferes with the divine inflowing.

**45. Question:** Well then, would you ever teach or advise centering prayer?

**Comment:** I would not promote it before a group. St. Teresa was wiser. There are no short cuts to contemplation. Using a word to re-focus attention can be useful for a person at a given time. For instance, it can be helpful for an individual usually receiving mystical prayer but who on occasion meets inner blank periods. Therefore, on a one-to-one basis, I may advise something like the centering idea but without oriental implications.

**46. Question:** What do you think of keeping a prayer journal? Is this beneficial or is it a distraction, another passing fad?

**Comment:** Whatever position one takes on this practice, a prayer journal is only a means to an end. It should be viewed and evaluated as such. To keep a record of one's prayer as a goal in itself could be a form of narcissism. Hence, if journaling really helps one grow, well and good. But if it subtly becomes a practice sought for itself, it is an encumbrance. St. Teresa took a dim view of writing about one's prayer. In her own down-to-earth sort of way she noted that if one has a real experience of God, it will not be forgotten. If it would be forgotten, she considered it not worth recording.

## LITURGY AND CONTEMPLATION

**47. Question:** Given that anyone's spiritual life, if it is patterned after the Gospel, is ecclesial and therefore communal, I should like to inquire about the interrelationship between public worship and private prayer. Would you advise lay people as well as clergy and religious to celebrate the Liturgy of the Hours?

**Comment:** Indeed, I would and do. But more important than my personal view is the mind of the Church which recommends that the faithful in all states of life join in this, the official public prayer of the Church of the Incarnate Word. All through Chapter One of *The General Instruction of the Liturgy of the Hours* we notice how it is assumed and explicitly asserted that this tremendously rich and official prayer of the Mystical Body is meant for everyone. While the clergy and religious are especially deputed to offer this worship, it "belongs to the whole body of the Church... and as far as possible the people should take part."[20] "Hence, when the faithful are invited to the Liturgy of the Hours and come together in unity of heart and voice, they show forth the Church in its celebration of the mystery of Christ."[21] Later in the same chapter while speaking of the various types of communal celebration the text recommends it even in the domestic church: "It is desirable that the family, the domestic sanctuary of the Church, should not only pray together to God but should also celebrate some parts of the Liturgy of the Hours as occasion offers, so as to enter more deeply into the life of the Church."[22] I would strongly urge you to read and ponder this entire instruction. If you embrace the habitual practice of the Liturgy of the Hours, you will find in your personal experience how immensely enriching it is to your sharing in Mass and to your growth in contemplative prayer. Not only is there no clash between liturgical worship and private devotion, the two mutually complement and enrich each other.

**48. Question:** While I readily grant this complementarity, I wonder what a person does who at times is so absorbed by the occasional intensity of the divine infusions of light, love, and delight that attention to the words and actions of communal prayer becomes very difficult, even impossible. How does one then participate?

**Comment:** Though this problem is not widespread, it is a marvelous difficulty, and it does occur. St. Philip Neri would on occasion be so profoundly absorbed in love at Mass that he could not speak, and thus had to interrupt the celebration for up to two hours. This happy problem can occur also during the recitation of the rosary either alone or in a group. One adjusts as one best can. God, after all, is the Lord both of liturgical worship and private communion. In a long chapter of his study, *Theological Dimensions of the Liturgy,* Cyprian Vagaggini, shows how thoroughly integrated in the case of St. Gertrude were her lofty mystical contemplation and her thoroughgoing liturgical spirituality. Not only was neither an impediment to the other, but actually they made one harmonious whole: each contributed to and nourished the other. After fifty pages of documentation, Vagaggini observes from the example of Gertrude that we see illustrated in her the truth "that the mystical graces, even the greatest, and contemplation, even the highest, in what is essential to them, are perfectly capable of being realized in the communitarian and public liturgical action without harm to normal active participation in it, to say nothing of their verification in the extra-liturgical part of a life dominated by liturgical spirituality."[23]

**49. Question:** You mentioned that liturgy and contemplation enrich each other. How can a mentor aid his disciple in seeing this and in living it?

**Comment:** A spiritual guide will, when the situation so indicates, direct his or her charge to suitable study and spiritual reading. These should provide the intellectual grasp of the relationships between liturgy and contemplation and of their mutual enrichment. I may mention a few briefly:

- The Catholic Church is most intensely herself when she gathers her members to celebrate the Eucharist, as Saints Luke and Paul imply (Acts 2:42; 1 Cor 10:16-17).

- The Eucharist, in Jesus' own teaching, deepens the indwelling presence and thus contemplative love (Jn 6).

- There is a close inner orientation between the Eucharist offered as sacrifice and our adoration of the Blessed Sacrament outside of Mass. The Lord's continuing presence in the tabernacle points both to the Sacrifice from which it proceeded and the next one in which he will again be offered and consumed.

- Contemplative prayer prepares us for a richer Eucharistic celebration (1 Cor 11:28).

- In silent adoration and petition we join the risen Christ now interceding for us before the Father (Heb 7:25).

Therefore, two observations may be added. "A liturgical movement unaccompanied by a contemplative movement is a kind of romanticism."[24] And further, priests, indeed all of us, "should prize daily conversation with Christ the Lord in visits of personal devotion to the Most Holy Eucharist."[25]

## COMMUNITY AND CONTEMPLATION

**50. Question:** What of the objection that in one's concern for contemplative solitude one neglects other people? While this aberration is possible, I suspect that it is rare. What do you think?

**Comment:** From what I have seen of human life—lay, religious, and clerical—you are right. A far more common aberration runs in the opposite direction: involvement with people, especially idle and trivial involvement, tends to eat up contemplative communion with God, the supreme Other. I have yet to live with a man who prays too much, but I am afraid I've seen only too many whose work and supernatural influence are anemic because of a lack of prayer. The final word on this question is Jesus himself with his habitual and long prayerful solitudes with the Father. And who will dare say he neglected people? We should likewise recall that due to our intimate closeness to one another in the Mystical Body, contemplative solitude, rather than excluding others, embraces all in the deepest sense, in the very heart of Christ.

**51. Question:** What about the benefits that the horizontal and vertical dimensions of the spiritual life bring to each other? To be more specific: how does loving my neighbor—husband, wife, children, friends, co-workers—contribute to my contemplative prayer?

**Comment:** I may begin with the theological core of the matter: there is only one virtue of charity by which we love God, ourselves, and our neighbor. If I am not loving others—although not necessarily liking them—I cannot have a deep prayer life, for its heart, love, is missing. My prayer will be no better than my love for others. No set of techniques, occidental or oriental, will be able of themselves to improve it.

**52. Question:** Is there not a psychological aspect to this relationship as well as a theological one? I mean that if we live in a loving atmosphere, prayer obviously comes more easily.

**Comment:** Yes, surely. Genuine love is the most effective healer of human wounds, and that in both directions. The person who gives love and the one who receives it are both made more whole. And the more whole we are, the better we do anything, and most of all, the better we pray. For instance, in a loving family (or convent or rectory) there is no need to 'shift gears' when we leave work or recreation to go to prayer. The whole of life is lived in the divine presence, which is an atmosphere of love. We are urged by St. Paul "to live through love in his presence"(Eph 1:4). St. Augustine also shrewdly noted that "in loving our neighbor the eye of our mind is purified to contemplate God."[26] Loving our associates requires that we practice other virtues: humility, gentleness, patience, obedience. Thus we are purified of our faults, each of which may be an impediment to growth in divine intimacy.

**53. Question:** This makes sense and deserves protracted pondering and self-examination. Does Scripture say anything about this relationship?

**Comment:** More times than once. In the sermon on the mount Jesus forcefully and concretely insists on love for others as an indispensable condition for praying as God wants us to pray. If I am on my way to worship at the altar and there recall that I have offended by neighbor, I am to get up, leave the church, and get reconciled with my brother or sister, husband or wife, friend or co-worker. Only then am I fit to return to prayer (Mt 5:23-24). Strong medicine. St. Paul likewise insists that worship is to happen in a community free of argument and conflict.[27]

**54. Question:** Now I should like to ask about the reverse influence: how does contemplation further community life in family, parish, convent, office, and shop?

**Comment:** Before I state what may be viewed as a thesis, I should like to note that I am supposing that we are concerned with normal people. My thesis may not apply to some of the mentally ill. My proposal is that deepening contemplation bestows and furthers universal warmth, forgiveness, long suffering, and cordiality. The man or woman of genuine prayer progressively grows in patience, forgiveness, and affection. Why this happens may be explained in three ways. First, a person immersed in divine beauty gradually becomes more and more sensitive to created beauty whether found in persons or in things. St. Francis of Assisi could sing exultingly to creation, as did the psalmist, because he was a mystic and not merely a naturalist. Theologian Josef Pieper somewhere remarks that the contemplative intuition sees a non-finite relation in the heart of created reality. St. John of the Cross fell into a deep and divine absorption when he gazed at the stars during the night or upon flowers in the sunlight because he saw 'much more' in these finite splendors than mere created artifacts. Saints are thus more perceptive of human beauty than the rest of us, and so have a higher regard for a companion or spouse, even for an obnoxious one. As the inspired word puts it, God "put his own light in their hearts to show them the magnificence of his works" (Sir 17:7-8). And the pinnacle of his works in visible creation is our brother and sister, including the annoying brother or sister.

**55. Question:** I've never thought of things in this light. How and why the saints were so exquisite in their love for others, including their persecutors, now becomes more clear. Yet there is more, for you mentioned three explanations. What would the others be?

**Comment:** The second is that in advancing prayer we gradually put on the mind of Christ and thus learn to suffer from and sacrifice for others as he did for you and me and for all other sinners. Our associates' faults become less and less formidable obstacles to our forgiveness and cordiality. The contemplative becomes more and more conformed to the crucified and risen Lord who showed the greatest of all human loves, "to lay down his life for his friends" (Jn 15:13). A mystic promotes a happy home, a grace-filled community, loving those who cause hurt and readily forgiving them. He or she repeats with St. Paul, "It makes me happy to suffer for you" (Col 1:24).

**56. Question:** It is hard to imagine that there is still another way to explain how contemplation promotes human love, but one more still remains.

**Comment:** St. Paul leads the way when he tells the Thessalonians that they have learned from God to love one another (1 Thes 4:9). While he probably was referring most of all to the teaching and example of Jesus, he might well have had in mind their learning from the very experience of *agapé,* the divine way of loving. Scripture tells us that the Lord's love fills the earth, that he comforts us, that he treats us tenderly (Ps 119:64, 76-77; 2 Cor 1:3-4). The prodigal son's father "clasped him in his arms and kissed him tenderly" (Lk 15:20). Mystics report receiving unspeakable intimacies and divine embraces in their prayer, spiritual embraces so tight at times that they could not live without God's aid. When sinners are so loved in advanced contemplation, we can hardly be surprised that they learn through sheer experience how to love friend and foe, spouse and co-worker. Indeed, there is no more powerful contribution to a harmonious marriage, or a happy monastery, or any other gathering of human beings—indeed to the world community—than contemplative prayer.

**57. Question:** Something just popped into my mind: would it not be correct to say that infused prayer contributes to community also in that it deepens communal worship? Since you touched on this only briefly in another comment, perhaps you could add a bit here?

**Comment:** Yes, what I said before this did not deal with what the individual indirectly contributes to marriage or convent or rectory living as a beneficial consequence of participation in group prayer. Each of us enhances our worship in several ways.

- By living a forgiving and cordial life together, we improve the atmosphere of prayer.

- Because of the communion of saints and our membership in the Mystical Body, when we deepen our private prayer we thereby enrich our communal worship. What affects one, affects all (1 Cor 12:12-27).

- When we come to Mass or the Liturgy of the Hours on time, indeed come earlier to recollect and prepare ourselves, we enhance the value of the celebration.

- For our part we improve common prayer also by attention to details: refusing to be annoyed by the mannerisms of others, by praying with proper deliberation, by unity of action as rubrics prescribe, by observing the appropriate pauses for silence, by uniting our intentions with the praise of the elect in their heavenly liturgy (Rv 8:2-4).

TEN

# Problems that Come up in Spiritual Direction

ONLY ONE WHO HAS ENGAGED extensively in the ministry of spiritual direction can appreciate the number and diversity of questions that are asked. While there seems to be no limit to the types of problems people wish to discuss, there are some common questions raised time and again. Here we shall touch upon a few of the former but devote most of our attention to the latter.

The robust spiritual life of the saints is not a vague, this-worldly do-goodism, not a mere ecological and environmental concern, not a religiosity that centers on creation with little attention to the hard sayings of the Gospel. Neither is it a mere winning of friends and influencing of people, nor the vain optimism that sees only 'institutional sins' and downplays, if not denies, individual sin: deadly mortal sin and the mediocrity of deliberate venial sin. We do not envision as a following of Christ the ill-placed and myopic thinking and seeking that St. Paul stigmatized as illusory desires (Eph 4:22).

Genuine spiritual direction is based on reality, on the revelation whose fullness is found in the Radiant Image of the Father and on a path leading from crucifixion to resurrection. Anything less is a wishful delusion doomed to disintegration and death. We shall explore, therefore, fundamental principles, some of which are highly unpopular in many quarters not only with irreligious men and women, but also only too often with others who sometimes worship in our churches.

We shall consider likewise some common confusions and misunderstandings found even in sincere people earnestly seeking God. What exactly, for example, are mortification and self-denial? Do they differ? Are they still necessary? If they are, how do married people as well as others practice them? What if we do not perceive in ourselves an attraction to the hard road and the narrow gate that open to life?

We shall look into the frustrations felt by large numbers of people who cannot tell the difference between feeling and willing and thus assume they simply cannot avoid sin. They will say, for instance "I can't control my impatience; judgments frequently pop into my mind; at prayer I am pestered by endless distractions, and only too often I experience a positive repugnance for any kind of communion with God; impure thoughts and desires assail me— how can I possibly be pure? I find it frustrating that I can't be good, so how can I ever become a saint? I almost feel like abandoning all these efforts to practice virtue."

Then there are the problems that center on conscience and confession. Directees are confused when they hear and read that their friends and some theologians appeal to conscience against the Catholic Church's teaching. They wonder what conscience actually is. They may doubt with reason whether their friends and the theologians know any more than they do about the matter. They ask if frequent confession is still recommended, for they may have heard the contrary within the celebration of the sacrament itself. And how does one overcome the bane of dull routine?

But first we turn our attention to the basic question: how does one seek God earnestly? What would a spiritual director say to a mere beginner?

## PROGRAM FOR PURSUIT

**1. Question:** I can think of no better starting place than the words you just used: how do I seek God earnestly? I do not mean merely sliding respectably under the wire, but rather what I once heard you refer to as a hot pursuit.

**Comment:** First note that the main problem is not finding a guru, a trendy novelty, or a set of techniques. God is manipulated by no one. The only way to seek God is to love and live truth and goodness. If you never sin against the light, even the imperfect light as you presently see it, and if you try to live according to that light, you will find God. If you persevere in loving truth and living it, you will become a saint.

**2. Question:** Yes, but how many really pursue truth? As far as I can observe most people at best accept what comes their way in matters of morality and religion. If they like some idea they see or hear about, they may accept it, and if they accept it, they may try to live it in a lukewarm way. I don't see much positive and protracted study to seek and find truth.

**Comment:** Neither do I. In my lifetime I have come across only a small percentage of people who will bother to get books, serious books, not bigoted diatribes or worldly popularizations, and then give themselves to serious study. On the other hand, large numbers of men and women knock themselves out to prepare for a profession in order to make money. Many spend hours before a mirror to attain bodily attractiveness. Many train themselves in grueling practice sessions to achieve fame in music or sports.

**3. Question:** If I go further and ask why so few of us zealously seek truth, I suppose that one of the reasons is sloth?

**Comment:** It is one reason, but by no means the only one, probably not the chief one. Truth tends to interfere with favored lifestyles. If I am serious about truth, about the way things actually are, I soon find out that I have to give up my pleasurable preoccupations, my vanity, and my pride. Any honest person who thinks about this for a moment will admit this is so. Hence, all bound up with pursuing truth is moral rectitude, at least, the sincere attempt to live a virtuous life of humility, chastity, obedience, patience, loving concern for others. It is not by accident that St. Paul declares that the only way to attain to the perfect knowledge of God and his will is to be converted from a worldly way of life (Rom 12:1-2).

Jesus himself made the point with dazzling clarity: only the pure of heart can see God (Mt 5:8). Only the humble are given divine light (Lk 10:21).

**4. Question:** Well, then, perhaps you could expand a little more on the implications of your point. The glitz and vulgarity welcomed as 'entertainment' by a jaded world seems to reflect an existential boredom in our society, wouldn't you agree?

**Comment:** Yes, I surely would. You are right to call it existential boredom, a dull and dreary boredom with human existence, not simply with some particular conversation or party or book. Bored people have no wealth of meaning, no lively sparkle, no consuming love in their lives, no concern for God. A saint is never bored.

**5. Question:** Earlier you made the point that a spiritual director is secondary, an instrumental aid to the directee, that the chief director is the Holy Spirit himself. The human guide assists a disciple in being rid of obstacles to the divine inner impulses toward truth and goodness and love. That means we have to be stripped of worldliness in order to have a vigorous spiritual life.

**Comment:** What you say is obvious, of course, when one envisions full scale worldliness but here we may consider the more subtle worldliness, the type captured by our current expression, a comfortable life. Blaise Pascal expressed the idea when he remarked that "the world naturally desires a religion, but a comfortable one."[1] Nature abhors a vacuum. We will be filled with one thing or another. If it is God, it will not be mammon. If it is mammon, it will not be God. Beginning with the Master himself, who was born in dire poverty and later in his journeys had no place to lay his head, Scripture offers no support to people who provide for themselves a cozy, comfortable life devoid of penance and self-denial. The Old Testament prophets lived austere lives, and the greatest of them, John the Baptist, lived in the desert on locusts and wild honey. The nomadic traveling of the apostles was one hardship after another—see the stark list of sufferings experienced by St. Paul in 2 Corinthians 11:23-28. Jesus spared no punches in his teaching that the wide, easy road leads to perdition (Mt 7:13-14), that it is harder for a rich man to enter the kingdom of heaven than for a camel to pass through the eye of a needle (Mt 19:23-26). The man who dines elegantly and is clothed in fine linen, who does not share with the beggar at the gate, ends up in hell (Lk 16:19-31). With necessary food and drink, we are all of us to be content (1 Tm 6:7-8). We are to take up our cross every day (Lk 9:23).

**6. Question:** But why are ease and comfort a danger? Why do saints, married as well as clerical and religious, deliberately choose a mortified life? Why does a saintly king or pope do private penance, why engage in fasting or wear a hairshirt? Are not created things that offer ease and comfort gifts of God? Is it not God who provides them for our benefit? Some people regard such sacrifices as misguided if not foolish.

**Comment:** Yes, created things are good, but the fact is that, due to our woundedness, we tend to seek them for themselves, to make idols of them, to be distracted by them from a burning pursuit of "the one thing." Clinging to anything for its own sake divides the heart. That is lethal if one aims at imitating the saints and living the universal call to holiness. "Nothing is so likely to corrupt our hearts," wrote Newman, "and to seduce us from God, as to surround ourselves with comforts—to have things our own way—to be the centre of a sort of world whether of things animate or inanimate, which minister to us; their very service and adulation will lead us to trust ourselves to them, and to idolize them."[2] Giving up what pleases and flatters us is painful, of course. It is not easy, especially at first. But there is no doubt, both on the word of Scripture and in the experience of those who try it perseveringly, that a willed surrender leads to life and joy. And in the long run it is a course of action that lessens suffering. Loving us perfectly and beyond our imagination, the Lord is not content with less than our entire sanctification. He loves us so much that if we do not correct ourselves, he will.

**7. Question:** Because it is so widespread and deeply imbedded in our culture, television is a touchy subject, and few there are who are willing to give up extensive use of the medium. Yet who can deny that habitual and frequent viewing erodes an earnest spiritual life? What do you say to directees who are more or less addicted to it?

**Comment:** As Sergeant Joe Friday of the TV show *Dragnet* comments, "The facts, ma'am, just the facts." I take it for granted that television is not bad in itself, and that it can be a powerful propagator of the divine message. St. Paul would probably be on prime time. But together with this there is another factor. The visual imagery together with the auditory output can exert a powerful pull to the ephemeral and the superficial, not to mention the downright immoral. Pascal, a man given neither to corner-cutting nor to ambiguous generalities, clearly saw the corrosive power of the visual and the auditory when they combine in an unholy alliance. "All the principal forms of amusement," he wrote, "are a danger to the Christian life; but of all those invented by the world, none is more to be feared than the theatre."[3] Had this remarkable thinker lived to see our contemporary abuses of film and television, he would in all likelihood have filled out his judgment with a stinging sentence or two. Should a spiritual director find a directee given even to small excess in TV viewing, he or she can hardly say less than Pascal about this principal form of amusement in our day. Not to do so would be to shirk duty.

**8. Question:** Those who pursue the comfortable life, even aside from blatant sin, tend to cut corners, wouldn't you say?

**Comment:** Yes, but also they lack a sense of realism—realism in the sense of perspective. They are shortsighted. Until we are fully converted, we all slip to some extent into a more or less unreal assessment of the value or lack of value of the concrete givens in our immediate circumstances. Seeing things as they actually are is one of the most precious and yet least common traits of fallen human beings. Those who assume that they see things realistically are often the most myopic. As we lie on our deathbeds one day, how trivial, indeed how ludicrous, will appear all sorts of happenings we thought so dreadfully important in our lives: winning a football game, being flattered for physical beauty, gaining popularity with the crowd, acquiring superfluous possessions, enjoying this meal or watching that television program, indulging in this dishonesty or that impurity, doing our own will or clinging to our own ill-founded opinion. One of the most effective aids to seeing things as they truly are, to acquiring perspective, is to imagine ourselves at the point of death and then ask, "How will it look then?" As the *Imitation of Christ* puts it, "When that last hour shall come thou wilt begin to have quite other thoughts of thy whole past life."[4]

## MORTIFICATION AND SELF-DENIAL

**9. Question:** Surrendering the comfortable life makes understandable what St. Paul meant when he called our inner renewal a spiritual revolution (Eph 4:23), nothing less. But isn't much more involved —that is, giving up more than indulgence in comfort alone?

**Comment:** Yes, that is right. This area of our discussion is among the least understood of all aspects of the Gospel. The common tendency is to shy away from it as from the plague. St. Paul himself was aware of the unpopularity of the cross when he observed that to the pagans it is madness and foolishness. The world has not changed in this respect even to our day. Even though the theme of self-denial occurs on almost every page of the New Testament, we who claim to follow Christ experience a decided discomfort with and resistance to the arduous sayings about the cross, hell, authority, the hard road, and the narrow gate. Many people wonder if mortification and penance and self-abnegation are still relevant. Some have bluntly declared them to be passé.

**10. Question:** Since we are living in our world and not some other, it would be helpful if you would address some of the problems our contemporaries have with all this—including people who are in our churches on Sunday morning. Indeed, including men and women engaged in religious work by profession. Am I being unreasonable or harsh in my last remark?

**Comment:** Not in my view of the matter. The evidence is plain for anyone to see, evidence both in the form of explicit statements and in willingly chosen lifestyles. The main point of your question, however, bears on the difficulties our fellow sojourners have with self-denial in the evangelical sense, the hard road and the narrow gate. I might specify these problems in a brief series of questions. Can we rightly reject or slight the goodness of this world, a world which Genesis itself terms "very good," a world which Vatican II also described as having much value?[5] It would appear that self-denial implies a rejection of this goodness. How can a Christian lay person be humanly involved in the world and yet be detached from it, "renouncing all that he possesses," and "minding the things above, not the things on earth"? Do recent findings in psychology suggest the harmfulness of the severe penances of past ages: discipline, hairshirt, and such like? Is it not sufficient in the spiritual life to accept the hardships that come our way in the ordinary course of daily duty? Why should we go out of our way to add sacrifices? Could this not be unhealthy, psychologically if not physically? We will be taking a look at these problems.

**11. Question:** They are honest questions, which express the very sentiments that I meet even among religiously-minded people. But there is another side to this whole matter. Candor requires that we acknowledge that side as well. I mean that we have an abundance of defects that must be cut away, or there will be no sanctity. Clearly, a life of holiness cannot be all peaches and cream. Still, people sometimes think they are doing very well in this department even though they have a multitude of spiritual defects. They see no need for self-denial.

**Comment:** I have found in the work of spiritual direction that the best of people are the very ones who progressively see more and more how deficient they are—and I am not referring to a weak or poor self-image. On the other hand, men and women who are far less holy often enough recognize very few defects in themselves. What I have in mind would include petty vanities; speaking too much; eating too avidly or to excess; seeking types of food and drink only for their taste pleasures, living in other peoples' minds; excessive desires for esteem; unreasonable pursuit of convenience and comfort; little impatiences with others or with oneself; trivial attachments (to a scratch pad, a holy card, a way of washing dishes, a choice of a chair); procrastinations; exaggerations in speech; too much recreation; gossiping; omissions of all sorts (a smile, a word of commendation, a helping hand, expressing an unpopular view); mixed motives. Both director and directee should be sensitive to these possibilities, and when they are operative, take determined means to overcome them. That obviously will require self-denial.

**12. Question:** Working on these defects looks like a lifetime program to me. We do not automatically grow out of them. As a matter of fact, I would imagine that without attention they grow progressively worse. But how in the world would a person begin? Just facing the matter discourages me.

**Comment:** I can understand your apprehension. At the risk of possibly adding to it, but with the hope of a more effective solution, let me note how emphatic and uncompromising Scripture is about faults like these. We are to have pure hearts, hearts cleansed of anything ungodly.... We are to try to be as pure as Christ himself.... We aim at being holy and spotless.... We are to be as unworldly as Jesus himself (Mt 5:8; 1 Jn 3:3; Eph 1:4; Jn 17:14-19). Nothing is to impede God's word working in us, and certainly not mere earthly thoughts (Lk 8:14; 2 Cor 4:18; Col 3:1-2). Hence we have to undergo a real exchange, a giving up of the world that will return to us far more than we have surrendered (Mt 7:13-14; 16:24-26; Lk 14:33). Some of this purification is active and can be done by our operating in a human way and with the grace of God (1 Cor 9:24-27; Eph 4:22-24; Rv 22:12-14). The deeper purification (what we cannot effect by human efforts) must be done by God who completes our work, if we allow him, by infusing the dark fire of contemplation (Mal 3:2-3; Rv 3:19; Jn 15:2; 1 Pt 4:12-13).

**13. Question:** I have problems about terminology in all this, and I think that many others are fuzzy about it too. What are detachment, penance, mortification, self-denial? They share one trait in common for most of us: they are dreary and forbidding. Are they pretty much the same thing?

**Comment:** No, these terms do not express the same reality. One of the chief reasons people have trouble with them is that they do not understand their actual meanings. *Detachment* is an inner matter of the will, that is, not seeking or clinging to created things for their own sakes, not making finite reality into little gods. Put positively detachment means using things as means to God for our own genuine good and thus for the divine glory (1 Cor 10:31).[6] The word *penance* has two common meanings today. One refers to *metanoia,* conversion. This is what Jesus had in mind when he said that we should do penance and believe the Gospel (Mk 1:15). The other is concerned with satisfaction for sin, one's own and others' (Col 1:24).

**14. Question:** So far, so good, but what about mortification? Many people use it interchangeably with penance and self-denial. Are these all the same?

**Comment:** No, they also differ, at least when one speaks properly and with theological precision. *Mortification* can be defined briefly and accurately as the correction of a disorder: laziness, pride, avarice, gluttony, lust. It is not an attack on anything good. Etymologically the word means a putting to death. But what we put to death is not our human nature but our aberrations. In this sense we could say that a doctor 'mortifies' a broken leg when he sets it. He is attacking neither the person nor the leg, but actually is righting what is wrong. Even a reasonable pagan will readily grant that mortification so understood makes complete sense. It will be admitted that any sensible and decent person should work at correcting, 'mortifying' immoral, unreasonable behavior.

**15. Question:** This simple definition immediately clears up any objection. Who can argue with getting rid of what is wrong? But I still have a problem with self-denial. How does one rightly deny his or her own being, one's own person?

**Comment:** Once again we have to understand what the term means as well as what it does not mean. Christian *self-denial* does not refer to an oriental type of ultimate denial of one's individual personality, nor does it relate to a false self-image. Rather it is an active entering into the paschal mystery of Jesus on his cross. Thus it extends further than does the mere correction of our defects. It is an anticipation of death, the most radical self-emptying. By this anticipation we give up in the bloom of health what everyone gives up at the moment of death. The three vows of religious life are instances of self-denial. Men and women thereby surrender a free use of material goods, a marital love for another, and the free disposition of their persons—all of which are surrendered in death even by the most worldly of people. Self-denial properly motivated indicates that one's center of gravity is transposed from earth to heaven, from finite reality to the bosom of the Trinity. Insofar as self-denial goes beyond mortification it can be known and permitted only by revelation.

**16. Question:** Does it follow from your example of religious vows that self-denial is meant only for religious and clergy? Or are lay people to incorporate it into their lives as well?

**Comment:** Just as Jesus died for all of us without exception, so all of us in each state of life are to join him on the cross. Everyone must both use the world and abstain from it. How and to what extent we use visible creation and deny ourselves the use of it vary according to one's vocation and generosity. We would expect the monk and nun and priest to use the world more sparingly, but the frugality and sharing with the poor found so frequently in Scripture are addressed to married men and women as well. When the Lord spoke of the matter, he did not distinguish among states in life: "If *anyone* wants to be a follower of mine, let him renounce himself and take up his cross every day and follow me" (Lk 9:23). And it is well to recall that self-renunciation concerns matters both immaterial and material. Husbands and wives, indeed anyone living in community, experience repeated and daily calls to self-renunciation, involving tastes, preferences, opinions, and conveniences.

**17. Question:** I don't see how a Christian could quarrel with this, but all the same how do you respond to the complaint that detachment, penance, mortification, and self-denial are negative realities? Many people who consider themselves religious reject them out of hand in favor of what they call a resurrection-and-joy spirituality?

**Comment:** My first remark is that these people have not thought carefully about the matter, for serious reflection shows how untenable that view is. Our human finitude demands that there be negative elements, repeated negative elements in anybody's life, no matter how secular that life is. Every choice we make implies the rejection of a host of possibilities incompatible with it. If I spend a thousand dollars on a few pieces of furniture, I must decline using that money for a trip or an act of charity. If a woman marries one man, she necessarily sets aside all other men as possible husbands. People who reject the negative aspects of the Gospel fail to understand even simple human reality, let alone the divine. They have spoken without thinking. We cannot serve God and mammon.

**18. Question:** I had never thought of it this way. Of course, I am not alone in this incomprehension. Yet our contemporary mentality of poll-taking assumes almost without question that community standards of human behavior are determined by the popularity or unpopularity of norms and ideas. As a spiritual director how do you counteract this assumption in your work?

**Comment:** Most of my directees entertain no such assumption. But for the others I would wish to counter the error by objective truth, by patient efforts to help them see reality as it is, not as most people would like it to be. Gospel morality simply may not be judged by polls or mere common sense or by the behavioral sciences or by sociological theories. Christ brought into the world what St. Paul called a revolution, not a mere polishing up of a naturalistic ethic. The person "of pure nature" spoken of in philosophy and common sense is a mere abstraction. No one exists as such. Concretely, here and now, we are fallen, dislocated. The natural sciences know nothing of this condition and thus they cannot

judge our genuine needs in an adequate manner. They have a contribution to make, but they are at best partial. For the same reason
penance, mortification, and self-denial may be judged correctly
only with the help of divine revelation. Common sense and philosophy see no point in fasting or in the hairshirt for the same reason
that to them the crucifixion is nothing but a horror. Only divine
light can reveal how all these are related to human woundedness
and final destiny. Hence, if my directees need further information,
I would recommend suitable reading. If what is lacking is knowledge of how to apply what they know, that is what we discuss.

**19. Question:** Both for deepening knowledge and its accurate
application surely Jesus himself is the perfect example.

**Comment:** Of course, you are right. He lived these negatives, not
only taught them. Though he had neither the tiniest sin for which
to make satisfaction nor the least defect to correct, he fasted in the
wilderness for forty days. He had no place to lay his head as he
traveled about Palestine. He practiced the self-denial of long hours
of prayer in solitude, and suffered the unspeakable tortures of the
passion and the cross. Pondering his life and death in prayer
teaches us more than hours of theoretical study.

**20. Question:** Another point to be considered is that the New
Testament does not present what we are calling the negative in
bleak terms. Quite the contrary. This, too, is part of the picture, is it
not?

**Comment:** Surely. What some of our co-religionists disdainfully
term 'a negative spirituality' Jesus himself and St. Paul considered a
joy and a blessing. We are to rejoice and be glad when we are persecuted and mistreated; the hard road leads to life and fulfillment;
the genuine Christian bears *anything* joyously, and he or she is glad
to suffer for others; suffering for Christ is a privilege, not a liability.
In all of his trials and tribulations Paul's consolation and joy over-
flowed through his mind and heart. Nothing dismal there. And I
might add that every one of the directees I have ever had who live

fully what Jesus, Paul, and the rest of the New Testament teach experience in their own lives the truth of the message. They find, with the saints, that the negative proves to be positive.

**21. Question:** If I may, I would like now to inquire about mortification as you have precisely defined it: correcting disorders in our moral and religious lives. As a directee how do I approach this major task? To be frank, the prospect is frightening. I doubt I can do it.

**Comment:** It may surprise you to hear me say it, but I find your fears encouraging. They tell me that you are serious. You have some insight into the task that lies ahead of you. Yes, you and I are incapable of correcting all of our disorders, even with God's grace. But he can do it, if we cooperate. The saints are witnesses that it can be done, for they were as natively weak as you and I are. How to approach this toilsome duty? Attitude, the right attitude, is very important. Excellence in human life cannot be attained without correcting what is wrong. In athletic endeavors one begins by strengthening flabby muscles and being rid of excess weight. Long hours, for weeks and months, are spent on improving defective coordination and lack of accuracy, not to mention remedying imperfect mental grasp of what excellence requires. St. Paul uses this very example of sports to illustrate how we who want God must train long and hard as the athletes in the stadium if we aspire to win an eternal crown that does not wither (1 Cor 9:24-27).

**22. Question:** Could you suggest a few more examples that I may get the feel of this idea—it is an unfamiliar one to me.

**Comment:** Fasting can be a mortification as well as a penance, for it can correct several forms of gluttony: eating too much, fussiness about quality and delicacies in dining, over-eagerness and speed in manner of eating. Engaging in extra work or exercise can serve to remedy physical laziness. Refraining from idle chatter and limiting time spent with newspapers and television can help to curb undue curiosity. Occasionally keeping to the background in group conversations tends to correct vain display and a desire to dominate a discussion by occupying center stage. You could add to these your own examples. The directee should bring up for consideration habitual defects, and a competent director presumably will have remedial suggestions.

**23. Question:** I have read somewhere or other a remark to the effect that we understand today that ascetical practices of the past damaged people either psychologically or physically. Consequently, we should abandon them. We know better now.

**Comment:** What you read is a prime example of chronological snobbery, the assumption that we today are so much wiser and more sensible than our ancestors. They knew as well as you and I do that excess in this area can do damage, just as in other areas. Yes, some individuals have gone too far in their asceticism even as vast numbers harm themselves and others in going too far in the opposite direction by indulging their vanity or avarice or lust. However, as you well know, excessive aberrations do not negate the value of practices good in themselves. Otherwise we would neither eat nor sleep. There is no evidence that sensible mortification or self-denial hurts anyone either physically or psychologically. On the contrary, they might improve one's health. Just as a football coach can go too far in training his players, so can one exceed in ascetical practices. But the basic value remains in each case.

**24. Question:** When most of us think of mortification we envision bodily practices: fasting, wearing a hairshirt, giving up coffee or desserts. But we have spiritual disorders that require correction too.

**Comment:** Indeed we do. You may have noticed that earlier I included spiritual disorders among my examples: undue curiosity, dominating conversations, vain display. Because each of us is made up of body and spirit, we need both external and internal mortifications. Because our wounds differ, one person from another, spiritual direction should be a help in determining the directee's needs, and consequently the types and amount of correctives which should be emphasized for a given person.

**25. Question:** I'd like to inquire about penance in the sense of satisfaction for sin. Could not one and the same action be both a mortification correcting an aberration and a penance making reparation for sin?

**Comment:** Your question is a good one and the answer is affirmative. Two good motives for one action brings a double value. Hence I may well wish to make satisfaction for my sins and those of others, and at the same time correct a disorder in myself. Lenten observances are meant both to correct what is amiss and to make reparation. Prayer and fasting have been called the wings of the soul. Without them we do not mind the things above, and we do not center our minds on heavenly pursuits, as St. Paul admonishes us to do (Col 3:1-2). Nor do we keep our eyes always on the Lord as the psalmist declares of himself (Ps 25:15).

**26. Question:** We read that the saints were attracted to doing penances and in a sense even loved them. I feel no attraction at all to fasting and the other penances. In fact, my nature shrinks from them as hard and painful. Does this show I am mediocre?

**Comment:** No, not at all. It shows you are human. Saints naturally shrink from hard and painful tasks just as you and I do. How we differ from them is that they love God so much and detest their sins so strongly that whatever can help make up for their aberrations they want to pursue. For this reason, and not for any sadistic tendency, they are drawn to make amends. Anyone who loves another much, even on a merely human level, wants to rectify any offenses against the beloved, no matter how much it hurts. Once again we see that the saints are the most consistent people in the world.

**27. Question:** I would like to ask some specific questions about self-denial insofar as it goes beyond what we are bound to do by duty. Is it right and advisable to take on sacrifices that are required neither by precept nor by circumstances? To put the question a bit differently, do you advise your directees to take on extra penances or mortifications, things they are not bound to do? Wouldn't this be going too far?

**Comment:** A legalistic moral outlook tends to be minimalistic, whereas an outlook based on love tends to be maximalist. What I mean is that people who love another intensely will instinctively aim to give and do more for the beloved, not less. Merely carrying out a law is not enough. A man who loves a woman deeply and genuinely wants to give her far more than any regulation requires. Keeping a law is praiseworthy, of course, and it should proceed from love. But if a person is content with the bare legal minimum, he or she does not love fully. This is why saints go beyond obligation. Furthermore, what are thought of as extras in the matter of self-denial are probably not extras, at least if one views them as matters of love. God has unique calls on each human person. He may invite me to do something to which he does not invite you— and vice versa. For one in love, responding to a call is not an extra. A competent guide is sensitive to this fact. While one should be careful to keep one's clients from imprudences, a director also leads them to a growing generosity.

**28. Question:** From what you have said elsewhere and from my own reading I know that right motivation is crucial for one following Christ. But it seems to me that in this area of self-denial we have to be especially careful that our asceticism is rightly motivated.

**Comment:** I agree. You have said it well. In addition to what we have already noted above let me suggest a few more thoughts regarding what our specific motives should be when we embrace the cross and even take on things toward which we have no general precepts. There are three types of specific motives here: redemptive and ecclesial; fruitful and lifegiving; and purifying. Our sacrifice is redemptive and ecclesial when we intend the benefit of our brothers and sisters, or as St. Paul puts it, to make up what is lacking in the sufferings of Christ by our sharing in his passion and death (Col 1:24). The apostle's expression does not mean that Jesus' offering on the cross was anything less than infinite, but that we must appropriate the Lord's redemption and make it our own. We join our sacrifices with his in the Mystical Body, which is the Church. Our self-denial is fruitful and lifegiving in that it brings healing and helping graces to us individually and to others as well.

We are grains of wheat which by our dying bring forth a rich harvest (Jn 12:24; Mt 7:13-14). Our oblations are purifying because they cleanse us from the residue of our sins, and they prune us to bear more fruit by cutting away superfluities (Jn 15:2). Together with these specific motives there is the general thrust directing everything to the glory of God (1 Cor 10:31). This thrust is love. Without love nothing we do can have supernatural value, not even giving away everything we possess, not even giving our bodies to be burned (1 Cor 13:3).

## FEELING AND WILLING

**29. Question:** What I bring up now I think I understand, but it seems many people do not. It took me years to grasp the point clearly, the main reason being that most priests seem not to explain the matter. In one way it is simple, in another frustrating and confusing. I refer to the question of feeling and willing. What is the difference?

**Comment:** You are not the only one to be frustrated. I am as well, though not for the same reason. All through my pastoral work I have met well-intentioned men and women, who apparently have never heard a simple explanation, together with lucid examples, of the differences between willing and feeling, the differences between temptations and guilt. They take it for granted that to feel something deeply is to have willed it. For them strong feelings equal guilt.

**30. Question:** This confusion is so prevalent that it may be well for us to discuss one case at a time. Perhaps the general principle will be more readily grasped if we consider different instances of it. Possibly the most common confusion is the interpretation of impatient and angry feelings as sins against patience and gentleness. I used to confess as sins against patience what I now know to have been nothing more than disturbing emotions with no will in them at all. Would you explain when there is will as well as feeling? When there is sin and when there is no sin?

**Comment:** It is often the case that people have never learned how to distinguish the one from the other. One way to tell a mere feeling is that you cannot control it when you want to. Someone annoys you and there arises with you, often necessarily and without your wanting it, the inner irritation we call impatience. There is no guilt in this inner surge because there is no free choice about it. Once you realize it is there and can choose how you will react, reasonably or unreasonably, you then act with freedom either in being harsh or gentle.

**31. Question:** Fine, but I still have a problem. Often the matter is not so clear cut as you seem to suggest. Often I don't know if my will has come into my sharp answer or not. Can there be partial freedom and thus partial responsibility?

**Comment:** Yes. When we teach, especially when we teach about distinctions among things, we should be clear. Feeling is not willing. But cases do arise when we may not be sure to what extent the latter is mingled with the former. For moral responsibility there must be some intellectual awareness of the moral dimension, of the impatient feeling. If you try to be gentle, even if firm, from the first moment you are aware of this moral dimension, there is no sin at all. You have grown in the virtue of patience.

**32. Question:** That helps. Now let's take the case of rash judgments. Suppose I see someone apparently misbehave and an unworthy motive pops into my mind. Have I committed a sin of rash judgment?

**Comment:** The mere popping up of the unkind thought is no sin. If you knowingly attribute the bad motivation to the person, if you freely choose to make the rash imputation, then, yes, you are guilty.

**33. Question:** How about when I feel a strong dislike, an antipathy toward someone who rubs me the wrong way? I don't want the feeling of dislike or hatred, but I cannot get rid of it despite all my efforts.

**Comment:** The same principle again applies. Your trying to be rid of the antipathy is proof that your will is not in it. There is nothing to confess, for there is no guilt. If, on the other hand, you knowingly and thus freely are cold or indifferent toward this person, you are guilty. But the feelings alone prove nothing.

**34. Question:** Does it follow then that this distinction is to be applied to all sorts of inner thoughts, desires, emotions: where there is no free choice, there is no guilt?

**Comment:** Correct. What we are saying applies to blasphemous ideas and to thoughts against faith, to impure feelings in one's body and to unchaste images and felt desires that may arise in a very pure person, to self-centered attractions to food and drink, to vain ideas about one's appearance or intelligence or education or accomplishments. None of these sully a person unless one knowingly and therefore freely makes them his or her own by an act of will.

**35. Question:** I wish to ask about one more concrete case that causes no end of confusion and anguish to sincere people, I refer to the question of forgiveness. Religiously-minded men and women who have been deeply and unjustly hurt by others, who may have been betrayed with no provocation at all, or who have been crushed by abuse or cold ingratitude in return for years of selfless service, will say that they can neither forget nor forgive, and yet they want to serve God. What do you say to them?

**Comment:** I apply to them the same principles we have been considering. Their feelings of hurt, resentment, betrayal, disillusionment are not sins as long as there is no free decision to judge or act unreasonably. I may feel deeply crushed and be unable to shake it off, but if because God so wills it, I want to forgive, I have forgiven. Forgiveness is not a feeling but an act of the will. An act of will cannot of itself be felt at all. Signs of our having willed to forgive include the willingness to pray for the offender, to come to the person's aid, to treat him or her kindly.

**36. Question:** Let me ask about confessing all these things. Could it be that confusing feeling and willing might explain why many people confess the same list of faults week after week, or month after month?

**Comment:** Yes, this is the case often with sincere individuals who are trying to serve God well. Others confess the same sins time and again for the simple reason that they are weak or because they lack in prayer or vigilance, or because they have no real intention to give up the sins. But at the moment we are considering the first group. These latter confess routinely and say the same things every time because they are overconfessing. By this expression, overconfessing, I mean accusing oneself of what has no guilt, what cannot be controlled, what has no will in it. For example, if a teacher confesses feelings of impatience in the classroom as though he or she were guilty of mere inner irritation when the pupils misbehave, the teacher is confessing what cannot be prevented and what entails no guilt. Naturally enough it will occur month after month, year after year. Thus such a person will be overconfessing in identifying it as sin. If, however, one willingly and knowingly is harsh, then one is rightly confessing a sin of anger or impatience. When we confess what we can control (in this case the harshness), we should not be mentioning the same sins each time we receive the sacrament, for we should be striving to avoid willed faults.

## CONSCIENCE AND CONFESSION

**37. Question:** What we have been discussing leads readily to the place of conscience in our spiritual life and its growing perfection through spiritual direction. Our contemporary world is a swirl of divisions, disagreements, and polarizations in matters of politics, religion, and morality—all areas that deal with how we ought to live. In most of these disagreements people appeal more or less explicitly to their consciences, yet they reach opposite conclusions. Something is wrong.

**Comment:** You will notice that the secular world is full of slogans about freedom and choice, while it says precious little about duties. Pro-choice jargon assumes that individual people are laws unto themselves. Without reference to objective reality pro-choice becomes a pseudo 'right.' This extraordinary superficiality loses sight of the fact that the Nazis were pro-choice in exterminating millions of Christians and Jews on the basis of religion and nationality. Choice and conscience are often assumed to be self-justifying, yet the idea is absurd. Murderers are pro-choice when they decide who is and is not worthy of living. Rapists are pro-choice in their lustful pursuits. Thieves are pro-choice when it comes to disposing of your property. Mothers are pro-choice when they decide to destroy their own babies. Often these barbarities are justified by appeals to conscience. If one has any doubt about this, one need only read statements of hardened criminals and those who have a long personal history of promoting and procuring abortions.

**38. Question:** It appears that before we go further we will have to define conscience, and I suppose that normal people do have one. By it we daily make dozens of decisions as we buy and sell, work and play, act and react, love or hate, worship the world or worship God. Just what is conscience?

**Comment:** Before we tackle that question I should like to note some of the popular norms for decision-making. Some decide largely by public opinion as it is reflected in the media—in polls, in slogans, in fashions, in public demonstrations. Others are heavily influenced by their inner feelings quite devoid of reasoned thought. These people and the former group as well experience no need to study, to look for evidence. In its blunt form this view is expressed in the saying, "If it feels good, do it." It is especially rampant in matters of sensate pleasures: eating, drinking, seeing, hearing, and sexual activity. The third popular moral norm is no norm at all. It is left to one's own sympathies and preferences. Like the second there is no felt need to study or seek evidences. Not only do these people fail to study ethical principles and problems, they assume that their sympathy is a sound guide all by itself. Contraception is a prime example. A large percentage of our modern population has strong views about the matter simply from what they prefer to think, even though they have given no time to study the question and have no desire to read or do research. Large numbers of men and women reject the Catholic Church's teaching on human sexuality without having read a single papal statement or sound theological study. Yet they will say they are following their consciences.

**39. Question:** I suppose then that they think conscience is a nebulous kind of inner feeling or personal preference. But surely this cannot be correct?

**Comment:** Even animals have feelings and preferences, yet no one infers that they have consciences. A mosquito experiences no guilt feelings at depriving you of your own lifeblood. Conscience, therefore, is a judgment of intellect deciding the morality, the goodness or badness, of an action or omission. In visible creation only we humans have this capacity. Only we feel guilt, shame, or regret. Only we perceive this unshakable oughtness regarding our actions —an oughtness that can come only from the Supreme Lawgiver. Because conscience is a moral judgment of intellect, it must be based on the way things are, on evidence. It has to be informed, instructed, and taught. It is not a mere feeling or preference devoid of rootedness in objective reality.

**40. Question:** Because conscience is an intellectual judgment, would it not follow that just as there can be erroneous judgments about all sorts of things so can there be erroneous consciences?

**Comment:** Yes, and that is why conscience must be informed, educated, and when necessary, corrected. Contradictory positions cannot both be true, for that is a logical impossibility. It necessarily follows that millions of people who hold contradictory moral views must have erroneous consciences regarding given questions, while other millions have correct consciences about these same matters. This is why Jesus established his Church to teach morality as well as doctrinal truths, all with his own authority: "Whoever listen to you, listens to me" (Lk 10:16, NAB).

**41. Question:** I don't see how we could avoid the conclusion that many men and women are naïve in trusting their own sympathies. What causes unfounded moral judgments?

**Comment:** There are a number of explanations. One is that many people have never received instruction in the principles of morality. Thus they are incapable of forming consistently sound judgments about justice, charity, sexuality, speech, rights, and duties. Hence, they fall back on their feelings and sympathies, both of which are notoriously prone to being out of touch with objective reality. Then, too, many have erroneous consciences because they disregard the Church God has established to keep our minds morally clear and correct: "Go, therefore, make disciples of all the nations.... I am with you" (Mt 28:19-20). When people reject the revealed assurance of right and wrong, what can they do but succumb to their own inner darkness and woundedness? We find here one reason among others why St. Paul was so pleased that the Thessalonians did indeed accept the teaching function of the infant Church: "Another reason why we constantly thank God for you is that as soon as you heard the message that we brought you as God's message, you accepted it for what it really is, God's message and not some human thinking" (1 Thes 2:13).

**42. Question:** Well and good, but it is also true that we must follow our consciences, even if they are mistaken. After all, John Henry Newman called conscience "the ab-original Vicar of Christ."[7]

**Comment:** True enough. But notice that he is talking about conscience, a judgment of intellect, not about mere feelings, preferences, sympathies—a vast difference. We—all of us—have a clear obligation before God to inform our consciences, to study and seek light, to accept the divinely authorized teacher of morality, the Church he founded. St. Paul spoke of this obligation to have a correct, informed moral judgment when he wrote to the Ephesians, "Live as children of light, for light produces every kind of goodness and righteousness and truth. Try to learn what is pleasing to the Lord" (Eph 5:8-10, NAB). We may add that one of the functions of spiritual direction is the further refinement of one's conscience, a function that is intimately related to the ecclesial mediation that a sound director affords the directee.

**43. Question:** Though we have touched on confession elsewhere in these pages, this may be the occasion well suited to clarify some basic ideas closely related to spiritual direction. Since one's confessor is often also spiritual director, and thus the two offices can be closely intertwined, let me raise the question: how can one make worthy confessions that foster growth in the spiritual life?

**Comment:** First of all, the account of one's sins must include all actions or omissions involving serious guilt. For the purpose of furthering spiritual growth, it is fitting to mention venial sins, especially those in which there was some deliberation. Absolutely essential for receiving this sacrament is sincere sorrow. Divine forgiveness is not a mere outward form, nor is it automatic. Without genuine sorrow no sin can be forgiven.

**44. Question:** How do we know that we are sincerely sorry, that we are not just going through a weekly or monthly routine, that our act of contrition is more than mere shame or no more than a wish to be better but with no real determination to change?

**Comment:** You have touched the very heart of this sacrament. Our God is the God of authenticity. He is not satisfied with appearances and poses. This is why Jesus was so hard on the Pharisees: they were strong on externals but devoid of inner goodness and genuine sorrow. How do we know our contrition is sincere? We need not foretell our future as to success in avoiding our faults, but we must firmly intend to stop them. This implies the intention to take the means necessary to overcome bursts of anger or impatience, to be resolute in avoiding what leads to impurity, to take steps to give up vanity and laziness and idle talk and overeating. Repeated confession of these sins with no real decision to stop them, to be firm about our amendment, does one little or no good.

**45. Question:** Would you tie this in with spiritual direction and the practice of frequent confession?

**Comment:** The tie-in is clear: a good confessor-director combines gentleness with firmness. Often there is no doubt that the disciple is determined to fight his or her faults. But when such is not the case, he needs to explain and insist upon what we have said here. To fail to do this is a cruel 'kindness.'

**46. Question:** What do you advise to a penitent who wants to change for the better, but is weak and falls into the same sins over and over again? What are the means for avoiding habitual sins?

**Comment:** A competent confessor-director, like any worthy doctor, adapts the remedies to the illnesses and the condition of the patient. Several types of advice are indispensable for a person who is serious about getting over faults, especially repeated ones. The first admonition for the repeat sinner is to make up his or her mind to stop committing the offense, to be determined and not wishy-washy about it: "This is it; I am going to stop with God's grace." The second requirement follows on the first: "I shall take the means to stop. I shall avoid what leads to my sin. Because I have fallen so many times, I know very well the circumstances and occasions that trigger my impatience or impurity or vanity or overeating. Like the recovering alcoholic, I shall not even put one foot into the pub." A ruthless cutting away of the occasions of sin proves sincerity of sorrow. Third, the sinner needs mortification, learning to say no even to legitimate pleasures, correcting his or her disorders even before they issue into concrete sins. If we take the word with precise accuracy, *mortification* is not the damaging or destroying of human nature but the correcting of a disorder in our being. Fasting as a mortification is rectifying the aberrations of overeating or craving at the table. A final admonition for overcoming sin is a deepening prayer life: daily meditation and contemplation; regular vocal prayer morning and evening, especially the Liturgy of the Hours; regular and frequent recourse to God in the midst of daily activities and in the spirit of Psalm 25:15: "My eyes are always on the Lord." The faithful guide will often recommend these indispensable aids to overcoming our moral lapses, mortal or venial.

**47. Question:** You did not mention the regular examination of conscience as a remedy for being healed of our aberrations. Why?

**Comment:** It is important enough that it merits being singled out. There are three types of examination of conscience which have parts to play in our pursuit of God: general examen in the evening, particular examen at another time of the day, and the examination with which we begin our immediate preparation for the Sacrament of Reconciliation. This is not the place to explain each one in detail. Other books and pamphlets and one's own spiritual guide can do that. But I may sketch each of them briefly. The general examen— usually part of one's night prayer, either in private prayer or during the Liturgy of the Hours—entails a mental running through of one's day to ascertain whatever falls there may have been and to express sorrow to God for them. As the name implies, particular examen, often done at midday, focuses on one fault to be eradicated or one virtue to be acquired. One goes over the previous twenty-four hours to check on that fault or virtue, and then plans for the next twenty-four hours in view of what has been learned. The examination of conscience before receiving the Sacrament of Reconciliation uses the results of the other two, and it covers the period since one's last confession. It is helpful for the directee to give a summary account of these reviews in the direction session itself. This accountability can serve as a spur to progress and as an occasion for the director to suggest useful bits of advice when and if they are needed.

**48. Question:** Should this summary account of one's examinations be given to both the confessor and the director when they are not the same person? Given that some directors are not priests would that be appropriate? Even if the director is a priest, would you advise discussing this with both director and confessor?

**Comment:** If the priest-director is not the confessor, then I think that the summary account should be shared with him as well. Otherwise, he will not understand the directee's situation fully. If the director is not a priest, sharing confessional material with him or her may be wise or unwise, depending on what it is and on how competent the director is regarding that particular matter.

**49. Question:** Why does the Church urge frequent confessions of devotion (that is, where there are no mortal sins to mention) when venial sins can be forgiven in other ways: for example, by personal sorrow, by virtuous actions, and by the reception of the Eucharist? If one goes to confession often could there not be an excessive concern with sin? What about the routineness problem: mentioning the same sins week after week, seeming to become mechanical?

**Comment:** The chief answer to your first question is the will of Jesus himself. It is he who decided on the value of confessing all sins, mortal and venial: "Whose sins you forgive, they are forgiven them..." (Jn 20:23, NAB). Even though venial sins are forgiven in the ways you mention, we do well to use the very sacrament the Lord instituted for the purpose. It is styled to give us the grace and strength to avoid the faults we confess in it. As to your second problem, yes, there could be an excessive concern about sin, but pastoral experience shows that frequent confession by no means prompts excessive worry or furthers scrupulosity in normal people. If such does develop, the confessor simply prescribes the needed remedy. A regular reception of this sacrament does sensitize the penitent to his or her faults, and this is an advantage in overcoming them. Your third difficulty, routineness, is a genuine problem for many sincere people, but it does have an adequate solution. I should like to deal with it further on after we have covered a few other items.

**50. Question:** I won't let you forget it. One reason is that I do not know the answer myself—and I have lots of company. But let me pursue our current line of enquiry. Jesus knew what he was doing, of course. But what would the inner reason be for a sacrament of forgiveness, when an act of perfect contrition obliterates the sin?

**Comment:** God takes our bodiliness seriously. He treats us as humans, not as angels. Hence he wants to heal us with a visible rite just as he has decided to bring us to himself through a visible Church. Catholic spirituality is ecclesial—incarnated. It is neither individualism nor an airy disembodied angelism. Furthermore, sin is a social offense against the Church (as it is first an offense against God). Hence, as theologian Karl Rahner pointed out, it is appropriate that it should be healed socially by confessing to a priest of the Church. We express our sorrow before him. We are absolved through his ministry. And we atone through a penance given by him. The sacramental system is an ecclesial system which stems from the will of Jesus. All of this makes clear to the penitent that his or her own contrition does not forgive sin. God's word spoken through his representative does the forgiving. It makes clear, too, that forgiveness by God is gratuitous, that we do not of ourselves merit it. All of this is important, and it should impress on those who reject the mediation of the Church how opposed they are to the mind of God.

**51. Question:** Isn't it another value of confession that it reminds us that we are sinners in need of divine mercy?

**Comment:** Right you are. As one of the recent popes put it, the characteristic sin of our century is the loss of a sense of sin. In our churches almost everyone receives Holy Communion. Yet in most parishes very few go to confession. No one, of course, claims that people today are on the whole more virtuous than they were three or four decades ago. You may notice, too, that when prominent people are caught in some financial or sexual scandal, they refer to their deed as 'bad judgment,' a 'mistake,' or an 'indiscretion.' Seldom do they say they sinned. Fornication is now commonly called being 'sexually active' and sodomy is defended as 'an alternative lifestyle.' Though it may sound harsh, it is true that many contemporaries are like the Pharisees so castigated by Jesus: they seldom admit that they are unchaste, dishonest, avaricious, corrupt. Those who go to confession, just as the publican so praised by Jesus, admit that they are sinners. Because God loves honesty, he loves people who seek healing in the Sacrament of Reconciliation. They are authentic and real about their plight.

**52. Question:** I think we can return now to my thus far unanswered question, the problem of routineness in many who receive this sacrament frequently. You did touch on this earlier, but there must be more to the matter than mistaking feeling for willing. People accuse themselves week after week or month after month of the same faults with little change or apparent improvement. What is the use of frequency, if we improve little or not at all?

**Comment:** It may startle you to hear me say that this routineness among sincere men and women is common but *not normal.* What do I mean? You have no difficulty understanding that many who confess regularly have this problem. But they have it because something is amiss in their manner of confessing, or in their examination of conscience, or in their determination to amend. I shall suppose here that the penitent honestly intends to give up the sins.

**53. Question:** I see dimly what you seem to have in mind, but suppose you explain your first two points one by one. What in the manner of confessing could cause penitents to say much the same thing time and time again?

**Comment:** As I have said earlier, it is the phenomenon I call over-confessing, that is, confessing things that have no guilt attached to them. The Sacrament of Reconciliation is for guilt, not for mistakes or oversights. Unfortunately many people, as we noted, do not see the difference between feeling and willing. They confess the former as though it were the latter. Because to a large extent we cannot control our feelings, it follows that these people confess feelings even when there is no will in them and thus no guilt: anger, impatience, impure images or sensations. The same may be said for unkind thoughts that pop into our minds or for missing Mass on Sunday when we have a good reason. When there is no free willing or consent, there is no guilt, nothing to confess. If penitents confess what they can control, what they freely will and do, there should be no sameness in confessing, for they should lessen and eventually overcome what they can control.

**54. Question:** Fair enough. Let me ask about your second explanation: something amiss in the examination of conscience. How can this lead to the routineness problem? What do you have in mind?

**Comment:** All of us have blind spots. We can get into a rut of examining our selves only in certain well-defined areas and lose sight of other possible infractions we scarcely think about. For example, how many men and women examine themselves on idle words? Yet Jesus made it clear that we shall give an account of even one such on judgment day. How many think of these omissions: failing to commend another when such is proper, not speaking up through human respect, lacking warmth toward an unattractive personality, failing to sing to the Lord in our hearts always and everywhere (Eph 5:19-20), not being cheerful? If we examine ourselves adequately, we will hardly lack real faults to confess.

**55. Question:** That makes sense. Do these blind spots show up in ways other than omissions?

**Comment:** Yes, they do. There is the whole matter of root attitudes, basic woundednesses that show themselves in various ways. For instance, if I have the fundamental attitude of coldness toward others, it is likely to manifest itself in my walking by others without noticing them, in being routine and mechanical in my greetings, in an indifference to what others think and say, in answering the phone in a dull manner, in being psychologically unavailable to people who may need me.

**56. Question:** Ouch! Who of us does not sin in some of these ways? I begin to see more and more that I have lots of possible offenses to confess without any overconfessing, plenty of things to work on. At the risk of more ouches, may I ask what some of the other root attitudes may be?

**Comment:** Yes, another is the lack of discipline which can turn up in different ways: procrastination; overeagerness in eating and drinking; laziness and neglect in carrying out personal duties; coming late frequently; criticizing ideas or programs without having done the hard work of acquiring a competency to speak; excessive time spent in amusements, recreation, television.

**57. Question:** It would seem to me that a pervasive root attitude that none of us escapes until we are fully purified is pride in all of its many ramifications, some obvious and some subtle.

**Comment:** Without overconfessing, most people can find in their lives at least some small slips, if not major ones, in succumbing to human respect, in too much talking about themselves, in vanities concerning appearance, dress, property, accomplishments, in resisting or rejecting admonition or correction, in sulking, in the arrogance of assuming an understanding of divine revelation superior to the very magisterium the Lord has established.

**58. Question:** I can see now that there is an abundance of material for fruitful examination of conscience, but let me ask if there is anything else to be added.

**Comment:** One more idea occurs to me. We should check the possibility of mixed motives in the good things we do. What I mean is that fairly often in our lives we have a solid reason for doing or omitting something but only too easily an unworthy motive can slip in. For example, I may decline a task because I just have too much to handle at a given time, but I may also want to decline this request because of laziness or a dislike for the person asking. On the other hand, I may be available for an extra job both out of a real love and out of a desire to impress. I may pray in the parish church both because I want to honor God and because I like to be seen praying. Once again, however, I should remind you that we ought not to overconfess. The mere passing through our mind of an unworthy motive is not laden with guilt, but if I knowingly make it part of my free motivation, then there is something to confess.

**59. Question:** Let us grant, then, that for a sincere person who examines sincerely and honestly according to what you have said, who avoids confessing what has no guilt, and yet works earnestly on real faults, there is little danger of repetitious confessions. Let me ask, finally, how often should most of us approach the Sacrament of Reconciliation?

**Comment:** I trust a person seeking spiritual direction is interested in more than the minimal annual confession required for those who have sinned seriously. Canon law says that religious men and women should confess "frequently."[8] That would seem a good norm for anyone, for we are all indeed called to holiness. Just what may be considered frequent in individual cases is probably best decided within spiritual direction itself.

# Part Three

## *Making Progress*

# ELEVEN

# How Can I Continue to Grow?

H OW DOES ONE ASSURE PROGRESS in the spiritual life? How does one prevent the slow slide into mediocrity? How do we fan the fire of fervor when the humdrum of everyday life, not to mention the dampening effects of the world and the mass media, tends to dim our vision and cool our love?

Devotion and fidelity to contemplative prayer is a huge part of the solution to these problems, but there are other helps as well, whether one has a director or not. For those who wonder, "How can I continue to grow in loving God?" this chapter provides some pointers.

Most of human life, even the life of a saint, is ordinary and unspectacular. While the "whole law and the prophets" is summed up in the simple double love of God and neighbor, the expressions and the conditions for that love are many, even if for the most part they are hidden and unknown to the casual observer.

The hints for holiness presented here may be used variously. For those who practice discursive meditation, they can serve as points to ponder and pray about. For anyone many of the points are apt subjects for particular examen, that is, for focused attention to what needs improvement here and now. They are likewise topics suitable for discussion with one's spiritual mentor and for special review during an annual retreat. Some of them may serve for the examination of conscience before receiving the Sacrament of Reconciliation.

We ask, therefore, what are the traits of men and women who are serious about their pursuit of God? What are the conditions for genuine progress?

**1. Determination.** Most of us assume that world-class excellence in music, scholarship, or sports is due mainly to extraordinary talent, but studies of the question find that while talent does play a part, the chief factor is drive and determination. So it is with sanctity. Saints are not born saints. They do not have a superior human nature. They are as weak and wounded as the rest of us. The difference lies in their resolution. Men and women on fire do not simply admire holiness or merely wish it were so. They make up their minds to take the Lord at his word and with no dilution of his message. Am I as determined in my pursuit of God as the worldly are in seeking prestige and power, fame and fortune?

**2. Totality.** St. Thomas Aquinas' sister approached him one day with the question, "What do I have to do to become a saint?" Thomas, who wrote brilliant volumes on the subject, gave her a two-word answer: "Will it!" His first word repeats what we have just said about determination. His second refers to totality, perfection, nothing less. The saint was telling his sister that respectability, avoiding serious sin, and going most of the way are not enough. A refined mediocrity, so common even among religiously-minded people, does not respond to the greatest commandment, a total love for God. Is my concept of holiness diluted, half-hearted, and pale? Or does it resemble the bright, full picture of the saints? Do I realize that if I aim at something less, it is likely that I shall not achieve even that?

**3. Radicality.** While we should follow the advice of our confessor or director in our choices of specific practices and penances, and thus avoid attempts beyond our present strength, we ought at the same time to shun half-hearted lukewarmness. Radicality (from the Latin *radix*, root) means here that we take means suited to the end, that we get to the roots of our problems and deal with them adequately. If we wonder what this means in practice, we need only read the lives of the saints. They are not timid. They do not operate by fractions. Do I?

**4. Being specific.** It is easy enough to aspire to great things in general, to entertain grandiose ideas of holiness in other circumstances or later in life, but it is quite another matter to live a perfect life in this present place, with this husband or wife, with this illness or weakness or handicap, in these circumstances. When St. Thérèse of Lisieux was interrupted in her work by a troublesome nun, she prepared herself specifically to react lovingly in coming episodes which she could foresee. Thérèse was not content with "I shall be better" in a vague sort of way. She thought out and decided what she had to do in particulars: smile and be gentle. She prepared herself in advance to do just that, to be ready for the annoyance. She was specific. Are my hopes for holiness nebulous and thus ineffectual? Or do I develop concrete plans to be rid of my faults and to acquire the virtues I lack? Do I plan?

**5. Particular examen.** Ideally suited to what we have just remarked is the practice promoted in many religious orders of a daily checkup on one specific virtue to be acquired or fault to be overcome. At a regular time each day a person, lay or religious, examines how he or she has done during the previous twenty-four hours regarding a fault (impatient reactions or idle words or coldness toward another) or a virtue (temperance at meals, thinking before speaking, recalling God's presence). Then, for a few more moments, the particular individual plans specifically how to improve on that point during the next day. The examen closes with a brief prayer for success. Fidelity to this exercise obviously is a great aid to steady growth.

**6. Frequent confession.** The mind of the Church as well as personal experience both indicate the advisability of receiving often the Sacrament of Reconciliation. As a visible and effective sign of inner healing and strength this sacrament is a powerful cause of holiness. The risen Lord explicitly related this causing sign to the giving of the Spirit of sanctity: "Receive the holy Spirit. Whose sins you forgive are forgiven them..." (Jn 20:22-23, NAB). As Chesterton remarked somewhere, a person emerges from this sacrament with the innocence of a tiny child. Even more, if one receives it with the fervor of a saint, one comes forth in a manner akin to the transformations of the great penitents: Magdalen, Augustine, and Matt Talbot. Do I receive this sacrament regularly? In the way I go about it is my reception changing my life? Significantly? If not, why not?

**7. Rendering an account.** Periodic reporting in to one's director or confessor on successes and failures in the spiritual combat can be of benefit for more reasons than one. It serves both as a check and as a motivational spur to continuing care and effort on the part of the directee. It may likewise trigger useful advice from one's guide, while it surely keeps the mentor aware of the overall picture. Spiritual direction or the Sacrament of Reconciliation are ideally suited to the need many of us have for accountability to someone who has our genuine progress sincerely at heart.

**8. Resolving to follow-up.** For most of us performance lags far behind profession. In our prayers we pronounce fine aspirations about "giving God everything." In our retreat or meditation resolutions we intend in no uncertain terms to eliminate this fault or acquire that virtue. Yet a month or two later we find little change. Five years later there still may be slight improvement, possibly none at all. Why? Malice or hypocrisy? Deliberate self-deception? No, most likely none of these. Then why? Often profession is only a wish with no real determination—see above numbers one through four. In other cases the problem is no effective follow-up, no plan to continue until victory is won. Life is a warfare, as Job remarked, and no war is won by mere wishes and haphazard efforts. Particular examen (see number five) is tailor-made to assure both focused efforts and persevering endeavor.

**9. Singlemindedness.** In the physical universe the dissipation of energies toward several goals obviously decreases their effectiveness

in any one given direction. So it is on psychic, mental, and voli-
tional levels. If I divide my attention or my intention toward two
or three different objects, all are weakened. Scripture tolerates neither divided love nor dissipated motivation. We are to pursue God
singlemindedly, to love him with no division of heart (Lk 10:27),
to do absolutely everything for his glory (1 Cor 10:31). This is all
for our own genuine good as well. We may not try to serve two
masters (Mt 6:24). Of course, this has nothing to do with the
monomaniac, the person of one idea who is so consumed with a
pet scheme that he or she sees nothing else which could condition
it and give it a context. Many of our current *isms* come close to
monomania. Biblical singlemindedness has nothing in common
with this mental illness, for it sees and embraces all reality. Only
people heroic in all the virtues, who love even enemies, who rejoice
in all of creation, are candidates for canonization by the Catholic
Church. Yes, the saints are men and women with one overwhelming love and focus. But all else is adequately cared for as well. All
else is seen, brought into, and nourished by and from the one fire.
People in love, fully committed to the beloved, are always focused
in this healthy manner.

**10. Purifying mixed motives.** A corollary of singleminded pursuit of God is the avoidance of mingling faulty motivation into our
praiseworthy words and deeds. Wounded as we are, it is only too
easy to give alms both out of genuine love for the poor and from a
desire to impress, to pray from a real devotion to the Lord but
without excluding the wish to be seen, to decline a request for help
both because time is lacking and because of thinly disguised laziness. What is wrong with mixed motives? The same thing that is
wrong with gold mingled with sand particles: one's authenticity is
diluted. Love is weakened. Fervor is cooled. Someone has observed that if a miser mixes a little more sawdust into the dog food
each day, eventually the pet dies. Or, as even C.S. Lewis' character
Screwtape once remarked, "The safest way to hell is the gradual
one." Hence, our program is clear: "With all whole heart I seek
you" (Ps 119:10, NAB).

**11. *Age quod agis*.** Little children live intensely in the present moment, neither in the past nor in the future. As the French writer LaBruyere once put it, "Children have neither past nor future; but they have something we seldom have—they rejoice in the present." This is a child-like trait which the New Testament would have us imitate. *Age quod agis*—literally, "do what you are doing." Jesus tells us not to worry about tomorrow and Paul forgets what is past as he races on to the finish (Mt 6:34; Phil 3:14-16). The future does not yet exist, and the past is gone forever. What we do have is the present moment. By it we are fashioning our eternity. When we work we should function enthusiastically, when we pray we commune fervently, when we recreate we play gladly, when we rest we relax fully—all peacefully for the glory of God. This program is conducive not only to emotional health but to sound spirituality as well. It is a wholeness in the present.

**12. Minding our own affairs.** While everyone appreciates people who avoid meddling, not everyone by any means practices what they admire. St. Paul was blunt: "Make a point of living quietly, attending to your own business and earning your living" (1 Thes 4:11). Following this advice not only frees us from misunderstandings and conflicts, but it also makes possible tending to our own lives, which is what we ought to be doing: loving our neighbor, keeping our eyes on the Lord (Ps 25:15), praying always and everywhere (Eph 5:20), avoiding our faults, carrying out duties in our state of life with fidelity. This, too, is solid spirituality, even if it is not spectacular.

**13. Sensitivity to the divine omnipresence.** Most of us consider it rude not to acknowledge another person's presence at least by a nod or smile, if not by verbal greeting. Hence, it is odd that most of us feel nothing amiss in failing to acknowledge by some conscious act the three divine Persons always present to us. Scripture is far more consistent: "Yahweh is in his holy Temple [of the universe]: let the whole earth be silent before him" (Hb 2:20). This is the silence of attentiveness, or as the poet Hopkins put it, "The Silence which stands open and listens for eternity." In the indwelling mystery we have even more than the natural omnipresence of God to his creation; we have the intimate, interpersonal, and mutual knowing-loving-delighting of our life of grace. God abides in us and we abide in him (1 Jn 4:16). This enriching, healthy silence is essential to a full human life. It should be fostered to the extent feasible in the family home as well as in the monastery.

**14. Continual prayer: mother of the virtues.** Scripture promotes this idea of continual communing with God over and over again not only because anyone in love spontaneously does this sort of thing with the beloved, not only because purest beauty, goodness, and love deserve abiding attention, not only because this practice with its varying degrees of intensity is the greatest of human delights, but also because an abiding awareness and experience of the Lord is a powerful generator of the virtues. What St. Thomas says of prudence, that it is *genetrix virtutum*, the "mother of the other virtues," we can say, in another application of the term, of continual prayer: it begets patience, fortitude, justice, temperance, humility, affability, gratitude, and all the rest.

**15. Renouncing trivialities.** The ideal of continual prayer is, of course, impossible in a life given to superficialities, to an overstimulation of the senses, to catering to artificial desires and passions, and to a neurotic compulsion toward glamour and excitements. Karl Rahner, in a telling passage, touches on this problem in our daily routine. He speaks of his soul as a "road crowded by a dense and endless column of bedraggled refugees, a bomb-pocked highway on which countless trivialities, much empty talk and pointless activity, idle curiosity and ludicrous pretensions of importance all roll forward in a never-ending stream.... Isn't it just like a noisy bazaar, where I and the rest of mankind display our cheap trinkets to the restless milling crowds?... How will I feel at the hour of my death? ... What will be the final yield?"[1]

**16. Renouncing idle gossip.** The wisdom literature of the Old Testament over and over expresses a dim view of what Rahner terms "much empty talk." A prime example is Proverbs 10:19: "A flood of words is never without its fault."[2] Endless chattering—a far cry from healthy, responsible speech—is indeed characterized by numerous aberrations: detraction, calumny, exaggerations, egocentricity, neglect of duties, indulgence in frivolities and useless curiosities, bypassing of opportunities for communion with God. Which is, of course, why Jesus made it clear that for every idle word we speak, we shall give account on judgment day (Mt 12:36). Unless our tongues are tamed, there can be no serious progress in holiness.[3]

**17. Fervent liturgical life.** The Eucharist and the other sacraments are powerhouses for progress. "Anyone who does eat my flesh and drink my blood has eternal life.... I live in him" (Jn 6:54, 56). Jesus has come that we may have life and have it abundantly (Jn 10:10), and he has chosen to communicate that life through his sevenfold channels of grace. We, the branches, either live from that Vine, or we do not live at all (Jn 6:53; 15:4-6). But the sacraments are not magic. They require authenticity in intent, care in preparation, and fervor of the will in reception. Human bumps-on-a-log profit little from presence at Mass. Sorrowless penitents might as well stay away from confession until they have made up their minds to break from their sins, or at the very least, they should wait until they are open to be persuaded by a priest to work earnestly toward repentance and returning "to the father" (Lk 15:17).

**18. Devotion to Mary.** Attention to and love for the Virgin Mother of God has for centuries been recognized in the Catholic Church as a sign of salvation. The Hail Mary implies this recognition in its closing petition that this gate of heaven pray for us sinners now and at the hour of our death. In all the vicissitudes of human life—sometimes violent enough to be compared to a small boat battered by huge waves in a gale and at the point of sinking—we should, as St. Bernard so eloquently sang in using this very comparison, look to Mary as the Star of the Sea and in her find our safety and security. Mary was and is always Christocentric: her function in the eternal divine mind was and remains to the end of time to give Jesus to the world and to bring the world to him. A fervent spiritual life will have the woman crowned with stars near its center, both in mind and in prayer.

**19. Love for the Church.** Love for Jesus' Mother cannot be divorced from love for his Church. The two loves are signs of authenticity, of attachment to the eternal Son. This was expressed in the early patristic saying that "he cannot have God as his father who will not have the Church as his mother." This truth flows directly from Jesus' own saying that they who reject the Church reject him, and they who reject him reject the Father as well (Lk 10:16). Despite all the defects of individual clergy, saints universally love the Church—passionately so. The main reason is that Jesus loves her and gave his blood for her (Eph 5:25)—that is reason enough. But in addition we owe love in simple gratitude. Under God we receive everything we need in the supernatural order through the Church: baptism, Eucharist, forgiveness of our sins, guaranteed truth in doctrine and morality, the saints, and our own final crowning in beatific vision and risen body. Most of all, we have Jesus himself, together with the whole New Testament, from and through her. Our spiritual life is ecclesial, or it is not Christian.

**20. Attachment to the Vicar of Christ.** For almost two thousand years devotion to the Lord's Mother has been coupled to a love for the Holy See as twin marks of faithful disciples. We read of these two traits repeatedly in the lives of the saints. From patristic theologians Ignatius of Antioch (c. A.D. 100-110) through Irenaeus and Augustine and on to our most creative and brilliant minds today, (for example, Hans Urs von Balthasar and Henri deLubac), we find a dutiful and welcoming response to the teaching and governance emanating from the primatial see of Rome. Because faithful disciples love their Lord Jesus beyond all else, they love also him to whom the keys of heaven have been entrusted, the rock on which the Lord chose to build his Church (Mt 16:18-19), the brother who strengthens us in the faith (Lk 22:31-32), the vicar shepherd commissioned to feed with truth and sacraments the lambs and sheep of the flock (Jn 21:15-17). He who has Peter has the Church, and he who has the Church has the Lord (Lk 10:16).

**21. Growing in Prudence.** Principles are universal and usually clear. Life in its concrete situations is immensely varied and complex—never exactly the same from one person's circumstances to another's. Norms and laws cannot legislate in fine details for the many specific circumstances that occur in every human life. Yes, we obey Gospel teaching and all just human regulations, but how to apply them in each unique case requires the first cardinal virtue, prudence, and the inner guidance of the Holy Spirit. Examples: how to combine a dutiful admonition with a loving manner, how to integrate prayer and work to the neglect of neither, how to be ascetic and yet care for health, how to tell the truth and yet keep confidences, knowing when and how to express an unpopular opinion. Growing in this virtue of judging rightly in particular circumstances is indispensable for growing in holiness. This leads us to our next two items.

**22. Making correct decisions.** Applying the Gospel message rightly in the many circumstances of life requires four conditions. The first is that we look for wisdom from the Lord and thus avoid the foolhardy self-trust of the illuminist or visionary who is sure he or she possesses an infallible insight denied to others (see Prv 3:5-7). Logically enough, the second condition is prayer for right and sound judgment. The third is mature deliberation, the amount of time being determined by the relative importance of the matter at hand. One, therefore, seeks adequate information, reflects on past experience, notes changed circumstances of time, place, and persons, profits from mistakes, foresees consequences, and asks advice. Lastly, one resolutely makes a decision without excessive hesitation or delay, and yet neither precipitously nor in anger.

**23. Maturing in prudence.** This virtue lacks material exactitude. While justice can be exercised precisely (there is a set price for a loaf of bread or a pound of meat), prudence implies a sense of proportion and a grasp of intangibles. Thus it matures in four ways. Humility invites a divine light, because God gives his wisdom only to the little ones, not to the learned and clever (Lk 10:21). Taking the long and ultimate view of things bestows a realism on present choices: "How would this problem, this criticism, this reaction, this suffering, this pleasure, look as I stare death in the face during my final minutes of life?" Recalling eternity contributes a sharp sense of reality to the present concern. Acquiring the habitual mind of the saints by reading their lives, works, and letters enables us to decide numerous questions not discussed in theology books. We slowly grow in thinking as they thought and in choosing as they chose. Finally, we mature in prudence through the guidance of a sound director or by sharing with a prayerful friend of good sense.

**24. Growing in self-knowledge.** Few of us realize the degree of our inner poverty. We tend to equate our holy thoughts and aspirations and our ability to discuss religious and moral questions with actual advancement in the spiritual life. We little realize how far behind our noble protestations lags our actual performance. The man in the Gospel declares, "'Yes sir, [I will go],' but he did not go" (Mt 21:30, NAB). Peter proclaims that he will die with the Lord and never disown him—a few hours later he thrice denies the Master (Mt 26:35, 69-75). On Palm Sunday the fickle crowds acclaim Jesus. Then on Good Friday they shout for his crucifixion. The Gospel has us well pegged. We tend to be prompt and ready of speech, but slow and slovenly in action. Illusion is no friend of sanctity. To grow, therefore, we need progressively deeper insight into ourselves, not such that leads to discouragement but rather promotes a realistic view and enkindles a conquering love.

**25. Spiritual reading.** From the earliest ages of the Church *lectio divina,* divine reading, occupied an honored and necessary place in the lives of men and women intent on going all the way with God. Since we have already dealt with this subject, we may content ourselves here with noting that the answers to two questions, what and how, determine how effective spiritual reading will be. If one selects mediocre books (usually because they have attractive covers or titles or because "everyone is reading them"), one can expect small benefit. If we nourish our souls with the very best, our minds will be enlightened and our hearts powerfully fueled with love and generosity. How we read likewise determines the extent and depth of the result. Mary is our model. She pondered in her heart, cherished, and prayed over the word as she received it into her life (Lk 2:19, 51).

**26. Reading the lives of the saints.** We have already noted that the main reason on the human level why saints become saints is their drive and determination. Being men and women on fire with total love for God and neighbor, they tend to ignite sparks in our own souls. As the popular saying has it, "One loving spirit sets another on fire." The frequent reading of saints' lives and works likewise fills us with their light and wisdom. "It has always been held," notes French theologian Yves Congar, "that the lives of the saints will help us to understand Scripture, as they are under the inspiration of the same Holy Spirit."[4] Their words, choices, and actions instruct us with thousands of concrete examples we cannot find in catechisms and theology books. Would they watch this television program? Would they eat as elegantly as I do? Would they wear the kinds of clothes I do? Would they react to annoyances as I react? Saints are models of prudence, the virtue by which we steer a right path through the multiplicities of human life and thus successfully attain our final destination.

**27. Practicing patience.** Every human life bristles with sufferings large and small: illnesses, failures, inconveniences, disappointments, disillusionments, harshness, indifference, coldness, injustice, criticism. Happily, however, these pains, no matter how tiny and unnoticed, can be sources of sanctity when they are embraced with love for the crucified Savior. Over and over we find this message in the New Testament: rejoice when you are abused and persecuted on Jesus' account (Mt 5:11-12).... the hard road leads to life (Mt 7:13-14).... to be a disciple we must take up our daily cross (Lk 9:23).... the grain of wheat that dies and is buried yields a rich harvest (Jn

12:24).... if we join the Lord in dying, we rise with him to new life (Rom 6:4).... having nothing, we possess everything (2 Cor 6:10).... to share in Jesus' sufferings is a blessing and a joy (1 Pt 4:13-14).... with his power we can bear anything joyfully (Col 1:11). The biblical message is borne out in practice. All through the ages and today as well sanctity is tested and deepened in the crucible of life.

**28. Growing in degrees of patience.** No skill, neither culinary nor scholarly, is achieved in a day. Nor are the virtues. Patience grows from the small victories of the beginner to the magnanimous triumphs of the heroic. We begin with a willed acceptance of trial, with a resignation that is emptied of bitterness. Feelings may lag behind, but the will is there. We then learn to suffer with equanimity and peace of soul, even if our nature shrinks (Lk 22:41-44). We come eventually to endure with the joy of a St. Paul (Col 1:11, 24), as did St. Thomas More during his 'holiday' in prison while awaiting a gruesome death. Finally, we grow even to the level of the saints who sought to suffer for the kingdom, who desired more of the cross than they had already experienced. In other words, as we grow in patience, we are progressively more and more conformed to the crucified and risen Lord.

**29. Reactions to suffering.** While we may trust that the readers of this volume are aspiring to holiness, like all members of our race, they too experience temptations in the face of bitter and lasting pain: discouragement, depression, even perhaps the feelings of despair without the sin of it. While temptation is not sin, it can be deeply disturbing to a sincere person. Feeling a momentary depression due to illness, conflict, or failure is no cause for concern, provided it lessens as the situation improves and one struggles to live by growing in patience. But clinical, lasting depression probably requires professional assessment. A feeling of being lost, a sense of "I can't be saved," calls for sound advice. It surely requires a firm will to accept that God is love, that he wills all of us to be saved, the sufferer included (1 Tm 2:4). The saints do four things in their acute sufferings: they correct what can be reasonably corrected;

they keep things in perspective; they embrace the cross with love; and they totally trust that God will care for them.

**30. Confidence in grace.** Our last words can bear development. Total trust in God is not merely a confidence in an abstract principle, true as that principle may be. It is an interpersonal certainty based on the entire integrity of persons we know well and love deeply. We have the repeated assurances in Scripture of exquisite divine care for the least of us, even to the falling of a single hair. We see in heroic people how impossiblities become possible through the power of grace—how humility is combined with towering talent (Aquinas and Bellarmine), how the chains of long indulged impurity are broken (Augustine), how love for worldly pleasure is dissolved like mist before the sun (Francis), how weak men and women are empowered to face death with joy (Maria Goretti, Thomas More). Of ourselves we can do nothing. With God we can do anything—anything noble, good, pure, worthy of praise (Phil 4:8).

**31. Maturing in levels of conversion.** Most people know well that conversion is an about-face, a shift of one's center of gravity from error and evil to truth and goodness. However, not everyone realizes that there are at least three levels of conversion, not only one. In addition to the fundamental rejection of mortal sin and "returning to the Father" (Lk 15:18, 20), there is a turning from an attachment to venial sins in any form: idle chatter, vanities, laziness, or excesses in eating, drinking, recreation. On the loftiest level, there is the turning to the total generosity we find in the saints, whereby one not only tries to avoid every sin no matter how tiny, but also assigns no limits to positive generosity. This degree of conversion is especially brought about by the purifications of advancing infused prayer. God effects it by the dark fire of divine love poured into our souls: "He will purify the sons of Levi and refine them like gold and silver, and then they will make the offering to Yahweh as it should be made" (Mal 3:3).

**32. Mortifying ourselves.** This condition for growth is highly unpopular in some quarters, something not to be mentioned, let alone practiced. The very term conjures up in many minds dark images of stark fasting, painful hairshirts, and perhaps the laceration of one's own body. Yet when the term is used correctly, it means not an attack on human nature but simply the correction of disorders in our own person. Fasting with proper motivation corrects overeating and other forms of gluttony; extra work lessens laziness; spare and careful use of words heals one's domination of conversations; a hairshirt (for one ready for it) can curb the flesh; using simple clothing curbs vanity in dress. What could be more reasonable than to right what is wrong? Growth in holiness clearly requires in us what St. Paul required in himself: "I run, intent on winning.... [and so] I treat my body hard and make it obey me..." (1 Cor 9:26-27). Athletes, scholars, and musicians intent on excellence do exactly the same thing. They 'mortify' themselves as they get rid of excess weight and flabby muscles, or as they daily study and work and practice. We can do no less if we aspire to the eternal wreath that does not wither.

**33. Cultivating poverty of spirit and fact.** God has a predilection for the little and the poor. They are his favorites, and on them he bestows his light and love (Lk 10:21; Jas 4:6). In the spiritual life, prayer and poverty are twins. This evangelical value is not destitution, but it is frugality. It paves the way to deepening contemplation. People who indulge in superfluities and luxuries but profess to be detached from them are deceiving themselves. If they were indeed free from egocentric clingings, they would share what they have with the needy. They would be glad to be rid of distractions that divide the heart. Anyone—married, religious, or priest—who wishes to run rather than crawl toward holiness must be intent on reducing to practice the many New Testament admonitions to be poor in spirit and in fact: Matthew 5:3; 6:31-34; 16:26; 19:23-26; Luke 6:20, 24; 2 Corinthians 6:16; 1 John 3:17-18; James 2:1-5, 14-17; 1 Timothy 6:7-8.

**34. Being faithful to our state of life.** Even though prayer is primary in any vocation, sanctity is incompatible with a conscious neglect of obligations inherent in one's way of life. A priest must be devoted to a fervent celebration of Mass and the sacraments, to proclaiming the word with animated fidelity, to visiting the sick and otherwise caring for his flock. So also husbands and wives, as well as religious sisters and brothers, cannot climb the mountain of perfection except insofar as they faithfully carry out the duties inherent in their respective states in life. While it is true that "action is subordinated to contemplation" for all in the Church,[5] there is no excuse for neglect of work and other vocational obligations.

**35. Being diligent in one's duties.** Among the tangible results of original sin are laziness and its cousin, procrastination. Even people who work hard at their active tasks are subject to a subtle lethargy that creeps in under the form of slowness in working at being rid of faults and defects. There are two types of laziness that can greatly impede spiritual development. One is an inertness, doing nothing. Or, as someone has defined it, laziness is resting before fatigue sets in. The second type is idleness, fiddling with trivialities and thus putting off duties to which one is not inclined. The man or woman given to either or both of these character traits makes little progress toward God. Industry and diligence require that, as Vatican II expressed it, we be "*eager* to act and *devoted* to contemplation."[6]

**36. Focusing the mind on God.** We human beings are distinguished from and elevated above all the other splendors of creation by our intellects and wills, which is why what goes on in our minds largely defines both the successes and failures of our lives and the happiness or misery we experience. While two individuals may have identical tasks on an assembly line, their experiences of a typical day may be radically different. One worker may be full of joy, while the other may be on the brink of despair. The difference lies not in what they are doing but in what is going on in their minds and hearts. This is why petty people with a narrow outlook on life tend to be dull and dreary, while magnanimous, largeminded souls are happy. Men and women who focus on God live exactly what St. Paul declared: they rejoice in the Lord always (Phil 4:4). Like the Mother of God, their souls magnify the Lord and they rejoice in God their Savior (Lk 1:46-47).

**37. Developing docility and openness.** A prime example of the thoughtlessness of worldly labels is the title of this condition for advancing in the spiritual life. Docility is, in certain quarters, highly unpopular, while openness is esteemed. Yet both words mean the same thing: a willingness to learn from another, a receptivity to truth. A follower of Jesus is no namby-pamby weakling characterized by a vague, amiable non-commitment to anything. He or she loves truth, which is to say the true disciple loves reality. This is to say that one is receptive to evidence, to being taught and changed by truth. St. Francis de Sales preferred that converts be "filled with all vices than with the sin of pride and vanity because in other offenses one can repent and get pardon, but the proud soul has in itself the principle of all vices... despising all the advice which is given it."[7] To attain sanctity, said St. John of the Cross, "Allow yourself to be taught, allow yourself to receive orders, allow yourself to be subjected and despised, and you will be perfect."[8]

**38. Joyful pliability in serving God and others.** Pastoral experience has taught me that the most frequently occurring problem serious men and women experience in pursuing God involves human relationships: misunderstandings, rash judgment, coldness, detraction, antipathies, conflicts. Some of these problems flow from differences in principles, others from mere tastes and preferences. We are concerned here with the latter. All of us are, at least to an extent, incompatible in some of our inclinations and sympathies. The virtues of patience and charity call for our yielding joyfully to the desires of others when no principle is at stake. One who loves wishes to please and delight others, following the Pauline admonition to "do all you can to preserve the unity of the Spirit" (Eph 4:3). Since we cannot love God without loving our neighbor, this joyful pliability is an indispensable ingredient not only in a harmonious home but also in progress toward the Lord himself.

**39. Readiness for paradox.** We humans have no little talent for setting truth on its head. We blithely assume as obvious that health is better for us than sickness, cozy prayer worth more than a dry waiting before God, power is preferable to obedience, acclaim more desirable than blame. Yet beginning with the Lord who declared that the first shall be last, we find that the saints uniformly contradict our assumptions. St. Ignatius Loyola considered sickness no less a gift than health. St. Teresa of Avila declared that arid, unsatisfying prayer may be a greater mercy from God than delight in him. St. Paul—and St. Francis of Assisi after him—judged that in having nothing he possessed everything (2 Cor 6:10). In the spiritual life we learn about reality from the lips of the Lord, not from the assumptions of the world. Only the radical, those who dare to be different, reach the summit.

**40. Accepting God's permissive will.** Kicking against the plans of providence is no trait of the faithful disciple. No human life is without its trials. While God never positively wills evil, he does permit it to occur—often for reasons we do not completely understand. Yet of this we can be sure, that whatever the Lord allows to happen is for our ultimate good, even if at the moment it may hurt a great deal. So convinced was St. Francis de Sales of this truth that he once remarked that if we knew all that God knows, we would will to happen whatever does happen. That is an observation worthy of careful pondering. It is because of our shortsightedness and inverted priorities that we are so inclined to object to and even rebel against the dispositions of God who loves each of us immeasurably more than we love ourselves. Our Lady's response to the angel suits each of us as a holy reaction to each disposition of divine providence: "May be done to me according to your word" (Lk 1:38, NAB).

**41. Cultivating an eternal perspective.** Looking death squarely in the eye promotes a sober realism about what is important in life and what is not. A major reason people are worldly is that their fevered round of pleasures, excitements, glitter, and glamour serves to shield them from honestly facing the simple fact that soon they are to die. The longest life is short. Even if hell were nothing more than never-ending boredom, it would be frightful. But it is more, much more. Pondering the possibility of eternal loss, unending disaster, brings a realistic perspective to our temporal problems and pursuits.

It brings a clarity to our spiritual life. Each of us needs to ask: do I entertain the horror of hell, eternal hell, as a real possibility for me, not simply for everyone in general but for me in particular?

**42. Meditating on eternal ecstasy.** In an opposite direction but for a similar reason, meditating on heaven is a powerful spur to progress. To take seriously the Pauline declaration that human eye has never seen, nor ear heard, nor can we imagine anything in this life that compares with what God has prepared for his faithful ones is to instigate a revolution in one's life (1 Cor 2:9). It is no exaggeration to say that heaven is an eternal ecstasy. If athletes, scholars, and artists will daily labor for years on end to attain pale human acclaim, we ought with far more zeal to labor to achieve the crown that never fails (1 Cor 9:25). Is the divine revelation of heaven an animating force that gives life to my daily choices and motivations?

**43. Fashioning eternity.** The transfiguring delight of the beatific vision in risen body is not attained by an artificial transaction, as though we were purchasing a ticket for a theater performance. There is no intrinsic, indispensable connection between money, ticket, and drama. There is on the contrary an inner and necessary relationship between our present pilgrim plodding and our transforming destiny in the homeland. He who receives the Eucharist worthily "*has* eternal life" (Jn 6:54, emphasis mine). At each moment we are, through our free choices, making ourselves to be what we shall be through an unending eternity. Our actions today, tomorrow, and next year are making us to be hateful or lovable forever and ever. To recall this reality on occasion is still another spur to persevering progress.

**44. Going beyond enthusiasm.** Healthy, normal youths brim with life. Young newlyweds delight in being in each other's company. A freshly ordained priest has a special earnestness about his homilies, baptisms, and confessions. Novices in authentic religious orders are typically joyous, happy, and full of energy. However, because the inner natural sources of enthusiasm tend to diminish with age, something deeper must take over. That something is a growing prayer life, a closer intimacy with God, the fire within. Even though the years take their physical toll, silver and golden jubilarians—religious, married, clerical—should be more earnest, committed, and joyous than they were on the days of their profession, wedding, ordination. A disciple of Christ should, if we may borrow St. Augustine's apt expression, become progressively more and more "an alleluia from head to toe,"... an incarnated whoopee.

# TWELVE

# Discernment: Assessing My Progress

A MONG THE BENEFITS a skilled director brings to the client is an objective view of progress or regress in the latter's spiritual combat. While this chapter may be useful to the mentor in making a sound assessment, our chief aim remains, as it has been throughout this volume, to aid directees in forming their own enlightened judgments regarding their growth—whether or not they enjoy a personal guide.

## DISCERNMENT IS DIFFICULT

One reason why coming to a sound judgment may be difficult is that biblical formulations of ideals can be misunderstood and misinterpreted. What does it mean to put on Christ Jesus? To be transformed from one glory to another (2 Cor 3:18)? To undergo a spiritual revolution (Eph 4:23)? To become as pure as Christ Jesus himself (1 Jn 3:3)? To be perfect as our heavenly Father is perfect (Mt 5:48)? To love God totally and without reservation (Lk 10:27)? To live a life acceptable to God in all its aspects, not just in some of them (Col 1:10)? To be filled with the utter fullness of God (Eph 3:19)?

A further obstacle to a valid assessment is an inadequate grasp of discernment itself. Can we, do we, actually receive inner light from the indwelling Spirit? In the various answers given to this question, it is anyone's guess which of two extremes has been, and probably remains, the more readily and widely assumed. At one end of the spectrum are those who reject out of hand, or at least strongly downplay as rare, any personal enlightenment given by the indwelling Spirit. At the other end, we find people who with little or no sound basis are convinced they are listening to the Spirit, even as they are likewise sure that their opponents are not.

It is unlikely that adherents of either extreme view have spent much time in a careful study of the sources of revelation on this question.[1] What careful investigation discloses is that, while the Spirit does enlighten the disciples, his wisdom is given to the extent of their fidelity to the Church's teaching and their generosity in living the Gospel message. Saints abound in divine light; sinners do not.

A third problem in self-evaluation is our tendency to equate our devotional protestations of intention and desire with our actual progress or lack thereof. We easily profess in our morning offering what far surpasses our performance throughout the day: "I love you with my whole heart.... I offer everything today to your glory. ... I want nothing for myself.... All my sufferings I embrace in union with yours on the cross." There may be nothing insincere in these professions, but a few moment's reflection will make clear that our actual performance often does not measure up to them. Most people strongly resist growing from ordinary to heroic sanctity. St. Bernard once remarked that it is much easier to find lay people converted from serious sin to the state of grace than to find religious move from good to better. Mediocre people because of their lowly standards are not reliable guides of their own growth.

Perhaps the most common mistake people make in assessing their progress is to judge it by the standard of feeling. If they detect a pleasing emotional experience at prayer, they conclude that all must be well. But if they are dry, distracted, 'empty' in their devotions, they assume something is wrong, perhaps gravely so. While Scripture surely speaks often of genuine experiences of God,[2] nowhere does it present feelings as decisive criteria of progress or dry 'emptiness' as an indication of fault or mediocrity. Yet this is how most people look at the matter.

What we do find over and over in God's word is the message that growth is shown in a concrete, down-to-earth identification of our wills with the divine will. "If anyone loves me, he will keep my word" (Jn 14:23).[3] The crucial commandment, the precept of love, includes all others for the simple reason that God never decides or acts arbitrarily (2 Jn 6). The divine commands always concretize what good is, what love requires in certain circumstances. At one time, for example, we should refrain from talking that others may pray or study or rest. At another, we should speak to impart information or to show affection and concern for a friend or a loved one. That specific ways of showing love have to be expressed via laws and rules is due to our sinfulness: "Laws are not framed for people who are good" but for criminals (1 Tm 1:9). Those who are led by the Spirit cannot be touched by laws (Gal 5:18). They are already doing in an entirely free way what the law indicates. By their fidelity to humility, love, chastity, patience, and all else, their wills are one with the divine will. In this chapter we detail what this conformity of wills actually entails and how it is shown.

## SIGNS OF PROGRESS

**God-centeredness.** Our first sign of growth comes from the lips of the Lord himself, and it strikes at the very heart of reality: "Where your treasure is, there will your heart be also" (Lk 12:34). Or as St. Paul expressed it: since you have risen with Christ, mind the things above, not those on earth (Col 3:1-2). Love is like gravity: everything in the lover's life tends toward the beloved. People growing toward God find that more and more the indwelling Trinity is their center of gravity. While they do not neglect duties toward others, their thoughts and choices are focused on their one love. When St. Francis of Assisi looked at a rose or a bird, he did not see only a remarkable artifact of the Creator. Deep in the center of the flower or the animal, he saw a glimpse of the divine glory, which is one reason why he and all the saints did indeed rejoice in the Lord always; they sought and found the supreme Beloved everywhere, even in hardships and suffering.

**An undivided heart.** "Too little does any man love you, who loves some other thing together with you, loving it not because of you." In this classic formulation of the undivided heart completely given to God, St. Augustine indicates the reason for Gospel totality: namely, the pure, unlimited lovability of God. In the very nature of our relationship to the Lord, anything less than everything is not enough. People on the right track may not be ready for canonization, but they are putting no realized limits on how far they are willing, even eager, to go in loving God and serving him totally. They are progressing day by day toward the singlemindedness recommended and lived by the saints. At the top of an imposing list of qualifications for appointees to the cardinalate, St. Bernard advised Pope Eugene III to select none but those "who will fear nothing except to offend God and hope for nothing except from God."[4] We are advancing when we can say with the psalmist, "With all my heart I seek you" (Ps 119:10, NAB), when we realize that it profits us nothing to gain the whole world and suffer the loss of our souls (Mt 16:26), when our joy lies in being close to God (Ps 73:28), not in obtaining what the world has to offer.

**Serving others.** Preferring another's advantage to our own (Phil 2:4) is an especially telling sign of progress, for it is a clear imitation of Jesus on the cross. He preferred our interests in the most striking way possible: he went to a tortuous death entirely for our sakes. Throughout his life he lived his own avowal that he came into the world to serve, not to be served. The more we are at the beck and call of others, the more we sacrifice ourselves for their sakes, the more we are conformed to the Splendor of the Father who chose to live among us as our ransom and our servant (Mt 20:28), the more we are his. "By this love you have for one another, everyone will know that you are my disciples" (Jn 13:35). This sign of progress is divinely proclaimed.

**Entering by the hard road.** "Enter by the narrow gate, since the road that leads to perdition is wide and spacious, and many take it; but it is a narrow gate and a hard road that leads to life, and only a few find it" (Mt 7:13-14). A stark saying to be sure and highly unpopular, rarely cited in our day. To choose the pleasurable road of serious sin obviously leads to eternal disaster, but even the superficial, comfortable path of a mild worldliness is fraught with danger. "If you examine the matter carefully," wrote St. Bernard to Pope Eugene III, "you will realize how few there have ever been whose minds did not relax in prosperity from their usual watchfulness and self-restraint, at least in some degree. And in the case of the incautious, has not prosperity always been to virtue what fire is to wax, sunshine is to ice and snow?... Indeed, there are more to be found who have preserved their balance in bad fortune than in good."[5] The person on the right track doubles earnest vigilance when things go well, that is, in success and health or when praised by others. In such situations the usual temptation is to be less careful in avoiding self-indulgence, less given to prayer, less earnest in serving God generously. With his usual illusion-dissipating insight Blaise Pascal noted that "the conditions in which it is easiest to live according to the world are the most difficult in which to live according to God; and the reverse: nothing is more difficult in the eyes of the world than the religious life; nothing is easier in the sight of God. Nothing, according to the world, is easier than to hold a great office and to enjoy a great fortune; nothing, according to God, is more difficult than to live like that, without participating in it and developing a taste for it."[6] Anyone can experience the truth of the simple fact that people who give themselves to worldly pastimes may keep themselves in the state of grace (and even that is problematic), but they do not and cannot approach the heroic virtue of the saints.

**Pilgrim frugality.** One of the most characteristic traits of the heroically holy, married as well as religious and clerical, is their disinterest in superfluous possessions, indeed their positive dislike for an accumulation of what they do not need. They rejoice to give up what does not lead to God (Ti 2:12), to renounce inwardly everything they possess (Lk 14:33). They are content with necessities and shun elegance and luxury (1 Tm 6:7-8). They are men and women in love. Understandably enough, they find all they need in loving their Lord. They make the Lord their only joy and he gives them what their hearts desire (Ps 37:4). As we grow in imitating the Master who had no place to lay his head (Mt 8:20), we take on the character of the poor pilgrim (1 Pt 2:11). We have one focus, our destination. We renounce any self-centered clinging to things and are inclined to share them with fellow pilgrims. We find in a freely chosen frugality both an unencumbered journey and a healthy sense that we have here on earth no lasting city. Pilgrims are themselves signs of the sacred, signs of the eternal.

**Suffering with love.** Affliction provides an acid test either of growth or of erosion in the spiritual life. A veneer of virtue is possible when all goes well, but its superficiality is exposed in the crucible. Distress and anguish of themselves improve no one. If we are grouchy, cynical, or complaining in difficulties, we are becoming worse, not better. If on the contrary we say yes to God's grace (always present) and unite our trials with those of Jesus on his cross, we grow rapidly in his ways. God can give "the strength, based on his own glorious power, to bear *anything* joyfully," and so St. Paul is happy to suffer for his flock (Col 1:11, 24). It is a sign of genuine progress when one finds love and peace in the troubles of life. Hardships and happiness are not incompatible. Love holds them together and causes us to flourish in the ways of the Lord.

**Hatred for sin.** While the holy person has only one deep fear, that of offending the Lord, the lukewarm individual is comfortable in mediocrity—it scarcely triggers a ripple on the stream of one's consciousness. Thus one's attitude toward venial sin is a barometer of spiritual health or illness. St. Teresa declared that she was ready to die a hundred deaths for the least ceremony of the Church; all the more was she prepared to die rather than commit a tiny venial sin. An abhorrence of sin is the other side of love for God—which is why it is so excellent an indicator of how far advanced one is in the ascent to the summit.

**Rejection by the world.** The Lord was blunt about this criterion of authenticity. If you are faithful to his word, you should expect rejection. You will be hated and attacked by worldly people: "If the world hates you, remember that it hated me before you. If you belonged to the world, the world would love you as its own; but because you do not belong to the world, because my choice withdrew you from the world, therefore the world hates you.... If they persecuted me, they will persecute you too" (Jn 15:18-20). And in Jesus' prayer to his Father: "I passed your word on to them, and the world hated them, because they belong to the world no more than I belong to the world" (Jn 17:14). St. Paul had the same message as his Lord: "Anybody who tries to live in devotion to Christ is certain to be attacked" (2 Tm 3:12). Dissenters seem innocent of the fact that their very popularity with the media is a self-condemnation: "the world loves [them] as its own." Speaking of false teachers toward the end of the first century, the first letter of John could not be more explicit regarding who are led by the Spirit and who are not: the latter "are of the world, and so they speak the language of the world and the world listens to them" (1 Jn 4:5).

**Fidelity to contemplative prayer.** Devotion to contemplative prayer is incompatible with continuing mediocrity. Over the years experience has taught me that while men and women can be more or less faithful to their vocal prayers and all the while remain mediocre and somewhat worldly, contemplation and lukewarmness cannot coexist for long. Either one sheds the mediocrity or gives up the contemplation. One can be perfunctory and merely rattle off prayer formulas, but in deepening communion this same person comes face to face with God and knows he or she is wrong and must change. Hans Urs von Balthasar has noted that an unwillingness to give up selfishness "is one of the main reasons why people so persistently avoid contemplative prayer.... Many Christians are well aware of this, and, if they are resolved not to effect any definite improvement in their lives, leave contemplation severely alone."[7] Because love brings with it all the virtues (1 Cor 13:4-7), and because love is the core of contemplation, as prayer deepens, one finds that the balance required for the moral virtues (*"in medio stat virtus"*) likewise becomes more and more obvious in one's life. Writing of moderation in eating, drinking, and sleeping, the author of *The Cloud of Unknowing* remarks that he "cannot believe that a person wholeheartedly given to contemplation will err by excess or default in these external matters."[8]

**Absence of egocentrism.** Little need be said of this sign of progress —it is obvious. Even on the merely human level the more the lover is enthralled in the beloved, the less focus there is on self. As we read in *The Cloud of Unknowing*, "a true lover not only cherishes his beloved more than himself but in a certain sense he becomes oblivious of himself on account of the one he loves."[9] This explains the remarkable selflessness we find in the saints. They appear to have lost any concern for their comfort and convenience. This growth is usually gradual. It ordinarily does not happen by leaps and jumps. As love deepens so goes self-centeredness weaken, even to the point of eventual disappearance.

**Delicacy of conscience.** People who love each other deeply experience a sharp pain on realizing that they have offended the other person. A saint has one fear only: offending God even in small matters. Yet a delicate conscience is far removed from scrupulosity, for this latter is characterized by unreality: making a venial sin into a mortal, or seeing a venial or mortal sin where there is no fault at all, or thinking one's confession is invalid for no sound reason. A delicate conscience, on the other hand, perceives things as they actually are. This individual is sensitive to infidelities that most people take for granted with no great concern: cutting prayer time short for frivolous reasons, idle chatter, snacking and munching without real need, occupation with trifles and superfluities, minor expressions of impatience, indulgence in unneeded comforts, wasting time with television. Delicacy of conscience is a strong sign of progress for the simple reason that one's will is becoming more and more identified with the divine will, more and more pure of the least obstacle to perfect union.

**Watching.** Both on the lips of Jesus and in the thought of his apostles, we find the admonition to watch and pray: "Wait here and keep awake with me.... stay awake.... be awake to all the dangers.... stay wide awake and sober.... keep a calm and sober mind.... happy is the man who has stayed awake" (Mt 26:38; Mk 13:35; 1 Cor 16:13; 1 Thes 5:6; 1 Pt 4:7; Rv 16:15). What is this wakefulness, this watching, this clear and sober mind? It seems to involve a negative element: being alert to danger. It also involves a positive one: attending to the one you expect and love. As the psalmist put it: "My eyes are ever toward the Lord" (Ps 25:15, NAB). The Virgin Mother is three times depicted as the one who watched and pondered (Lk 2:19, 51; Acts 1:14). The traditional term, being recollected, literally being gathered together, focusing on God, captures some of the idea: "Think of what is above" (Col 3:1-2, NAB). Or we might say, living in the divine presence always (Eph 1:4), being a genuine pilgrim who attends to the sacred shrine.

**Obedience.** This sign of growth is surely one of the least popular ideas of our day. In a negative way, this is an indication of its rightness, for the world does not like divine revelation. (See Lk 10:16; 1 Jn 4:1-6). Our economy of salvation is, by the explicit and many times repeated will of God, an obediential one. God wills that we be led to him through other human beings, who, by his delegation, take his place and speak in his name. He does not look kindly on the rebellious, dissenting mind.[10] Why is the humble, obedient spirit so strong a sign of progress toward God? One cannot please God without the basic yes of faith and acceptance (Heb 11:6), not only to the content of the divine message but also to the manner in which he chooses to present it, that is, through a teaching Church which speaks in his name (Lk 10:16). This is why St. John of the Cross rightly sees spiritual direction as ecclesial. The guide acts not merely as a private friend or as a secular counselor does, but as a legate of the Lord. For this reason St. Teresa obeyed her confessor-director rather than a vision, if there was a clash. And the Lord himself assured her that this was his will.

**Humility.** Everyone instinctively recognizes that genuine humility is a mark of authenticity. We find attractive the unassuming, docile person who is content to be unknown and unrecognized. People who magnanimously do what is right, who perhaps show extraordinary skill and talent, yet have not the least care that others either notice or applaud, are very dear to God. They can say with the psalmist, "I look to no one else in heaven, I delight in nothing else on earth.... My joy lies in being close to God" (Ps 73:25, 28). The Book of Proverbs several times extols the wisdom of the person who welcomes admonition. St. John of the Cross saw in a willingness to be corrected a clear sign of holiness: "Allow yourself to be taught, allow yourself to receive orders, allow yourself to be subjected and despised, and you will be perfect."[11]

**Speech, a reflecting mirror.** One of the most simple and obvious indicators of progress in the spiritual life is reflected in one's own speech, for "from the fullness of the heart the mouth speaks" (Mt 12:34, NAB). While it is true that one can be deceived by pious professions and protestations, and likewise that it is action that betrays the quality of a person, it is also true that if one talks long enough and to receptive listeners, what captivates the heart will eventually come out: money, pleasures, prestige, or God.

**Holy dissatisfaction.** "He has ceased to be good whosoever does not desire to be better," declared St. Bernard.[12] In the gospel account of the Pharisee and the publican, the former listed his virtues, mentioned no personal defects, and was well content with his state before God, while the latter declared himself a sinner in need of mercy (Lk 18:9-14). Jesus' judgment of the two was withering: contrary to appearances, the Pharisee was far from God, while the publican had set things right. Anyone making genuine progress is unsatisfied with his present state. The fact is that as we grow we have more divine light, we see God's purity more clearly, and we perceive how far we still fall short of our goal. People who are well content with their position before the Lord are either beginners or grievous sinners. The latter have a blunted conscience and little concept of sanctity and no lively desire for it. The former have little experience with their mixed motives even in doing good ... hardly understand the demands of total love... do not yet see their many defects, willed and unwilled... are unacquainted with heroic virture... and do not grasp what it means to be "perfect as

[our] heavenly Father is perfect" (Mt 5:48). Hence, a calm discontent—not to be confused with the unrealism of a poor self-image—is an encouraging sign of progress in our journey to God.

**Joy.** "Rejoice in the Lord always," declared St. Paul, "I shall say it again: rejoice!" (Phil 4:4). Sinners experience pleasures but not joy. The more they are immersed in avarice or lust or gluttony or pride, the more they find that the pleasure eventually fades. Eventually jadedness sets in, even disgust. Hence, we see the never-ending thirst for new stimulations and excitements. But never do sinners experience the thrill of real delight, the sparkle of a happy conscience, the ecstasy of genuine love, a "joy so glorious that it cannot be described" (1 Pt 1:8, NAB). Again and again the biblical word speaks of delighting in the Lord, and saints find in their complete generosity that they do rejoice even in severe trials (Col 1:11, 24). St. Thomas Aquinas pointed out that delight is the normal crowning of a good action, the flower of doing what is right, the brilliance of a gem. For this reason an abiding joy is a token of growth.

**Love for truth.** In matters that touch on lifestyle (morality, religion, politics) many people, if not most, embrace views that accord with their preferences rather than what objective evidence shows to be true. Four reasons may be advanced for stating that love for truth is a sound index of sanctity. One is that it shows a personal integrity, a desire to fit one's life to reality, not to attempt to adjust reality to accord with personal desires. A second is that loving truth demonstrates an acceptance of the divine plan for the world and for oneself. Third, from a negative point of view, sins of the mind are worse than those of the body (Mt 10:14-15). Preferring one's own will rather than objective reality is a fundamental dishonesty, not a momentary weakness. Dishonesty and sanctity are incompatible. Lastly, when people love truth, they are on the path to God, the supreme Truth. If they persevere, they are bound to find him.

**Love for the Church.** Among the most plain and tangible indicators of holiness is this last one: all saints whose lives I have read stand out in their love for the Church which Jesus so loved that he gave his life for her (Eph 5:25).

This mark of authenticity was cited by Vatican II in a classic sentence borrowed from St. Augustine: "A man possesses the Holy Spirit to the extent of his love for Christ's Church."[13]

Readers who find these signs becoming more prominent in their lives—gradually but steadily—may rest content that they are progressing on the path. Despite feelings of emptiness or discouragement, despite sufferings and difficulties, they are climbing the mountain of perfection. Their wills are becoming more identified with the divine will. In this supernal union, not in something less, is the holiness we seek.

# Notes

ONE
## Getting Our Bearings

1. Peter Kreeft, "C.S. Lewis' Argument from Desire," in *The Riddle of Joy*, ed. Michael H. MacDonald and Andrew A. Tadie (Grand Rapids, MI: Eerdmans, 1989), 267.

2. Arnold Lunn, *Now I See* (New York: Sheed and Ward, 1937), 118.

3. Hans Urs von Balthasar, *The Glory of the Lord*, Vol. 1 (San Francisco: Ignatius, 1982), 247.

4. "Chastity, the Common Good, and True Worship," *Fellowship of Catholic Scholars Bulletin*, March, 1991, 14.

5. Thomas Dubay, S.M., *Fire Within* (San Francisco: Ignatius, 1989).

TWO
## The Key Principle of Mediation

1. Von Balthasar, *Glory*, Vol. 1, 193.

2. This mediation is frequently found in the Old Testament: Nm 16:28; Ex 24:3; Lv 10:11; 24:33; Nm 5:4.

3. See for example Jer 35:14-17; Gn 22:1-18; 2 Mc 7, especially v. 30; Lk 2:51; Mt 17:24-27; 23:1-3; 1 Tm 4:11-12; Ti 2:15; 3:1, 8; 1 Pt 2:13-17; 5:5; Rom 13:1-7.

4. John Henry Newman, *Parochial and Plain Sermons* (San Francisco: Ignatius, 1987), 917.

5. Newman, 1445.

6. Newman, 1102.

7. See also Proverbs 28:26 for a similar idea.

8. See *Fire Within*, ch. 14.

9. See *Ascent of Mt. Carmel*, bk. 2, ch. 19, no. 10, *The Collected Works of St. John of the Cross* (Washington: ICS Publications, 1973), 167. See also *Fire Within*, 260-261.

10. Vatican Council II, *Sacrosanctum Concilium*, no. 2. Unless otherwise stated, citations from Vatican Council II are taken from the Flannery translation, *Vatican Council II* (Northport, NY: Costello Publishing Co., 1988 rev. ed.).
11. Von Balthasar, *Glory*, Vol. 1, 241.
12. Von Balthasar, *Glory*, Vol. 1, 165.

THREE

## What Is Spiritual Direction?

1. There is an opposition between the flesh and the spirit in the Pauline sense: between embracing sinful worldliness and being led by the Holy Spirit. See Rom 8:1-13.
2. *Lumen Gentium*, no. 34.
3. St. John of the Cross, *Ascent*, in *Collected Works*, bk. 2, ch. 22, nos. 7 and 11, 181, 183.
4. St. John of the Cross, *Ascent*, bk. 2, ch. 22, no. 16, 185-186.
5. St. Teresa, *Interior Castle*, trans. E. Allison Peers (New York: Doubleday, Image ed., 1961), mans. 6, ch. 9, 189.
6. Von Balthasar, *Glory*, Vol. 1, 348.
7. Newman, 823.
8. Cited by Bishop Kallistos (Ware) of Diokleia in his introduction to Irénée Hausherr, *Spiritual Direction in the Early Christian East* (Kalamazoo, MI: Cistercian Publications, 1990), x.
9. Cited by Joseph Ratzinger, "The Transmission of Divine Revelation," in *Commentary on the Documents of Vatican II*, edited by Herbert Vorgrimler, Vol. 3, (New York: Herder and Herder, 1969), 193.
10. *Commentary on the Documents of Vatican II*, 194.
11. See D. Dee, "Manifestation of Conscience," *New Catholic Encyclopedia*, Vol. 9 (New York: McGraw-Hill, 1967), 160c-162b.
12. St. Teresa, *Book of Foundations*, ch. 4. St. Teresa remarks in passing that both men and women have come to her "in great numbers" about their spiritual lives. *The Complete Works of St. Teresa*, Vol. 3, trans. E. Allison Peers (London: Sheed and Ward, 1963).
13. Ailbe J. Luddy, *Life and Teaching of St. Bernard* (Dublin: M.H. Gill, 1937), 77.
14. Von Balthasar, *Glory*, Vol. 1, 177.

FOUR

## Do I Need Spiritual Direction?

1. St. Francis de Sales, *Introduction to the Devout Life*, trans. Michael Day (Westminster, MD: Newman Press, 1956), 1:4, 16.
2. Thomas à Kempis, *Imitation of Christ*, trans. Richard Challoner (New York: Benziger Brothers), 1:4, 22.

3. Thomas à Kempis, 1:8, 30.

4. St. John of the Cross, *Sayings of Light and Love,* in *Collected Works,* no. 7, 667.

5. St. John of the Cross, *Sayings of Light and Love,* no. 11, 667.

6. St. Teresa, *Testimony 3,* no. 13, *Collected Works of St. Teresa of Avila,* Vol. 1, trans. Kieran Kavanaugh and Otilio Rodriguez, (Washington: ICS Publications, 1976), 322.

7. St. Teresa, *Way of Perfection,* trans. E. Allison Peers (New York: Doubleday, 1964), ch. 39, 259.

8. K.A. Wall, "Direction, Spiritual," *New Catholic Encyclopedia* (New York: McGraw-Hill, 1967), Vol. 4, 889b.

9. Hausherr, 112.

10. Hausherr, 165.

11. Hausherr, 169.

12. Newman, 829.

13. For background information and what the advice might be see *Fire Within,* ch. 14.

14. *The Cloud of Unknowing,* author unknown, trans. by William Johnston (New York: Doubleday, Image edition, 1973), ch. 45, 105.

15. *Cloud,* ch. 46, 106.

16. Ian Ker, *John Henry Newman* (Oxford and New York: Oxford University Press, 1990), vii.

17. Thomas à Kempis, 1:13, 43.

18. Thomas à Kempis, 1:16, 52.

19. St. John of the Cross, *Spiritual Canticle,* in *Collected Works,* stan. no. 36.

20. Ker, 42.

21. *Centesimus Annus,* no. 11, *Origins,* May 16, 1991, 6.

22. Paul VI, *Evangelization in the Modern World, Evangelii Nuntiandi* (Boston: Daughters of St. Paul, 1975).

FIVE

## Spiritual Directors: Ideal and Real

1. *Presbyterorum Ordinis,* no. 3.

2. *Optatam Totius,* no. 16.

3. *Optatam Totius,* no. 15.

4. *Presbyterorum Ordinis,* no. 9.

5. *Presbyterorum Ordinis,* no. 9.

6. *Presbyterorum Ordinis,* no. 12.

7. *Presbyterorum Ordinis,* nos. 14, 15

8. *Presbyterorum Ordinis,* no. 16.

9. *Presbyterorum Ordinis,* no. 17.

10. *Lumen Gentium,* no. 41.

11. *Presbyterorum Ordinis,* no. 18.

12. *Optatam Totius,* no. 19.

13. *Presbyterorum Ordinis,* no. 6.

14. Ker, 118.

15. *Verbum Caro,* 172-173, in *The Von Balthasar Reader,* ed. Medard Kehl and Werner Loser, trans. Robert Daly and Fred Lawrence (New York: Crossroad, 1982), 114.

16. Peter Kreeft, *Making Sense Out of Suffering,* (Ann Arbor, MI: Servant Publications, 1986).

17. Dr. Zeno, *John Henry Newman: His Inner Life* (San Francisco: Ignatius Press, 1987), 38.

18. St. Teresa, *Foundations,* in *Complete Works,* ch. 19, 92.

19. St. Teresa, *Life,* ch. 34, no. 11, *Collected Works,* 231-232.

20. St. Teresa, *Interior Castle,* mans. 5, ch. 1, 100-101.

21. Von Balthasar, *Glory,* Vol. 1, 76.

22. Ker, 276.

23. Hausherr, 53.

24. Joseph De Guibert, *The Theology of the Spiritual Life* (London: Sheed and Ward, 1956), 168.

25. St. Teresa, *Interior Castle,* mans. 4, ch. 1, 72-73.

26. St. Teresa, *Life,* ch. 13, no. 18, 95.

27. St. Teresa, *Interior Castle,* mans. 6, ch. 8, 183.

28. *The Letters of St. Teresa of Jesus,* trans. and edited E. Allison Peers (London: Sheed and Ward, 1951), two vol., continuous pagination, letter 74, 178-180.

29. *Letters of St. Teresa,* letter 65, 161.

30. St. John of the Cross, *Living Flame of Love,* in *Collected Works,* stan. 3, no. 30, 621.

31. St. Teresa, *Testimony 58,* in *Collected Works,* no. 13, 352.

32. St. Teresa, *Interior Castle,* mans. 2, ch. 1, 51.

33. St. Teresa, *Life,* ch. 13, no. 6, 90.

34. St. Teresa, *Life,* ch. 13, no. 6, 90.

35. *Sacramentary,* October 15, opening prayer—as the original Latin has it.

36. *Cloud,* ch. 72, 141.

37. St. John of the Cross, *Flame,* stan. 3, no. 43, 626.

38. St. John of the Cross, *Flame,* stan. 3, no. 46, 627.

39. St. John of the Cross, *Flame,* stan. 3, no. 54, 631.

40. St. John of the Cross, *Flame,* stan. 3, no. 56, 632.

41. John G. Arintero, *The Mystical Evolution* (Rockford, IL: Tan, 1978), Vol. 2, 82-83.

42. St. John of the Cross, *Ascent,* prologue, no. 4, 71. For the differences between the nights and depression see the author's *Fire Within* 163-164, 295.

43. See *Fire Within*, 7-8, 54, 57.

44. See *Fire Within*, chap. 11, "The Universal Call," 199-216.

45. St. John discusses this mistake in *Flame*, stan. 3, nos. 57-61, 632-633.

46. St. Francis de Sales, *Introduction*, 1:4, 17.

47. Arintero, Vol. 2, 258.

48. *Letters from Baron Friedrich von Hugel to a Niece* (J.M. Dent, 1965), xxix.

SIX

## Key Concerns in Spiritual Direction

1. St. Francis de Sales, *Introduction*, 1:4, 16-17.

2. See, for example, Prv 9:7-9; 15:31, 32; 19:20.

3. St. Teresa, *Foundations*, ch. 17, 80; *Life*, ch. 26, no. 3, 171 and no. 5, 172.

4. Blaise Pascal, *Pascal's Pensées*, trans. Martin Turnell (New York: Harper, 1962), no. 737.

5. Cited in Hausherr, 197.

6. De Guibert, 162.

7. De Guibert, 162.

8. St. John of the Cross, *Flame*, stan. 3, no. 57, 632.

9. *Letters of St. Teresa*, Letter 10 to Doña Juana de Pedraza, January 28, 1589, 691.

10. St. Teresa, *Way*, ch. 5, 63.

11. St. Teresa, *Life*, ch. 5, no. 3, 46-47.

12. St. John of the Cross, *Flame*, stan. 3, no. 62, 634.

13. St. Francis de Sales, *Introduction*, 1:4, 16.

14. St. John of the Cross, *Flame*, stan. 3, no. 30, 621.

15. Hausherr, 235.

16. Hausherr, 236.

17. In Hausherr, xiii.

SEVEN

## Can I Direct Myself?

1. The conversational format will be resumed after this introduction.

2. See also the vigorous judgments in the books of Proverbs, Sirach, and Wisdom regarding this folly.

3. *Lumen Gentium*, no. 1.

4. We mean also, of course, to aid those who enjoy the blessing of having competent directors.

5. Newman, 210.

6. Thomas à Kempis, 1:3, 19.

7. St. Teresa, *Life*, ch. 34, no. 11, 231-232.

8. Michael Sharkey, "Newman's Quest for Holiness," *Newman Today*, ed. Stanley L. Jaki (San Francisco: Ignatius, 1989), 181-182.

9. Cited in Luddy, 90.
10. A book-length answer to this question is given in the author's *Authenticity: A Biblical Theology of Discernment* (Denville, NJ: Dimension Press, 1977).
11. St. John of the Cross, *Ascent,* bk. 2, ch. 11, no. 9, 135.
12. Newman, 128.
13. *New Oxford Review,* April, 1981, 11.
14. Compare for example Eccl 1 and 2 with 1 Cor 2:9 and 2 Cor 4:17-18.
15. Hans Urs von Balthasar, *Prayer,* (New York: Paulist Press, 1967), 162-163.
16. G.K. Chesterton, *The Common Man* (New York: Sheed and Ward, 1950), cited in *The Quot-able Chesterton,* ed. George J. Marlin, Richard P. Rabatin, John L. Swan (San Francisco: Ignatius, 1986), 42.
17. Hans Urs von Balthasar, *Thérèse of Lisieux* (New York: Sheed and Ward, 1954), 38.
18. Richard Partill in *The Riddle of Joy,* 31.
19. *Cloud,* 43-44.
20. A. Sertillanges, *The Intellectual Life,* 107. I would recommend in this work especially ch. 7, sec. A, on reading.
21. Newman, 881. The Scripture text cited by Newman is Jn 1:5.
22. "Hans Urs von Balthasar: A Portrait," in *The Von Balthasar Reader,* 35.
23. *Liturgy of the Hours,* August 20. For an example of this illumination see the Office of Readings on the same day, reading no. 2.
24. See Luddy on St. Bernard, 140.
25. *New Oxford Review,* December, 1982, 9.

EIGHT

## The Role of Prayer in the Spiritual Life

1. Von Balthasar, *Prayer,* 23.
2. *National Catholic Reporter,* October 8, 1971, 20.
3. See *Fire Within* on infused contemplation, chs. 2, 5, and 6, and also ch. 14 on locutions and visions.
4. For those marks see *Fire Within,* 235-242.
5. *Dei Verbum,* no. 8.
6. *Sacrosanctum Concilium,* no. 10.
7. Hausherr, 41.
8. St. Augustine, *Confessions,* trans. John K. Ryan (New York: Doubleday, Image edition, 1960), bk 8, ch. 1, 181.
9. St. John of the Cross, *Spiritual Canticle,* stan. no. 22, no. 6, 498.
10. St. John of the Cross, *Spiritual Canticle,* stan. no. 3, 497.
11. St. John of the Cross, *Spiritual Canticle,* stan. 11, no. 1, no. 4, 448-449.
12. St. Augustine, *Confessions,* bk 10, ch. 27, 254.
13. For example, see Ps. 34:5; Is 61:10; Jn 15:11; Rom 14:17; 1 Pt 1:8.

14. St. Augustine, *Confessions,* bk 10, ch. 40, 272.
15. St. Augustine, *Confessions,* bk 9, ch. 4 and bk 13, ch. 9, 210, 341.
16. See 1 Cor 2:4-5; 4:19-20; 2 Cor 4:7; Phil 3:10.
17. Lunn, 76-83.
18. St. John of the Cross, *Sayings of Light and Love,* no. 14, 667.
19. See the author's *Pilgrims Pray, God Dwells within Us,* and *Fire Within* for more complete answers to this question.
20. *Cloud,* chs. 24, 80.
21. Von Balthasar, *Prayer,* 18-19.
22. In *Theology Today: Hans Urs von Balthasar,* ed. Martin Redfern (New York: Doubleday, 1972), 54, 63.
23. Literally *activus* is an adjective, but I prefer to comment on the noun form.
24. *The Von Balthasar Reader,* 327.
25. There is an extended treatment of this point in the author's *Caring: A Biblical Theology of Community.*
26. Raissa Maritain, *Raissa's Journal,* presented by Jacques Maritain (Albany, New York: Magi Books, 1974), 15 July, 1971, 51.
27. *Cloud,* ch. 54, 117.
28. Von Balthasar, *Prayer,* 68.
29. *Sacrosanctum Concilium,* no. 2.
30. *Optatam Totius,* no. 8 and no. 11.
31. *Perfectae Caritatis,* no. 15; see also Eph 5:18-20.
32. *Perfectae Caritatis,* no. 7.
33. Von Balthasar, *Prayer,* 83.
34. Von Balthasar, *Prayer,* 69.
35. Von Balthasar, *Prayer,* 89.
36. See *Fire Within,* ch. 10.
37. *The Book of Privy Counseling,* (New York: Doubleday, 1973), ch. 11, 169.

NINE
*Practical Problems and Questions about Contemplation*
1. *Cloud,* ch. 16, 69. Jesus' remark is found in Lk 7:47.
2. For an extended explanation of this transitional phase of growth see *Fire Within,* 86-87.
3. Heb 1:1-3; 1 Jn 1:1-2. See also the preface for Christmas in the liturgy.
4. Von Balthasar, *Prayer,* 132.
5. See Lk 2:19, 51; Acts 1:14.
6. *Lumen Gentium,* no. 65.
7. *The Book of Privy Counseling,* ch. 15, 176.
8. Thomas à Kempis, 2:1, 103.
9. *Raissa's Journal,* May 23, 1920, 120.

10. Von Balthasar, *Glory,* Vol. 1, 274.
11. *Cloud,* ch 3, 48-49
12. *Cloud,* ch. 41, 101.
13. Von Balthasar, *Prayer,* 36.
14. Rom 1:7: "God's beloved..."; see also 1 Jn 4:9.
15. *Sacrosanctum Concilium,* no. 2.
16. St. John of the Cross, *Ascent,* prologue, no. 6.
17. Kilian McDonnell and George T. Montague, eds., Heart of the Church Consultation, *Fanning the Flame* (Collegeville, MN: The Liturgical Press, 1991).
18. See *Fire Within,* ch. 9.
19. "The First Blind Guide: John of the Cross and Spiritual Direction," *Spiritual Life,* Summer, 1991, 72.
20. *The General Instruction of the Liturgy of the Hours,* ch. 1, no. 20.
21. *The General Instruction of the Liturgy of the Hours,* no. 22.
22. *The General Instruction of the Liturgy of the Hours,* nos. 25-27.
23. "The Example of a Mystic: St. Gertrude and Liturgical Spirituality" (Collegeville, MN: The Liturgical Press, 1976), 740-803, 791.
24. Von Balthasar, *Prayer,* 98.
25. *Presbyterorum Ordinis,* no. 18.
26. *"Diligendo proximum, purgat oculum ad videndum Deum."* See *Liturgy of the Hours,* January 3, Office of Readings.
27. 1 Tm 2:8. For the Old Testament on this same point see Is 58:6-10.

TEN

## Problems that Come up in Spiritual Direction

1. Pascal, *Pascal's Pensées,* no. 779
2. Newman, 1464.
3. Pascal, *Pascal's Pensées,* no. 713.
4. Thomas à Kempis, 1:23, 81-82.
5. See Gn 1:31; Vatican II document, *Gaudium et spes, (passim)*.
6. See *Fire Within,* ch. 8.
7. Newman, ch. 5.
8. Canon 664.

ELEVEN

## How Can I Continue to Grow?

1. *Encounters with Silence,* 45-46.
2. See also Prv 17:27; 20:19; Eccl 5:1-2.
3. See the striking rebuke to our sinful tongues in James' letter, ch. 3.
4. Yves Congar, *Tradition and Traditions,* 451.
5. *Sacrosanctum Concilium,* no. 2.

6. *Sacrosanctum Concilium,* no. 2.
7. St. Francis de Sales, *Letters to Persons in Religion,* Letter 13 to an abbess, bk. 1 (London: Burns and Oates, 1909), 78.
8. St. John of the Cross, *Maxims,* in *Collected Works,* no. 33, 676.

TWELVE
## Discernment: Assessing My Progress

1. For a book-length discussion of discernment one may consult the author's *Authenticity: A Biblical Theology of Discernment* (Denville, NJ: Dimension Books, 1977).
2. E.g., Ps 34:5, 8; 73:25-28; Jn 14:15-17, 21, 23; 1 Pt 1:8, 2:3.
3. See also Mt 7:21; Jn 14:15, 21.
4. Luddy, 629.
5. *De Consideratione,* Luddy, 613.
6. Pascal, *Pascal's Pensées,* no. 705, 325.
7. Von Balthasar, *Prayer,* 176.
8. *Cloud,* ch. 42, 101.
9. *Cloud,* ch. 43, 102.
10. See 1 Pt, the whole of ch. 2, a striking condemnation of those who teach contrary to the official Church. See also Heb 13:17; Rom 13:1-2; Lk 22:42.
11. St. John of the Cross, *Maxims,* no. 33, 676.
12. Luddy, 137.
13. *Optatam Totius,* no. 9.

# Index